RUSSIA OBSERVED

ANECDOTES OF THE RUSSIAN EMPIRE

William Richardson

ARNO PRESS & THE NEW YORK TIMES

New York • 1970

Reprint edition 1970 by Arno Press, Inc.

Library of Congress Catalog Card No. 79-115580
ISBN No. 0-405-03059-2

Russia Observed
ISBN for complete set 0-405-03000-2

Reprinted from a copy in
the Harvard College Library

Manufactured in the United States of America

ANECDOTES

OF THE

RUSSIAN EMPIRE.

ANECDOTES

OF THE

RUSSIAN EMPIRE.

IN A

SERIES OF LETTERS,

WRITTEN, A FEW YEARS AGO, FROM

ST. PETERSBURG.

LONDON:

PRINTED FOR W. STRAHAN, AND T. CADELL

IN THE STRAND.

MDCCLXXXIV.

TO

THE RIGHT HONOURABLE

WILLIAM SHAW LORD CATHCART,

THESE LETTERS

ARE,

WITH GREAT RESPECT,

INSCRIBED,

BY

HIS LORDSHIP's

MOST OBEDIENT AND

DEVOTED SERVANT,

W. RICHARDSON.

GLASGOW COLLEGE,
Sept. 17, 1783.

ADVERTISEMENT.

THE Author of the following Letters, during the ſpace of four years that he paſſed in Ruſſia, had opportunities of obſerving many circumſtances that appeared to him remarkable in the manners of the Ruſſians; and of knowing ſome particulars, that ſeemed to him intereſting in the characters of eminent perſons. He does not pretend, however, to have compiled a complete Account of the Ruſſian Empire. He has only mentioned ſuch facts as he had occaſion to witneſs; or ſuch as had been communicated to him by perſons on whoſe information he could depend: and for this reaſon, as the term *Anecdote* may perhaps apply to a nation in general, no leſs than to individuals, he has entitled his Work ANECDOTES.—Chiefly ſolicitous of conveying ſuch information as might be uſeful or amuſing to his Readers, he has kept every thing reſpecting himſelf as much out of view as poſſible; and this muſt account for abruptneſs in ſome of the Letters; and for his preſenting others in the form of Extracts. At the ſame time, the Reader may probably remark, that ſeveral of the following Letters have little relation either to the manners of the Ruſſians, or to the characters of eminent cotemporaries. Some of them contain enquiries ſuggeſted to the Author, or his Correſpondents, concerning facts or events which he took occaſion to mention. Others have a connection ſtill more remote; and are ſcarcely any otherwiſe related to his ſubject, than that they were written during the time he remained in Ruſſia. It is hoped, however, that, in a Publication in which a very cloſe method is not propoſed, the ſlight connection between thoſe Letters, and the profeſſed deſign of the Volume, will not be conſidered as a great defect.

CON-

CONTENTS.

CONTENTS.

ANEC-

ANECDOTES OF THE RUSSIAN EMPIRE.

LETTER I.

Journal of a Voyage from England to St. Peterſburgh.

DEAR SIR, St. Peterſburgh, Aug. 16, 1768.

I HAVE the pleaſure of informing you of my arrival in Ruſſia. The paſſage was expeditious; but not intirely without ſome hazard: and the following Journal of the Voyage, in which, however, I have only marked thoſe days when any thing particular occurred, may perhaps afford you ſome amuſement. Nor ſhall I haraſs you with *larboard* and *ſtarboard*, and *fore* and *aft*.

We are neither of us ſeamen; why, therefore, ſhould I trouble either you or myſelf with the affectation of naval terms?

Auguſt 2. I embarked, in the evening, along with Lord C.* and his family, on board the Tweed Frigate at the Nore.

Auguſt 3. Early in the morning the veſſel was under ſail. The wind very favourable. The Tweed carries thirty-two guns: and, including forty marines, her full complement of men is two hundred and twenty.

Auguſt 6. Very ſtormy. The weather, hitherto, had been remarkably pleaſant. This day we entered the Categate.

Auguſt 7. The weather fine, and the wind favourable. We ſailed along the coaſt of Zealand.——Nothing of the kind could be more delightful than the verdure and variety of hill and dale, diſplayed in that beautiful iſland. In the afternoon we paſſed a ſmall palace belonging to the King of Denmark.

* His Lordſhip was appointed Ambaſſador Extraordinary and Plenipotentiary to the Empreſs of Ruſſia.

It is diſtant about two miles from Elſinore; is flat-roofed; has twelve windows in front, and is built, as I was told, on the very place formerly occupied by the palace of Hamlet's father. In an adjoining garden, the very ſpot is ſhewn where that Prince was ſaid to have been poiſoned.—We came to anchor in the evening, in the Sound, between the oppoſite fortreſſes of Elſinore and Helſingburgh.

Auguſt 8. Remained at Elſinore.

This town ſtands upon a ſmall bay: it contains about five thouſand inhabitants; commands the Sound; and was formerly the place of reſidence of the Daniſh Princes. The ſtreets are narrow, and ill-paved: the houſes are of brick or wood, and are covered with tiles. The caſtle ſtands on the weſt point of the bay: it is fortified with works of earth, on which are mounted three hundred and ſixty-five pieces of cannon; and the ſubterranean apartments are ſaid to be ſo very ſpacious, as to be capable of containing more than a regiment of men. In other reſpects, the caſtle itſelf ſeems to be a place of very little defence: it is a ſquare edifice, built of free-ſtone brought from the coaſt of Sweden; and is ſo adorned with ſpires, as at a diſtance to reſemble a church. The rooms are lofty; and contain many coarſe hiſtorical pictures, relating chiefly to the wars of Denmark.—The altar-piece, in the great church of Elſinore, is alſo ſhewn as a curioſity. It is made of oak, very richly gilt and carved; and the figures, in different groups, repreſent the hiſtory of our Saviour.—The Sound, at this place, is about three miles broad; and the toll, levied from merchant ſhips, was firſt impoſed to defray the expence of light-houſes erected along the coaſt by the King of Denmark.—The ſoil in Zealand, though the ſea-coaſt appears very beautiful, is light, ſandy, and not very fruitful. The grain it produces is chiefly rye; and any cattle I ſaw were remarkably ſmall. The carriages, in which the inhabitants carry turf for fewel, and other neceſſaries, are drawn by horſes, go upon four little wheels, are narrow, and have their ſides wattled.

The opening of the Sound, and the ſitua- of the Tweed this evening, diſplayed a very beautiful landſkip. The view to the eaſt was bounded

bounded by the isle of Ween, formerly the residence of Tycho Brahe. This little island is of a circular form: the shore is higher than the neighbouring coast of Zealand; and even higher at that particular place than the coast of Sweden. We were just able to distinguish its agreeable verdure, and to discern the spires of Copenhagen, which seemed very near it. The sea-coast from Elsinore to Copenhagen, finely diversified with cornfields, meadows, woods, little hills, and summer-palaces belonging to the King and the Nobility, was happily contrasted by the black rocks on the opposite and mountainous coast of Sweden. The sea was quite smooth; and the castles of Elsinore and Helsingburgh, with the numerous vessels that lay at anchor, and all the other circumstances of the scene, were embellished by a glorious setting sun, whose rays were reflected from a multitude of gilded clouds.

The only disagreeable circumstance I met with here, was a whispered account of the royal family. I am afraid you will soon hear of "something rotten in the state of Denmark."

Auguſt 9. We paſſed the iſland of Bornholm. The coaſt appeared high, without wood or cornfields; but covered with verdure. The weather fine.

Auguſt 10. We ſailed along the coaſt of Gothland, a very beautiful iſland. The land riſes gently towards the middle. The country appeared fertile and woody; and, from the number of ſpires and houſes, and from the vaſt ſwarm of fiſhing-boats which came around us in the evening, it ſeemed very populous. The number of iſlands in the Baltic, diſplaying a variety of different appearances conſtantly ſhifting, and ſucceeding one another, renders the navigation of that ſea, in ſummer or autumn, remarkably agreeable.

Auguſt 11. A very ſtormy day. At noon we came in ſight of Dago, an uncouth, black, and diſagreeable iſland; the firſt ſpecimen of the Ruſſian dominions. At night we left the Baltic, and entered the gulf of Finland.

Auguſt 12. A fine day. The ſea perfectly ſmooth. We paſſed Revel in the morning; and as the evening was uncommonly pleaſant,

ſant, for the light continued with us longer than in more ſouthern latitudes, we remained upon deck till paſt eleven at night. Our voyage, which hitherto had been ſpeedy and agreeable, was near an end; and we retired, in perfect ſecurity, to our cabins.

Auguſt 13. At one o'clock in the morning an alarm was given. The ſhip had ſtruck on a rock. All upon deck was tumult: all below conſternation. Expecting every moment that the ſhip-boats would be ſent off with the paſſengers, we held ourſelves in readineſs for that event. The morning was perfectly calm; and the ſea ſmooth as a mirror. Theſe circumſtances were peculiarly favourable; for the leaſt gale of wind would have daſhed the veſſel in pieces. To the north-eaſt, within two or three miles of us, lay ſome little iſlands; and to the north-weſt was a beacon, to which our pilots, for we had two of them, had not attended. Our ſhip, in the meantime, was ſo cloſely wedged in between the rocks, that ſhe ſeemed incapable of any motion. The rocks at the fore-part were hardly two feet under water.

The firſt attention of Mr. Colingwood, the Captain, was to lighten the veſſel: and, accordingly, ſeveral of the ſhip-guns, and ſome heavy caſks, were thrown into the ſea. A large anchor was carried out by the ſtern; and an united effort was made by the ſhip's crew, to force back the veſſel. But the anchor having taken faſt hold of a rock, and having its flook torn off, our effort failed. We now expected to leave the ſhip, leſt a ſudden gale ſhould put it out of our power. But to this meaſure, ſeveral reaſons were oppoſed. Signals of diſtreſs had been hung out, and ſix or ſeven guns had been fired; but though in the neighbourhood of ſome iſlands, no boats had come off to our aſſiſtance: if, therefore, thoſe iſlands were inhabited, it muſt be by barbarous Fins, who, living on the confines of the Ruſſian and Swediſh dominions, were hardly ſubject to either power, and might prove no leſs formidable than the gulf itſelf. If they were not inhabited, we muſt run the hazard of wanting proviſions, as we knew by our charts, that we were twelve leagues from the coaſt of Finland. Beſides, our leaving the ſhip, might have diſcouraged the crew, who had hitherto exerted

erted themſelves with the utmoſt ſpirit and alacrity.

In the meantime, the ſun roſe moſt ſplendidly, without a cloud. It reſembled a blaze of fire riſing from the midſt of the ſea; and the gulf, to the diſtance of many leagues, ſhone with refulgent beams. The ſcene was glorious; and all of us ſeemed to receive new ſpirits from the view of that radiant object. More guns and caſks were thrown overboard: another anchor was carried out: another effort was to be made; and the attention and expectation of all were excited. But the anchor having broke, like the former, we remained in our former poſition. Add to this, that the increaſing light, by having ſhewn us the wreck of a veſſel that had been loſt on theſe very ſhelves, ſcattered among the rocks and under water, heightened our ſenſe of danger. Yet no unbecoming feelings appeared.

Soon after, the appearance of ſails at ſome diſtance, revived our hopes. Signals of diſtreſs were repeated: we fancied they were ſteering towards us: we expected they would put us on ſhore at Revel, or ſome neighbouring

ing harbour: we every instant imagined they were coming nearer: every one was eager to impart the joyful intelligence: but when those who were gone below deck on this good-natured errand returned, and expected to see those friendly vessels at hand, they saw them with difficulty; the sails were lessening, and disappeared. Whosoever they were to whom those vessels belonged, and I trust they were not our countrymen, they did not choose to involve themselves in our misfortune. Thus, fastened as we were, to a solitary rock in the gulf of Finland, we had the additional distress of feeling ourselves abandoned.

We had now been struggling no less than eight hours in this critical and forlorn situation. It was nine in the morning: and the sea, owing, very probably, to an approaching gale, seemed to swell, and have a tremulous motion. Not a moment was to be lost. Our sheet anchor was laid on a raft, and carried out like the former: more guns and casks were thrown into the sea, and the remaining guns were loaded, that by their discharge, the concussion given to the ship might assist us. The effort was made: our anchor broke as before: but

but at that interesting moment the ship got off. It was now our fortitude seemed to leave us: we had been more careful in arming our minds against any thing adverse, than in guarding against the joy of deliverance; and our apprehensions never appeared but in our mutual congratulations, when we thought ourselves safe. Our honest Captain, steady as he appeared to be during the time of our danger, and who was just about giving orders for cutting down the masts, shewed emotions, when he saw us out of danger, which did him honour.

About half an hour after the Tweed was in motion, we discovered a small vessel, with a sail, coming towards us: but on seeing us clear of the rocks, it put about, and the persons on board seemed afraid of approaching us: circumstances which gave us no favourable opinions of their designs, had our ship been wrecked. We obliged them to come on board. They were Fins from a distant island, who had set out on hearing the first signals of our distress. They assisted in piloting us from among the rocks, and were very happy in being allowed to pick up the casks floating upon

upon the water. One of the midſhipmen gave the chief perſon among them an old laced hat, with which he ſtrutted upon deck with great conſciouſneſs of ſuperior rank.

We were not above an hour under ſail, when the ſky became cloudy, and the ſea very rough: and, what is very ſingular, we were in no leſs danger the ſucceeding night: but the hazard to which we were expoſed was inſtantaneous; and we ſcarcely knew of it till it was paſt. Coming with a briſk wind right upon a ſteep rock on the coaſt of Hogland, the ſhip was within a few minutes of being daſhed in pieces; and was called to by a trading veſſel, juſt time enough to tack about.

The rocks we ſtruck upon are about fifty-five leagues from St. Peterſburgh, and in the ſixtieth degree of north latitude. The iſlands are named Pelting Scars; they are ſituated off the coaſt of Nyland in Finland, and almoſt directly ſouth from the city of Borgo. Between Nyland and the Pelting Scars, is Pelting Sound, a ſea full of rocks and barren iſlands.

August

August 14. We paſſed the iſland of Hogland or Hochland, ſignifying, in the language of thoſe parts, Highland. The coaſt is rocky, mountainous, and covered with heath. At night we lay at anchor at Cronſtadt, in the iſland Scutari.

In this place are the principal dock-yards of the Ruſſian Empreſs. The iſland itſelf is four miles in length, and two in breadth, and has ſome wood upon it. The town of Cronſtadt is very ſmall, and ill-built. It is diſtant about eighteen miles from St. Peterſburgh.

Auguſt 15. This day we left the Tweed, and arrived at St. Peterſburgh in one of the Empreſs's yachts. The weather was very fine: and we had, in ſailing along, a full view of the neighbouring coaſt of Æſthonia. The palaces of Oranibaum and Peterhoff have a magnificent appearance to the ſea; and the face of the country is agreeably diverſified with woods and little hills. The country around St. Peterſburgh is very woody: ſo that in approaching it, the ſteeples and ſpires, which are covered with tin and braſs, and ſome

ſome of them gilt, ſeemed as if they aroſe from the midſt of a foreſt.

I ſhall write you again in a few days, either by poſt, or by the Tweed, on her return to England.

Adieu.

LETTER II.

The Empreſs of Ruſſia, and the Great Duke, lay the Foundation of a magnificent Church.

DEAR SIR, St. Peterſburgh, Aug. 19, 1768.

I AM juſt returned from witneſſing the ceremony of the Empreſs's laying the foundation-ſtone of a church dedicated to St. Iſaac; and which is intended to be the largeſt in St. Peterſburgh. St. Iſaac is held in eſteem by the Ruſſians, not ſo much for any diſtinguiſhed character of his own, as that the day conſecrated to him was the birth-day of Peter the Great. As the Ruſſians apprehend that every day of the year is conſecrated to ſome particular Saint, they are convinced that every individual is under the peculiar protection of that holy perſon, on whoſe day he happened to have been born; and all of them carry about them a ſmall metal image of their tutelary Saint. Herodotus, if I rightly recollect, gives a ſimilar account of the Egyptians.

He tells us, that they believed every day ſacred to ſome. particular God; that they were under the peculiar protection of that divinity on whoſe day they were born; and that they rendered him particular homage. So much alike are all ſuperſtitions.

As the ceremony I ſhall now deſcribe to you was reckoned of great importance, it was performed with great pomp and magnificence. All the ſpace to be occupied by the church had been previouſly railed in; and into this place, only perſons of high rank, and thoſe who had a particular permiſſion, were admitted. An immenſe multitude of people were aſſembled without. An arch, ſupported upon eight pillars of the Corinthian order, and adorned with garlands, was raiſed immediately over the place intended for the altar. Beneath this arch was a table covered with crimſon velvet, fringed with gold; upon which was placed a ſmall marble cheſt, fixed to a pully directly above the table. On a ſide-table, fixed to one of the pillars, was a large gold plate, with medals and coins to be depoſited at the foundation, and a gold box to contain them. On another ſide-table was another

other gold plate, containing two pieces of marble in the form of bricks, a gold plate with mortar, and other two plates of the ſame metal, in which were two hammers and two trowels of gold.

The proceſſion began with the Grand Duke and his retinue. This young Prince, the heir apparent of the Ruſſian empire, is of a pale complexion, with dark eyes, more remarkable for their good colour, than expreſſion; and of a ſhape more delicate than genteel. He ſeems of a chearful diſpoſition, of affable and eaſy manners. He was dreſſed in the uniform of the navy, which is white turned up with green, and wore a blue ribbon of the order of St. Alexander Newſky. He was attended by Count Panin, his governor, who is alſo prime miniſter.

Soon after his arrival, the approach of the Empreſs was announced by the beating of drums, and a diſcharge of the cannon at the Admiralty, which continued firing at regular intervals during the whole time of the ceremony; and the Grand Duke, who had been converſing with the courtiers, returned with his retinue to meet his mother, and fall in with her train. It was now that the principal parts of the proceſſion approached. It was preceded by prieſts of inferior orders, in long purple or dark-coloured garments of woollen cloth, with wide ſleeves; having their heads uncovered, their long hair hanging looſe about their ſhoulders; ſcattering incenſe from ſmall cenſers, which hung in chains; and carrying flags, on which were repreſented, in glaring colours, the deeds, and, I believe, the martyrdom of St. Iſaac. Theſe were followed by prieſts of a higher order, with their heads uncovered like the former; but having their flowing robes, of flowered ſilk, adorned with gold and ſilver; and carrying ſplendid croſſes, burning tapers, and a large portrait of the Saint. Immediately after theſe came a band of Choiriſters, ſinging hymns; the muſic was deep-toned, ſolemn, and even ſublime. After them came the dignified Clergy, with garments of gold and ſilver ſtuffs, adorned with precious ſtones; and having their lofty mitres ornamented in a ſimilar manner. They had, in general, a

very

very venerable appearance, with grey locks and long beards: they ſeemed like ſo many Socrateſes and Zenos; though, ever and anon, you might have ſeen an excellent Silenus, appearing rather ſurpriſed at his becoming a biſhop.

Some large wax tapers were carried immediately before her Imperial Majeſty, who came next, attended by a great number of ladies and gentlemen. The Empreſs of Ruſſia is taller than the middle ſize, very comely, gracefully formed, but inclined to grow corpulent; and of a fair complexion, which, like every other female in this country, ſhe endeavours to improve by the addition of rouge. She has a fine mouth and teeth; and blue eyes, expreſſive of ſcrutiny, ſomething not ſo good as obſervation, and not ſo bad as ſuſpicion. Her features are in general regular and pleaſing. Indeed, with regard to her appearance altogether, it would be doing her injuſtice to ſay it was maſculine, yet it would not be doing her juſtice to ſay, it was entirely feminine. As Milton intended to ſay of Eve, that ſhe was fairer than any of her daughters, so this great Sovereign is certainly fairer than any of her subjects whom I have seen *.—She wore a silver stuff negligee, the ground pea-green, with purple flowers and silver trimming. Her hair was dressed according to the present fashion. She also wore a rich diamond necklace, bracelets, and ear-rings, with a blue ribbon of the highest order of Knighthood; and the weather being very warm, she carried in her hand a small green umbrella. Her demeanour to all around her seemed very smiling and courteous.

After the whole procession arrived at the proper place, divine worship was performed with prayers, vocal music, and all the pompous ceremonies of the Greek church. A crucifix, after being immersed by a Priest of high rank in a silver bason filled with water, was carried to the Empress and Grand Duke. Bowing, and crossing their breasts, in testimony of adoration, they kissed it. Holy water was

* I have seen no pict.re, medallion, or print, excepting one picture, in which she is painted in men's clothes, that does her justice. In most of them her features appear too strong, and her air too masculine.

 sprinkled

ſprinkled on all who were preſent, and a cenſer ſmoking with incenſe was carried round. Then, after ſome ſuitable paſſages of the Greek ſervice had been read aloud, accompanied with prayers and muſic, another dignified Clergyman, laying the medals on a crimſon velvet cuſhion, fringed with gold, lifted them on his head, and carried them round the altar-place. After they were in this manner conſecrated, and laid in the marble cheſt, the Empreſs giving her umbrella in a very eaſy manner to an attendant, and taking a hammer very gracefully in one hand, and a piece of marble in the other, ſhe put it into the cheſt. Then, with the trowel, ſhe put in ſome mortar. The ſame ceremony was performed by the Grand Duke and the dignified Clergy. Some of the Nobility, and Foreign Miniſters, alſo put in ſome mortar. The marble cheſt was then ſhut up, and raiſed by the pulley; at that inſtant the table, ſinking down through a trap door, was very quickly removed; and her Imperial Majeſty letting down the pulley, the cheſt ſunk gently down through the platform into its place. When this was done, the Court Chaplain, aſcending a pulpit, which was faſtened to a pillar, delivered, with fervent, and almoſt declamatory, elocution, a ſhort diſcourſe in the Ruſſian language. I could only judge of his manner, which was not diſagreeable; and of the ſound of the language, which was liquid and pleaſant. The whole ceremony concluded by the Empreſs's allowing the dignified Clergy to kiſs her hand, which they did with good-will and a loud noiſe; and ſeemed rather happier with ſuch an opportunity, than her Imperial Majeſty herſelf, notwithſtanding her ſmiles.

Adieu.

LETTER III.

Anecdotes of the Empreſs of Ruſſia.

DEAR SIR, St. Peterſburgh, Nov. 7, 1768.

I PERCEIVE, by ſome ſevere expreſſions, in a letter from our friend ——, that our northern Semiramis has but little chance of exciting his admiration. Not to him, therefore, but to you, who have more indulgence for the "weaker veſſel," though on the preſent occaſion no indulgence is neceſſary, I tranſmit the following diary of the Empreſs, as I heard it from the Counteſs Romanſoff, a very reſpectable old lady of the higheſt rank in this place, and mother to Count Romanſoff.

Her Majeſty, according to this authority, riſes at five in the morning, and is engaged in buſineſs till near ten. She then breakfaſts, and goes to prayers: dines at two: withdraws to her own apartment ſoon after dinner: drinks tea at five: ſees company, plays at cards, or attends public places, the play, opera, or maſquerade, till ſupper: and goes to ſleep at ten. By eleven every thing about the palace is as ſtill as midnight. Whiſt is her favourite game at cards; ſhe uſually plays for five imperials * the rubber; and as ſhe plays with great clearneſs and attention, ſhe is often ſucceſsful: ſhe ſometimes plays too at picquet and cribbage. Though ſhe is occaſionally preſent at muſical entertainments, ſhe is not ſaid to be fond of muſic. In the morning, between prayers and dinner, ſhe frequently takes an airing, according as the weather admits, in a coach or ſledge. On theſe occaſions, ſhe has ſometimes no guards, and very few attendants; and does not chuſe to be known or ſaluted as Empreſs. It is in this manner that ſhe viſits any great works that may be going on in the city, or in the neighbourhood. She is fond of having ſmall parties of eight or ten perſons with her at dinner; and ſhe frequently ſups, goes to balls, or maſquerades, in the houſes of her nobility. When ſhe retires to her palaces in

* Ten guineas.

the

the country, eſpecially to Zarſkocelo, ſhe lays aſide all ſtate, and lives with her ladies on a footing of as eaſy intimacy as poſſible. Any one of them who riſes on her entering or going out of a room, is fined in a rouble *: and all forfeits of this ſort are given to the poor. You will eaſily perceive, that by her regular and judicious diſtribution of time, ſhe is able to tranſact a great deal of buſineſs; and that the affability of her manners renders her much beloved. But I will not yet ſay any thing very poſitive concerning her character and principles of action. For, ſhe may be very ſocial, and very affable, "and ſmile, and ſmile, and"——you know the reſt.

I may, however, very ſafely affirm, that a great number of her actions, ſo great indeed as to conſtitute a diſtinguiſhing feature in her character, proceed either from the deſire of doing good, or the love of fame. If from the laſt, it muſt alſo be acknowledged, that the praiſe ſhe is ſo deſirous of obtaining, is, in many inſtances, the praiſe of humanity.

* Four ſhillings.

Some-

Sometimes, indeed, there is a ſort of whim or affectation of ſingularity, in the manner of conferring her favours, that looks as if the deſire of being ſpoken of, fully as much as the deſire of doing good, was the fountain from which they flow. For example—A young officer who attended the court, fell in love, as was natural, with a young lady. The lady, as was alſo natural, appeared not inſenſible to his worth, nor diſpleaſed with his aſſiduity. But want of fortune on both ſides, was an obſtacle to their union. The Empreſs, however, perceived their attachment; and ſent, one day, for the young gentleman to a private conference. She told him, ſhe had obſerved that M— and he entertained great tenderneſs for one another; that the whole Court obſerved it; and hinted ſomething like regret, that ſuch things ſhould have been remarked. The young man was diſconcerted; but had firmneſs enough to avow the ſincerity of his paſſion. " Then," ſaid her Majeſty, " you " muſt forthwith be married." This was ſudden: the young man ſhewed ſome heſitation; but not from any motives that were improper: " he had no fortune, and could " not

" not maintain the lady in a manner ſuited " to her rank and merits." The Empreſs was peremptory. They were married as ſpeedily as the forms of the church permitted, and ſent off in a coach to St. Peterſburgh; for the Court was at that time at Zarſkocelo. They knew not whither they were going, nor how they were to ſubſiſt; nor were they very certain of their not having incurred their Sovereign's diſpleaſure. Meantime, the perſons who conducted them, and who would give them no information, ſet them down in the * Galerhinhoff. Here, to their utter aſtoniſhment, they were carried into a houſe elegantly furniſhed; they met with a numerous company of their friends; they found a ſplendid entertainment; and the bridegroom was told by a meſſenger from the Empreſs, that her Majeſty had given him that houſe as he found it, and had appointed him to an office " ſuited to his rank and merits."

* * * * * *

Adieu.

* One of the fineſt ſtreets in St. Peterſburgh, inhabited chiefly by Engliſh merchants.

LETTER IV.

Deputies aſſembled by the Empreſs of Ruſſia, from different Parts of her Empire, for making Laws.

DEAR SIR, St. Peterſburgh, 1768.

I WAS lately preſent at a meeting of the deputies ſummoned by the Empreſs from all the nations of her empire, and who have been aſſembled to aſſiſt her Majeſty in forming a ſyſtem of legiſlation. There is ſomething magnificent in this idea: and if ſhe really intends what ſhe profeſſes, to give equitable laws to all her ſubjects and dependents, from the Baltic to the wall of China, and from Lapland to the Caſpian, ſhe deſerves admiration. The deputies, in their firſt addreſs, ſtiled her "Great, wiſe, "and the Mother of her People;" titles which, excepting the laſt, ſhe declined, telling them at the ſame time, "None can be "called great before death; none wiſe that

"are

"are mortal; I hope I ſhall act as the Mother
"of my People."

The meeting conſiſts of about ſix hundred members. They meet in the palace, where they have one large hall for the whole aſſembly; and ſeveral adjoining rooms for committees. They conſiſt of repreſentatives of the nobility, the peaſantry, and the inhabitants of towns or cities. Count Panin is deputy for the city of Moſcow. The chief officers in this aſſembly are a Mariſchal, who preſides; and a Procureur General for the Crown. Out of the aſſembly, ſix committees, each conſiſting of five perſons, are choſen by ballot: and their buſineſs, according to their various departments, is to regulate the form and order of thoſe matters, concerning which the whole aſſembled deputies are to deliberate.

In tranſacting buſineſs, the following method is obſerved. The Procureur lays before the deputies ſome principle or ſubject of law propoſed by the Empreſs, and concerning which they are to give an opinion. They then adjourn; and the committee to whom that

that ſubject particularly belongs, prepare it for the next general meeting. Then all the members are permitted to deliver their opinions in a written ſpeech, and to determine the point before them, by the plurality of votes. But whatever their determinations may be, it remains with the Empreſs to ratify them or not, as ſhe pleaſes. Two of the ſubjects lately diſcuſſed in this aſſembly were, "Whether any but the nobility had a right "to buy lands?" and, "Whether any but "the nobility had a right to buy ſlaves?"

I have heard that freedom of extemporaneous ſpeaking was allowed in ſome of the firſt meetings of this aſſembly; but that being likely to occaſion too much diſorder, it was diſcontinued. At preſent, it is expected that no perſon, unleſs his views be very well known, ſhall deliver a ſpeech without previouſly conſulting the Mariſchal; and if he diſapproves of it, the orator, though he had the powers of a Cicero, muſt keep his ſpeech in his pocket. Indeed, this aſſembly has no pretenſions whatever to freedom of debate, and ſcarcely any tendency towards eſtabliſhing political liberty. The members, in general, are chosen by the will of the sovereign: by her the subjects of debate are proposed: she keeps in her own hands the right of ratifying every determination: and the assembly, convoked by her sole authority, may be dismissed at her pleasure.

All the deputies have gold medals, as badges of their office, fastened to their breasts: and as they come here from the remotest parts of the empire, the variety of their dresses and appearance is very whimsical and amusing.——I have several times heard the following anecdote of the two Samoid deputies. I give it you as nearly as possible, in the very words in which I have heard it. The Empress asked them to suggest such laws as they apprehended would promote the welfare of their nation. One of them replied, that they had very few laws, and did not desire any more. "How," said the Empress, "have you no crimes! Are there no persons "among you guilty of theft, murder, or "adultery? If you have crimes, you must "have punishment; and punishment supposes law." "We have such crimes," answered the deputy, "and they are duly "punished.

" punished. If one man puts another to
" death unjustly, he also must suffer death."
Here he stopped: he thought he had said
enough. " But what," resumed her Majesty,
" are the punishments of theft and adultery?"
" How," said the Samoid, with a good deal
of surprise," " is not detection sufficient pu-
" nishment?"——One would imagine, from
this anecdote, that the Samoids are, or resemble, the nation of whom Tacitus says,
" *Plusque ibi boni mores valent, quam alibi*
" *bonæ leges:*" " and virtuous manners have
" there more efficacy than good laws else-
" where."

LETTER V. (EXTRACT.)

Thankſgiving for the Recovery of the Empreſs and Great Duke from the Small-pox.

December 3d, 1768.

* * * * DIVINE ſervice was performed this day in the Empreſs's chapel, on account of her recovery, and that of the Great Duke, from the ſmall-pox; for which they had undergone inoculation by Dr. Dimſdale. The ceremony was very ſolemn and magnificent.

On each ſide of the chapel, which is a very lofty and ſpacious room in the winter-palace, is a row of gilt Ionic pillars. The walls are covered with glaring and ill-executed pictures of Ruſſian ſaints. On the roof over the altar*, the Supreme Being is repreſented as an old man in white apparel. On the inſide of a rail which extended acroſs the room, and cloſe by the pillar which was next the altar,

* Or rather, the place correſponding to the altar in Engliſh churches.

on the ſouth ſide, ſtood the Empreſs and her ſon: and alſo on the inſide of the rail, and on each ſide of the altar *, was a choir of muſicians. All the reſt who witneſſed, or took part in the ſolemnity, excepting the prieſts, ſtood on the outſide of the rail.

The ceremony began with ſolemn muſic; and then were pronounced the prayers and ejaculations which conſtituted the firſt part of the ſervice. This having laſted ſome time, two folding-doors cloſe by the altar were opened from within, and diſplayed a magnificent view of the interior and moſt holy part of the chapel. Oppoſite to us was a large picture of the taking down from the croſs: on each ſide, a row of gilt Ionic pillars; in the middle, a table covered with cloth of gold; and upon the table were placed, a crucifix, a candleſtick with burning tapers, and chalices with holy water. A number of venerable prieſts, with grey hair, flowing beards, mitres, and coſtly robes, ſtood in ſolemn array on each ſide of this magnificent ſanctuary. The whole ſuggeſted an idea of the Temple of Jeruſalem.

* See the preceding note.

From

From this place advanced a prieſt, with "ſlow and ſolemn pace," carrying a lighted taper: he was followed in like manner by another, reciting prayers, and carrying a cenſer ſmoking with incenſe. Advancing towards her Majeſty, he three times waved the cenſer before her; ſhe all the while bowing, and very gracefully croſſing her breaſt. He was ſucceeded by another prieſt, who carried the Goſpel; out of which having read ſome part, he preſented it to the Empreſs, who kiſſed it.

The prieſts then retired; the folding-doors were cloſed; the choiriſters ſung an anthem: they were anſwered by muſical voices from within: the muſic was deep-toned, and ſublime. The folding-doors were again ſet open: the ceremonies of the taper and incenſe repeated: two prieſts then advanced, and carried the bread and wine of the Euchariſt, veiled with cloth of gold. Having adminiſtered theſe, they retired. The doors were cloſed, and the ſolemn muſic reſumed.

The doors were ſet open a third time, with the ſame ceremonies as before; and a prieſt

 aſcending

aſcending a pulpit fixed to the pillar oppoſite to the Empreſs, delivered a diſcourſe. In this he celebrated her fortitude and magnanimity; and took occaſion to remark, "That "the Ruſſians had borrowed aſſiſtance from "Britain, that iſland of wiſdom, courage, and "virtue." After this, ſome prieſts came from the inſide of the chapel, and concluded the ſervice with prayers and ejaculations. * * * *

LETTER VI.

Diſtribution of Prizes by the Great Duke to Students in the Academy.—The Repreſentation of a Ruſſian Tragedy by young Ladies.

St. Peterſburg, January 1769.

I ASSURE you, my dear Sir, I do not find it an eaſy matter to obtain information concerning the ſtate of Ruſſia. Very little can be reaped from mixed converſation; for the topics uſually diſcuſſed in large companies are either very general, or ſuited, as indeed they ought to be, to promote preſent amuſement. Beſides, it is an unpleaſant thing to aſk queſtions. The enquirer is ſo much in the power of the perſon he addreſſes, that the ſituation is diſagreeable; or he puts people ſo much on their guard againſt him, that he defeats his own purpoſe, and receives not even accidental or indirect information. They entertain ſuſpicions of your deſign;

they think you wiſh to be a profound politician, or that you are carrying on a treaſonable correſpondence; or, ſtill more atrocious, that your purpoſe is to publiſh a book; or, laſtly, they may perchance have read Horace, and have ſaid to themſelves, in the words of that exquiſite poet,

Percontatorem fugito, nam garrulus idem eſt*.

Beſides, no intelligence of a political nature, but ſuch as the court chuſes to communicate; no views of men and manners, and no anecdotes of incidents in domeſtic life, can be collected from the news-papers. How unlike England! that land enlightened by the radiance of Chronicles, Advertiſers and Gazetteers. The half of Ruſſia may be deſtroyed, and the other half know nothing about the matter. I cannot imagine how travellers coming into this, or indeed any foreign country, and who, beſides other difficulties, may be ignorant of the language, and who ſtay only a few weeks or months, are able to give an exact circumſtantial account of perſons, manners,

* Th' impertinent be ſure to hate;
Who loves to aſk, will love to prate. FRANCIS.
Avoid the queſtion-aſker, for he prates. ANON.

govern-

government, political interests, improvements, and all those particulars which draw the attention of strangers. I marvel at their abilities, or at their boldness.

I have to contend too with another difficulty. I perceive that the same objects are seen in very different lights by different persons. I will give you an instance; and to an Etonian, daily versant in the works of instruction, the circumstances I shall mention may afford some amusement.—I was lately present at a distribution of prizes to students educated in the Academy of Arts and Sciences. I passed through two large rooms, where the boys, dressed in white uniforms, were drawn up in two ranks; and went into a third, where the Great Duke, and other Academicians, were seated round a table, on which were placed specimens of hand-writing and drawing, executed by the scholars. There were also present many ladies and gentlemen of the Court. Count Betskoy began the ceremony, by addressing a speech to the Grand Duke, in which he recommended the seminary to his protection. To this his Imperial Highness replied, " As

" the welfare of Ruſſia ſhall ever be the ob-
" ject neareſt my heart; and as the proper
" education of youth is of ſo much conſe-
" quence in every well-ordered ſtate, it
" claims, and ſhall ever obtain, my moſt
" conſtant attention." He ſpoke ſlowly, and with propriety, yet not without the diffidence of an amiable boy. On ſitting down, he turned ſmiling to Count Panim, his governor, with the air of one aſking, Have I acquitted myſelf aright? The Count ſeemed to aſſent, and I thought a tear roſe in his eye. I was told that the Empreſs was preſent among the ladies; but though this might be known to them, ſhe did not chuſe upon that occaſion to be acknowledged as Empreſs. The mother wiſhed to obſerve her ſon. It was the firſt time he had ſpoken in public; and the mother's heart muſt have thrilled with pleaſure *. I almoſt wept for joy.——After this the company paſſed into another room, where the prizes were diſtributed. They were firſt preſented to the ladies, and by them to the little boys. The ſcene was amuſing; and was enlivened at intervals by a band of muſicians in an adjoining receſs.——Tell me

* Latonæ tacitum pertentant gaudia pectus. Virg.

now,

now, would not a ſtranger, on witneſſing ſuch a ſcene, on ſeeing one of the moſt powerful Sovereigns on earth, and the preſumptive heir of this mighty empire, ſo attentive to the welfare and improvement of their people, would he not feel rapture, approve, and applaud? Yet when I expreſs thoſe sentiments, there are perſons who ſhake their heads; who tell me, this Academy has ſubſiſted for many years, and what have they done? It may be mentioned, with oſtentatious pomp, in a news-paper, or by Voltaire, and nothing elſe is intended.—Such ſpeeches are mortifying; and, notwithſtanding their authority, I muſt ſay, that even admitting the love of fame to be the ſole motive, the means uſed are far more laudable than thoſe practiſed by princes who purſue the objects of their ambition, by adding one inhuman act to another.

The Academy mentioned above was founded in a former reign. But at a convent, a few verſts from St. Peterſburgh, there is an eſtabliſhment for the education of young women, by her preſent Majeſty. It ſomewhat reſembles that of St. Cyr, founded by M. Maintenon;

Maintenon; and the Empreſs maintains in it two hundred girls, from ſix to eighteen years old. They are divided into two claſſes: the firſt conſiſts of the children of officers, above the rank of Major, incluſive: and the ſecond conſiſts of the children of inferior officers: the firſt are inſtructed in elegant and polite accompliſhments; and the ſecond, together with muſic and dancing, are taught to work in all female employments. All their expences, comprehending even their dreſs, are defrayed by the Empreſs.

I was preſent, ſome time ago, at an entertainment, conſiſting of dances of different kinds, which they exhibited in preſence of the Grand Duke, and many of the Nobility. It began with dances by girls of the ſecond claſs, who were dreſſed uniformly in brown petticoats, blue jackets, white aprons, white caps and handkerchiefs. They were ſucceeded by thoſe of the firſt diviſion, who were dreſſed in court-dreſſes, of different colours; excepting that the younger part were dreſſed uniformly in white, trimmed with blue.——But the moſt amuſing exerciſe I have

have ſeen them exhibit was the repreſentation of a Ruſſian tragedy. It was repreſented not only with propriety, but with elegance; and not only ſo, but with great theatrical ability. The flowing hair, the ſparkling blue eyes, the fine figure, and graceful motions, of the young lady who performed the principal character; her melodious voice, and exquiſite but well-regulated ſenſibility, charmed, and even tranſported, her audience. Near where I ſat was an old venerable officer: during the firſt ſcenes, his ſolicitude and anxiety were very apparent; they were ſoon changed into joy; his emotions flowed out in tears:—ſhe was his grandchild.

Yet blue eyes, fine figure, and melodious voice have no effect on thoſe who ſhake their heads, and make ſage remarks. They chill the ardour of your applauſe by aſking, What proviſion is made for theſe young ladies after they leave the convent? And whether their education be ſuited to their fortune or expectations? And whether, if they ſhould not ſoon get huſbands, they will be inclined, after all this muſic, and dancing, and tragedizing, to ſubmit to the rigid laws of a nunnery?

nunnery ?——Queſtion-aſking, as I obſerved at the beginning of this letter, is no pleaſant buſineſs; and the above queſtions ſeemed to me particularly diſagreeable, as I was not juſt furniſhed with fit replies. I ought to have mentioned that the nuns reſident in this convent, ſome of whom were preſent at the above-mentioned entertainments, have it in charge, to inſtruct the young ladies in religious knowledge.

Adieu.

LETTER VII.

Causes of the Turkish War.

DEAR SIR, January, 1769.

YOU are in the right; Russia is at present in very critical circumstances, and will furnish the Gazettes of Christendom with more interesting intelligence, than any other nation in Europe. The Empress has, within these few days, declared war against the Turks; and the preparations that are making on both sides seem to announce a very violent struggle. The following circumstances, I am credibly informed, have occasioned this unfortunate rupture.

Count Poniatowsky, the present King of Poland, was, at an early period of his life, appointed Envoy from his own country to the Court of Russia. During his residence in that empire, he attached himself to the great Duchess, who is now Empress, and insinuated

ſinuated himſelf into her favour. This Princeſs, poſſeſſed of eminent talents, and actuated by an unbounded ambition, having dethroned her huſband, who ſucceeded to the Empreſs Elizabeth, and having inveſted herſelf with the Imperial dignity, reſolved to eſtabliſh her credit at home, and her importance abroad, by governing the affairs of Poland. Accordingly, connecting herſelf with the King of Pruſſia, and in ſpite of the efforts of France, Auſtria, and the Saxon Princes, ſhe advanced Poniatowſky to the throne, hoping, perhaps, that he would cooperate implicitly in her deſigns, or imagining that he poſſeſſed greater abilities than he has hitherto diſplayed. Surely no prince has had a finer opportunity of diſtinguiſhing himſelf as a warrior or politician: he was celebrated by Voltaire, who alſo celebrated the King of Denmark, and who celebrates all princes that are free-thinkers, and that pay him for his adulation: yet Poniatowſky, like ſome others, to whom he has offered incenſe, has done little credit to his panegyric. He has ſhewn neither ſpirit nor patriotiſm, and is ſaid to be chiefly deſirous of amaſſing treaſure, and of ſecuring to himſelf an indepen-

dency

dency in ſome foreign country, ſhould he, like another Staniſlaus, be forced to abdicate his unmerited dignity. The Empreſs of Ruſſia, having ſucceeded in giving a King to Poland, continued to act with authority in the affairs of that kingdom. To render herſelf popular at home, and to leſſen the influence of Catholic Princes among the Poles, ſhe encouraged all thoſe, who adhered to the tenets of the Greek religion, or to the principles of the reformation. This party, known in the Gazettes of Europe by the appellation of Diſſidents, poſſeſſed at a former period very conſiderable privileges. They not only enjoyed the free exerciſe of their religion, but had voices in the legiſlation, and were inveſted with public offices. Supported by the power of Ruſſia, and the favour of the King, they revived their pretenſions, and demanded a reſtoration of their rights. The Catholics took the alarm. The French fomented the quarrel, and thus concurred with the Empreſs Queen, who had married her favourite daughter to one of the Saxon Princes, and who flattered herſelf, that, by encouraging the diſaffected party, and by dethroning Poniatowſky,

towſky, ſhe might exalt her ſon-in-law to the throne. Mean while, the Empreſs of Ruſſia, depending on the greatneſs of her power, and not ſufficiently aware of conſequences, or miſinformed by her miniſters, acted with violence and precipitancy. One outrage led to another. The Diſſidents were alarmed; they foreſaw the ruin of their country; and willing to content themſelves with having the free exerciſe of their religion ſecured to them, withdrew their claim to ſuperior privileges. But Ruſſia having maintained the juſtice of their demands, thought her honour intereſted in aſſerting them, and determined by force of arms to ſubdue the obſtinacy of her opponents. King Staniſlaus wavered; he abandoned himſelf to the advices of the Czartorinſkys, who are his relations, and, without connecting himſelf with the confederates, incurred the ſuſpicions of the Empreſs. Mean time the French were indefatigable; they laid out immenſe ſums in Poland, and were no leſs active at Conſtantinople. They painted in the livelieſt colours the growing power of the Ruſſians, and repreſented how dangerous they would be to the Ottoman Porte, ſhould they become ab-

ſolute

ſolute in Poland. The Poliſh confederates added weight to their repreſentations; they ſupplicated the protection of the Sultan, and offered to indemnify him with a part of their dominions. The Turks have been eaſily perſuaded. Inſtigated by their ambition, and ſeduced by the policy of France, they have determined to interfere in the affairs of Poland. Nor are they without expectations, that a diverſion may be made in their favour on the ſide of Sweden. The Empreſs of Ruſſia, on the other hand, is no leſs determined to aſſert the rights, and maintain the dignity, of her Imperial diadem.

As the time ſeems big with important events, I may, perhaps, from time to time, give you ſome information concerning them.

Adieu.

P. S. I need not inform you that the Ruſſian army is reckoned inferior to none in Europe. It is not, however, on her army alone that the Empreſs means to depend. At the time that the war is to be carried on with great vigour in Moldavia and the Crimea, ſome conſiderable exertions will be made by

 ſea.

ſea. The command of the great army, to act on the frontiers of Poland and Moldavia, is given to Prince Galitzen: and it is reported that an Engliſh Admiral is to have a conſiderable command in the fleet intended for the Mediterranean.

LETTER VIII.

The Russian Winter.

February, 1769.

COLD! desperately cold! We have had winter without the least abatement of its rigour since the first of November; and it may continue, we are told, without the least mitigation, till the beginning or the middle of April. The frost has been all this while uninterrupted. The wind has blown almost constantly from the north-east. It comes howling and cold from the heights of Siberia, and has brought with it immense quantities of snow. In the beginning of winter the snow fell, without intermission, for several days. In the country, nothing appears but a boundless white desart; and the rivers are almost one chrystalline mass.——I refer you, however, for a better account of a Russian winter than I can pretend to give you, to your

your favourite Virgil. In his third Georgic you have the following account, which I ſhall lay before you, circumſtance by circumſtance; and which deſcribes the objects I have now in view with great exactneſs.

——Neque ullæ
Aut herbæ campo apparent, aut arbore frondes.

O'er the unfruitful ſcene
Nor fields nor trees are cloth'd in lively green.

Yet the feathered appearance of the boughs and little branches, is beautiful and romantic.

Sed jacet aggeribus niveis informis, et alto
Terra gelu late, ſeptemque aſſurgit in ulnas.
Semper hiems, ſemper ſpirantes frigora cauri.

One waſte of ſnow the joyleſs landſcape lies;
Seven ells in height the ridgy drifts ariſe;
There ſtill the bitter blaſts of winter dwell.

The repetition of the word "ſemper" in the laſt line has an admirable effect. Virgil could not have expreſſed himſelf more feelingly on the banks of the Neva. There is no circumſtance ſeems to me ſo dreary as the "ſpirantes "frigora cauri,' the cold-breathing blaſts. No tranſlation can do the paſſage juſtice. The conſtant monotonous melancholy ſound of of thoſe howling blaſts make me almoſt low-ſpirited.

> Tum ſol pallentes haud unquam diſcutit umbras.
>
> Nor the ſun's rays the paly ſhade diſpel.

This ſeems to you ſurpriſing. You think, perhaps, that we have conſtant clear weather. Far from it. We have had, ſince the beginning of winter, a great deal of hazy, miſty weather; and the cold, on thoſe occaſions, has frequently been very intenſe. The ſky, however, has been much clearer ſince the middle of January, than before that time. I have remarked a circumſtance here which I never obſerved in Britain: in the coldeſt and brighteſt weather you ſee an infinite multitude of little ſhining darts or ſpiculæ, flying in all directions through the ſky. They ſeem to be about a quarter of an inch in length; they have not more thickneſs than the fineſt hair; and their golden colour, glancing as they ſhoot through the deep azure ſky, has a great deal of beauty. If the weather were warmer, and if the climate were more genial, and if we had any belief in ancient mythology, we ſhould take them to be an immenſe multitude of arrows, diſcharged by ſome miſchievous Cupids. Nor would ſuch an explanation be without evidence in the character of the Ruſſians.

> Concreſcunt ſubitæ currenti in flumine cruſtæ:
> Undaque jam tergo ferratos ſuſtinet orbes,
> Puppibus illa prius patulis, nunc hoſpita plauſtris.
>
> Th' encroaching ice the loitering current feels,
> And on its boſom bears the ſtudded wheels:
> Where erſt the ſtately bark was wont to ride,
> Waggons thro' paths unknown ſecurely glide.

All this is very juſt, excepting in one particular, namely, that of the wheels. What the ancient Scythians might have done, I know not; but the modern Ruſſians take the wheels off their carriages in the winter, and, in their ſtead, uſe ſledges. When the ſnow has fallen in its greateſt quantity, and that the roads are beat ſmooth, the motion of the ſledge is very eaſy and agreeable. It is drawn in this country by horſes, and the ſwiftneſs with which they go, even upon ice, is aſtoniſhing. The horſes here are ſmall, but very nimble and beautiful; and the Ruſſians, in general, are excellent horſemen. Driving in ſledges is one of the chief amuſements that perſons of rank can have without doors in the winter; and accordingly, they endeavour to diſplay

diſplay their fancy in the form and embelliſh-ments of theſe whimſical carriages. They are quite open, and the moſt elegant I have ſeen have the appearance of ſhells, painted with ſhowy colours; ſo that the ladies and gentlemen who drive in them reſemble Divinities of the ſea. Thoſe uſed by perſons of any diſtinction are drawn by two horſes; but thoſe that ply in the ſtreets are drawn only by one. They fly with aſtoniſhing ſwiftneſs; ſo that in the ſpace of five or ten minutes you can be tranſported to any quarter of the city.

Stiriaque impexis induruit horrida barbis.

Their matted beards by the keen climate frore,
With hanging icicles are hard and hoar.

The circumſtance, though true, is almoſt ludicrous; but not inconſiſtent with the freedom of didactic poetry. In addition to it, I have heard of a circumſtance ſtill more ludicrous; namely, that two Ruſſian peaſants, ſaluting one another, have, by the ſuddenneſs and intenſeneſs of the froſt, had their beards unexpectedly frozen together. I do not, however, atteſt the fact.

Interea toto non fecius aëre ningit.

Meanwhile the ſkies are dim with falling ſnows.

The tranſlation here does not expreſs the fact ſo ſtrongly as the original. For ſeveral days together, in the beginning of winter, as I mentioned above, the ſnow falls without the leaſt intermiſſion.

——— Confertoque agmine cervi
Torpent mole nova, et ſummis vix cornibus exſtant, &c.

In growing heaps benumb'd, the crowding deer,
Scarce from beneath their branching antlers rear, &c.

I cannot take upon me to confirm what the Poet deſcribes with ſo much ſpirit and fancy concerning the deer; but I have heard a ſimilar account of bear-hunting. The bear, when the ſnow begins to fall, ſeeks ſome hollow, lays himſelf down, and is ſoon covered many feet deep. The peaſants diſcover him by a ſmall opening through the ſnow, by which he breathes. The huntſmen immediately gather around, and puſhing a long pike through the wreath or heap, they pierce his body. He wakes, ruſhes forth, and immediately the dogs aſſail him.

Ipſi in defoſſis ſpecubus, ſecura ſub alta
Otia agunt terra, congeſtaque robora, totaſque

Advolvere

Advolvere focis ulmos, ignique dedere:
Hic noctem ludo ducunt, et pocula læti
Fermento atque acidis imitantur vitea sorbis.
Talis hyperboreas septem subjecta trioni
Gens effræna virum Riphæo tunditur Euro:
Et pecudum fulvis velantur corpora setis.

In caverns deep, with oak up-pil'd, they raise,
And many a branching elm, the crackling blaze.
From cold secure, around the flaming hearth,
Waste the long dreary night in social mirth.
Guiltless of wine, the goblet still goes round,
With Ceres' juice, and sparkling cyder crown'd.
Such is the race of savage swarms that lie
Beneath the regions of the polar sky;
And, sore afflicted by the piercing east,
Their limbs with furs, and brinded skins invest.

Some part of this description is more applicable to the northern and more uncivilised parts of Russia, than to the neighbourhood of Petersburgh or Moscow. Perhaps in Siberia, and near the White Sea, some of the inhabitants may have their habitations, during the winter, under ground and in caverns. The fuel here, agreeably to what the poet says, consists chiefly of wood; but it is usually burnt in stoves built in the wall; so that in a Russian house you never see the flame, nor have the comfort and chearfulness of a blazing fire. With regard to the pastime, drink and

and dreſs of the Ruſſians, the Poet is as well informed as though he had lived at Archangel.

You will no doubt remark, in the lines I have quoted, an example of that beautiful gradation and progreſs of thought, that occur ſo frequently in the works of Virgil. His deſcription conſiſts of three parts. He begins with inanimated nature; leafleſs foreſts, the froſt, the ſnow, and the frozen rivers. He then exhibits living objects, but irrational: "corpora magna boum:" "conſertoque agmine cervi." In the third part he deſcribes the manners of intelligent and rational beings.——I am ſure you will thank me for having animated ſo cold and ſo dreary a ſubject with ſo much excellent poetry.

Adieu.

LETTER IX.

Religion of the Russians.—Russian Clergy.—Anecdote of a Priest.

To the REV. MR. W——.

REV. DEAR SIR,

I CAN offer you nothing very interesting on the article of Religion. You are acquainted with the tenets of the Greek Church. It is pretended that its principles are pure and rational: the practice, I'm sure, is different. I may tell you of pompous ceremonies, magnificent processions, rich dresses, showy pictures, smoking censers, and solemn music; but I cannot tell you that the clergy in general are exemplary, or the laity upright. On no consideration would a Russian peasant omit his fastings, the bending of his body, and the regularity of his attendance on sacred rites: scourge him if you will, yet you cannot oblige him to cross himself with more

more than three fingers; but he has no ſcruple to ſteal or commit murder. Were I not an eye-witneſs, I could ſcarcely conceive it poſſible, that men ſhould ſo far impoſe upon their own minds, as to fancy they are rendering acceptable ſervice to Heaven by the performance of many idle ceremonies, while they are acting inconſiſtently with every moral obligation. Judge of their religion by the following anecdote.——A Shop-keeper came on ſome buſineſs to the houſe of an Engliſh Merchant, on the evening before the day conſecrated to St. Nicholas. The Merchant was engaged, and begged he would return on the morrow. "To-morrow," ſaid the pious Ruſſian, "you are doubtleſs an in-"fidel! The very Tartars have more de-"cency: each of them will ſpend his rouble "to-morrow; and, in honour of St. Nicho-"las, get becomingly drunk."

The Ruſſians obſerve four faſts in the year. Of theſe, Lent is of the longeſt duration: and one of the moſt ſolemn ceremonies of their religion is performed at Eaſter, in honour of the reſurrection of Chriſt. In ſome churches, the very act of reſurrection is dramatically

matically reprefented; and all the miniftering priefts, moving in proceffion, cry with a folemn voice, "Chrift is arifen!" The ceremony begins about two in the morning, when all the churches are crowded with vaft multitudes of people. The following week is fpent in revelry and rejoicing. Hardly any bufinefs is done; for the Ruffians of all ranks and opinions, nobility and peafantry, believers and unbelievers, betake themfelves with the utmoft licentioufnefs to the pleafures of the table. They all embrace one another, faying, "Chrift is arifen," and prefent eggs to one another, painted with various figures, and infcribed with different devices. Some of thefe devices are religious; fome amorous; and fome both together: fo that it is no unufual thing to fee St. Athanafius with a crofs, on one fide of an egg; and on the other, a lover falling at the feet of his miftrefs. Wherever they meet, whether they are acquainted with one another or not, they embrace and give the cuftomary falutation. Nor is it unufual to fee two drunken peafants, announcing the glad tidings, embracing, and tumbling into the kennel. In the vacant places of the city, vaft crowds affemble, and fing ſing in their flying chairs, and partake of every ſort of amuſement. Mean time, every perſon who chuſes, goes into the churches, rings the bells as long as he thinks fit, and believes that he is thus glorifying God, or making expiation for his ſins. The week before Lent is in like manner dedicated to riotous diverſion; with this difference, that when they part with one another on the evening before the faſt commences, they take leave as if they were going on a far journey.

You aſk me particularly about the Ruſſian clergy. They are, in general, very ignorant. There are, no doubt, among them men of ſome learning and ingenuity; but their number is very ſmall. No more learning is uſually required of common officiating pariſh Prieſts, or Popes, as they call them, than that they be able to read the old Ruſs or Sclavonian language. They ſeldom or never preach: and their chief duty conſiſts in the knowledge of forms, and in reading prayers and portions of ſcripture. You may judge of their improvement by the following fact, which happened indeed in the reign of a former

former ſovereign, but which, without miſre-preſenting the religious manners of Ruſſia, might have happened at preſent.—At the end of Lent, as I mentioned above, all ranks of people abandon themſelves to feaſting and rioting: but this they are not permitted to do till the clergyman of the place viſits their houſes, and gives them his benediction. It happened that a Prieſt, having had ſome diſpute with one of his flock, intentionally paſſed his houſe, when making his progreſs through his pariſh, and omitted giving him the benediction which he had given the reſt of his pariſhioners. The man was exceedingly afflicted, to be obliged to faſt, and to ſay prayers, while all his neighbours were feaſting and getting drunk, was not to be borne; it ſeemed ſtill more inſufferable to his wife. In all emergencies of this kind, the fair ſex are good at giving good counſel. Softened by the admonitions of his help-mate, the huſband waited upon the Prieſt; acknowledged his fault; implored his forgiveneſs, and craved his bleſſing. But the holy man was inexorable. His ſuppliant was forced to employ his laſt reſource; it was his corps-de-reſerve; a gooſe, which he had concealed under his cloak. Its eloquence was irreſiſtible; its interceſſion was powerful; and the effect inſtantaneous. For immediately, on ſight of it, the countenance of the holy man was changed; his ſeverity was ſoftened into complacency, and, from the extreme benignity of his nature, he was diſpoſed to grant remiſſion to a repenting ſinner, who had given ſuch evidence of his contrition. But one difficulty remained: the Penitent's houſe was ſeveral miles diſtant; the day was far ſpent; next day was Eaſter; and the Clergyman was obliged to attend in church. What was to be done? for it was eſſential, in giving the uſual benediction, that it ſhould be pronounced cloſe by the four corners of the houſe. But the gooſe quickened his invention, and ſeemed like inſpiration to the man of God. An expedient was immediately ſuggeſted to him. "Hold your cap," ſaid he, to the wondering Penitent. He religiouſly held open his cap. Then the Prieſt, croſſing himſelf, bending, and holding his mouth over it, pronounced the benedictions and exorciſms, which he would have pronounced at the man's houſe. "Now," ſaid he, "hold it

"cloſe;

" close; get home as fast as you can, and at " every corner of your house, crossing your-" self, open a corner of your cap, and my " presence may be dispensed with." The man obeyed; thanked God, and got drunk.

But, with all the superstition and ignorance of the Russian clergy, it must be acknowledged in their favour, that they are tolerant, and very charitable to those of a faith different from their own. They say, all men may go to heaven; but that the chief place will be assigned to the Russians. This tolerating spirit seems to me very wonderful: I shall attend to it more minutely: and if I shall think myself able to say any thing satisfactory concerning its causes, I will very frankly, as on former occasions, lay my opinion before you. * * * * *

LETTER X.

The Russian Spring.

DEAR SIR, May 12, 1769.

I EMBRACE the opportunity of a courier going to London, to inform you of my health. Though the winter has been very ſevere, and the climate very different from that of England, I have had no ſort of ailment. Our weather for ſome days paſt has been very warm, yet we have ſcarcely any appearance of vegetation; and while the woods with you are filled with primroſes and hyacinths, we ſee not a green leaf. Indeed, when the wind blows from the eaſt, the cold returns with it; and the river is filled with large fragments of ice from the Ladago. Till the beginning of April, the ice was as firm on the Neva as in the middle of January. It broke up a few weeks ago, and announced its departure with a dreadful noiſe.

If

If climate could have any effect on national characters, the proofs ought to be manifest in Russia. The heats and colds are excessive; and the transition, from the one extreme to the other, sudden. A fortnight ago the ground was covered with snow; this day the heat is almost insufferable: at present scarcely a bud appears; but we expect, in a few days, to see the fields and trees invested with verdure.——A short letter this, you will say, and a short account of a Russian spring. It is so;—but a long description would be unsuitable, when a Russian spring is the subject.

LETTER XI.

State of Agriculture in Ruſſia.

DEAR SIR, June 14, 1769.

I AM juſt returned from an excurſion of thirty verſts * into the country. I was at a place called Craſnocelo, where an Engliſhman, who has been ſome time in this country, has eſtabliſhed a manufacture of printed cloth. The weather was very fine, and the province of Ingria, ſouth and eaſt from St. Peterſburgh, appeared delightful. The country is perfectly green; varied with woods, conſiſting chiefly of birch and fir; and interſperſed with a number of riſing grounds.

I travelled a conſiderable way along the banks of a beautiful little river, bordered with wood. In the neighbourhood of Craſnocelo is ſituated a romantic round hill, co-

* About 20 miles.

vered

vered with birch, larix, and other trees; and in the middle of it, a dell, about a quarter of a mile in length. The ſides of the eminence that ſurrounds it are very ſteep; nor is there any acceſs to it but by a ſloping entry to the weſt, and not more than twenty feet wide. This delightful little ſpot is the immediate property of the crown; it is laid out like a garden, and has in the middle an elegant ſmall pavilion. Yet I ſhould have liked it better unadorned, or adorned only by the hand of nature.

The ſoil, in this province, ſeems tolerably good; in ſome places a deep clay, and in others ſandy. It is, as you may ſuppoſe, very little improved. A Ruſſian plough is, indeed, a ridiculous object; ſo light, that you may lift it in your hand: it is drawn by one ſmall horſe; the plough-ſhare is no bigger than a large carving knife, and ſerves no other purpoſe than to looſen the ſurface of the earth. Yet, in ſome places, you ſee tolerable crops of barley, rye, and buckity wheat; and, in many places, extenſive meadows, luxuriant with natural graſs.

Indeed, as agriculture is ſtill in its infancy in Ruſſia, on account of the ſlavery of the peaſants, the preſent Empreſs endeavours to promote ſome knowledge of this neceſſary art, by forming colonies of ſtrangers. A few verſts from this city, there is a ſettlement of Germans, conſiſting of about a thouſand people; and the following, I have been informed, is the manner and terms of their eſtabliſhment:——One of the coloniſts receives from the Empreſs a horſe, an ox, a cow, four or five hundred rubles, and a portion of crown lands. Theſe lands he muſt cultivate; and, at the end of ten years, he muſt repay the crown the ſum of money which he has received. He is then at liberty to leave his farm, and ſettle wherever he pleaſes. If he remain, the farm, on paying a ſmall annual rent to the crown, becomes his property for ever. There are ſeveral of theſe colonies in different parts of Ruſſia: they conſiſt chiefly of German Lutherans, and are indulged in the free exerciſe of their religion.

I hope

I hope to hear from you ſoon; and am, &c.

P. S. On the fourth of this month, at twenty minutes paſt three in the morning, I had the good fortune to ſee the tranſit of Venus.

LETTER XII.

Progress of the War.

IT is really impossible for me, my dear Sir, to give you a circumstantial account of all the rencontres, and various acts of hostility committed, I might rather say perpetrated, in the present barbarous and complex war. I doubt much whether it will ever be possible for the clearest and most accurate historian to deliver them in a regular, particular, and complete detail. You will see the propriety of this remark, by observing the present situation of the different combatants and opponents. The whole of Poland is in a state of distraction. There are confederacies and associations of armed men in every quarter; and almost in every quarter there are Russian troops, or such as are inlisted under the royal banner. Of consequence there are constant encounters: sometimes the one party, and sometimes the other, is successful. These conflicts contribute nothing to the

the re-eſtabliſhment of public affairs: they are bloody and barbarous: all the effect they produce is, to extend and diverſify the miſeries of the country; nor, in any of them that ever I heard of, is there, even in individuals, any ſuch diſplay of conduct, military talents, and heroiſm, as, independent of their effects, would render them intereſting. It is really wonderful, that the preſent civil war in Poland has called forth in that nation, no gallant ſpirits to draw upon themſelves particular attention, and to riſe above the general maſs of furious and fierce partizans. No ſupereminent abilities have appeared among them. How different have been the effects produced by the civil wars both in France and in England! On the frontiers of Ruſſia too you have the ſame uniform and ſhocking ſpectacle. You ſee in one quarter, parties of ſavage Tartars committing cruel depredations on New-Servia; and parties of no leſs ſavage Coſſacks, perpetrating bloody outrages in Wallachia and Beſſarabia. Fertile provinces rendered deſolate, towns and villages in flames; numerous herds of cattle rapaciouſly driven away; the inhabitants butchered, or carried into captivity, conſtitute the dreadful features of Ruſſian and Tartarian

Tartarian warfare. When you consider these things, I persuade myself you will not regret my disinclination, and indeed inability, to lay before you circumstantial details. One event, however, has happened on the eastern frontier, which may be of singular importance in the progress of the war. The Russians have taken possession of Asoph; and as it may be of great service in assisting them to carry on a naval war with their adversaries, they have employed a number of men in repairing the fortifications.

As far as I am able, I shall give you a more particular account of the motions and atchievements of the great armies under Prince Gallitzin and the Grand Vizir. The great Russian army, in the present campaign, seems to direct its chief operations against Moldavia. Perhaps, as this Province is contiguous to Poland, it may be the intention of the Empress to prevent, or cut off, as early as possible, any intercourse between the Turks and the Poles. Accordingly, Prince Gallitzin led his army, as soon as he was able, to the banks of the Neister, intending, by a sudden attack, to seize Chotzim, the frontier town. He crossed the river,

river, and on the thirtieth of April attacked an army of above twenty-five thousand Turks, in their entrenchments under the walls. They were defended by the artillery of the fortress. Caraman Pacha, who commanded them, made his cavalry charge the right wing of the Russians; but notwithstanding the valour of their attack, and the advantages of situation, the Turks were totally routed and driven out of their camp. General Ismaelof pursued them, and it is said, that the bloodshed, both in the battle and the pursuit, was very considerable. About the same time some considerable advantages were gained by Prince Prosorowsky over a detachment of the enemy, at no great distance from Chotzim. These successes you may be sure, and this happy commencement of the war, occasion much rejoicing in the capital. I heard Te Deum sung before the Empress in the Casan church, on account of them. Indeed, the issue of this war may be of great consequence, not only to the Russian empire, but to the Empress in particular. Her elevation to the throne was not auspicious; and there are, no doubt, many persons in the empire not yet reconciled to her government.

Many

Many of the nobility choose rather to reside at Moscow, than with the court at St. Petersburg. The Russians are in general fickle, and fond of change. The Great Duke will soon be of age, and it was understood by many, when the Empress was crowned, that when her son was old enough to reign, she was to resign. An unsuccessful foreign war tends to impair the authority of all despots; and this is the first foreign war she has ever waged. To her, therefore, in circumstances so particular, the issue of the war is of the greatest importance. Accordingly she exerts every effort; and, actuated in this manner, we are not to expect a languid, slow, and protracted contest, but a war of spirited and vigorous operation. The reduction of Chotzim, it is expected, will be the immediate consequence of Galitzin's victory; and in the mean time a considerable fleet is preparing at Cronstadt, to attempt some important stroke in the Mediterranean or Archipelago. One of the best officers in the Russian fleet, is Commodore Greig, a native of Fifeshire. His naval abilities are reckoned very great; yet that simplicity and modesty of deportment which usually accompany, and too

often

often veil, the most distinguished merit, may with a people, so fond of shew and glare as the Russians are, and so apt to judge of men, according as they seem to entertain a high opinion of themselves, keep out of sight for a time, and even lessen the value of his abilities. * * *

LETTER XIII.

Anecdotes of Count Munich.

Island of Caminioiostrow, July, 1769.

"ISLAND of Caminioiostrow," methinks I hear you repeat with terror, after observing the date of my letter, recollecting yourself, turning over to a map of Russia, and with an anxious eye looking towards Siberia. No occasion, my good friend, for your fears; I have not been guilty of treason, and am neither banished to the frozen Sea, nor to the borders of China. The place I write from, is an island in our river, where Lord C. and his family are to pass the weeks, you will observe I don't say months, of the summer.

It is indeed a delightful recess; distant no more than three miles from St. Petersburgh. It is the northmost of a numerous cluster

of

of iſlands formed in the mouth of the Neva, where it enters the gulph of Finland, and is joined to Peterſburſky iſland by a bridge of nine boats. It is ſcarcely two miles in length, and not more than half a mile broad. This, and all the neighbouring iſlands, and the banks of the river, are adorned with wood, chiefly with birch, which grows very tall and buſhy, and whoſe fine ſilver bark makes a beautiful contraſt with the deep verdure of the leaves. Our little iſle, for there are ſome much larger, is finely interſperſed with lawns and meadows; and its fields and ſhores are diverſified with a number of flowers. The wild flower, which ſeems to grow here in the greateſt abundance, is the lily of the valley. The river, branching out into many clear deep ſtreams, laves the green borders of the different iſlands: and the fragrance wafted from the trees, eſpecially in an evening, heightens the pleaſure of the ſcene. Nothing can be more agreeable than to row around this and the adjacent ſhores, in a fine morning, or in a moon-light night. The Ruſſian bargemen uſually ſing as they row; they ſing in choruſes;

rufes; the mufic is fometimes accompanied with a horn; and in the ftillnefs of the night, and, when heard at fome diftance, it has a folemn effect.

In this ifland is a fmall palace belonging to the great Duke, which Lord C. poffeffes during the fummer; and adjoining to it is a little garden, laid out with arched and gravel walks. It was built by Count Beftuchef, who was Chancellor during part of the reign of the late Emprefs. While he continued in favour, he was regarded as Prime Minifter, and the foremoft man in the empire. His door was daily befet with coaches; and all the nobility looked up to him, almoft as to their fovereign: his fmile conftituted their happinefs, and his frown their mifery. But having fallen into difgrace, he was inftantly ftripped of his honours, offices, and eftate; and was exiled into fome remote and inhofpitable corner of that empire which he formerly governed.

Oh how wretched
Is that poor man that hangs on princes' favours!
There is betwixt that fmile he would afpire to,
That fweet afpect of princes and his ruin,
More pangs and tears than war or women have;

And

And when he falls, he falls like Lucifer,
Never to hope again.

Reverſes of this ſort are not unuſual here, and in other countries that are governed by deſpots. In the life of no great man in this empire were they illuſtrated more remarkably, than in that of the famous Count Munich. The old age of this celebrated General was marked by ſome ſtriking circumſtances, which are not very generally known, and of which the following account may afford you ſome amuſement.

Count Munich was Prime Miniſter of Ruſſia, in the reign of the Empreſs Anna Ivanowna, and in that of her ſucceſſor Ivan; was condemned to ſuffer death by the Empreſs Elizabeth, but received a pardon on the ſcaffold; and, inſtead of being beheaded, was baniſhed into Siberia. Count Oſterman, his political rival, was to have ſuffered death at the ſame time, and in the ſame manner: he aſcended the ſcaffold; ſaw the axe and the executioner; committed his ſoul to heaven; laid his head upon the block; expected the deadly blow; was lifted up; had his eyes uncovered; and was told that the Empreſs had ſpared his life, but that he muſt go into baniſhment. One might aſk, whether, in this inſtance, mercy wore the vizor of cruelty, or cruelty the vizor of mercy?——The Counteſs Munich had the liberty of chooſing, either to accompany her huſband into a wild and dreary region in the north of Aſia; or to remain with her acquaintance and friends in Peterſburg. Without heſitation or reluctance ſhe choſe to follow her huſband.

The commanding officer of the fortreſs where the Count was confined, was ſtrictly enjoined to allow him no more than the mere neceſſaries of life; and was ordered to indulge him in no alleviation of his ſufferings. But, fortunately for Munich, the Officer had ſerved under him in the Turkiſh war, and was a perſon of a generous and humane diſpoſitions. Moved by veneration for his General, whom he had ſeen performing ſo many gallant exploits, and conceiving himſelf out of the reach of information, by his great diſtance from the capital, he did every thing in his power to ſoften the rigour of exile; and, among other indulgences, permitted him the

uſe

uſe of materials for writing, and to have ſome intercourſe with the inhabitants of the country. The Counteſs found amuſement, and pleaſure, and relief, during many ſolitary years, in inſtructing the children of the neighbouring peaſants. For this alleviation of her misfortune, ſhe was indebted to the ſame goodneſs of heart, that carried her from the gaiety of ſocial life into the midſt of a lonely deſart: for had ſhe been proud and ſelfiſh, ſhe could not have ſubmitted to, or been capable of, any ſuch employment; and muſt conſequently have been deprived of the comfort which it afforded her. Even the diſcharge of her duty to her huſband, and his affectionate gratitude, could not otherwiſe have preſerved her from pining. The Count found amuſement in the exerciſes of a well-regulated underſtanding; he employed himſelf in writing the memoirs of his life, and in drawing plans of ſieges and fortifications.

But theſe alleviations of their captivity were interrupted. A Ruſſian officer paſſing through the country, and ſtaying ſome days at the fortreſs, obſerved the liberty enjoyed by Munich, and had the ſingular inhumanity, on his return to St. Peterſburg, to inform Elizabeth of all he had ſeen. The diſpoſitions which led him to inform, led him alſo to exaggerate. He inſinuated, that the Count was plotting miſchief againſt the Empreſs, or againſt the ſtate: and that his plans and writings were not matter of mere amuſement. Accordingly, the friend of Munich was ſuddenly recalled, diveſted of his authority, and threatened with the puniſhment of treaſonable diſobedience. But the Count, in order to exculpate his benefactor, ſent all the papers he poſſeſſed, thoſe memoirs, and thoſe plans which were the objects of his affection, and his ſolace for many winters of diſmal ſolitude: he ſent them with the utmoſt readineſs to St. Peterſburg. This effort coſt him a grievous pang. They were burnt. But they were an oblation offered on the altar of grateful friendſhip; for he had the conſolation of learning, that they had been the means of preſerving his friend from rigorous puniſhment. He had not, however, the happineſs of ſeeing him return to Siberia.

On the acceſſion of Peter the Third he was relieved from his captivity; and, after an exile of of twenty-five years, was reſtored to his former honours. One of the firſt perſons he met with at Court, after his reſtoration, was his old enemy and rival Count Oſterman, who, as was above mentioned, had been exiled at the ſame time with himſelf, and was now alſo at Court, for the firſt time, ſince his recal. What, do you apprehend, were the ſentiments of theſe two remarkable men, on this extraordinary and unexpected meeting? They had been equally ambitious; had poſſeſſed ſimilar political abilities; had been engaged in the ſame purſuits; competitors for the ſame pre-eminence, and of courſe in violent oppoſition to each other: they had both been diſappointed, had ſuffered ſimilar puniſhment, and were now, after a long period, in the ſame manner, and at the ſame inſtant, releaſed. Would any remains of their old animoſity ſtill lurk in their boſoms, and ſtill darken their hearts? Or, rather, cured of the ambition which had formerly ſet them at variance, would they not regard one another with ſome complacency? Would they not feel as if they had met in heaven? And, deſpiſing the littleneſs of their former diſſenſions, would not the recollection unite their affections? Such, perhaps, would have been the tendency of their feelings, if the presence of so many spectators, who beheld them with gazing curiosity, had not impressed their minds with the dread of impropriety, and so restrained their emotions. The circumstances were indeed disagreeable; and the Emperor, by whose clemency they were restored, would have shewn a delicate, instead of a whimsical generosity, if he had prevented a situation so very painful. I am indeed persuaded, by the following anecdote, that if the heart of Munich had been allowed to flow unrestrained, it would have flowed in a full stream of complacency.—Soon after his return to St. Petersburg, the person who had so maliciously informed against the Officer who had shewn him so much attention in Siberia, sought an early opportunity of waiting upon him, threw himself at his feet, and craved his forgiveness. "Go," said the old man, "were my heart "like yours, perhaps I might seek for re- "venge; but as I am out of your reach you "have no reason to be afraid." An anecdote of the same kind is related of the Emperor Adrian. After his elevation to the imperial dignity, meeting a person who had formerly been his most inveterate enemy: "My good friend,"

friend," cried he, " you have eſcaped, for I " am Emperor."

Munich died not long after the acceſſion of Catharine the Second: and I have heard, that though much ſolicited, he would never accept of any marks of her favour. " I am an old " man," he would ſometimes ſay: " I have al- " ready ſuffered many misfortunes; and if I " purchaſed a few years of life by the proſtitu- " tion of my opinions, I ſhould make but a " bad exchange." He had, at the time of Peter's dethronement, given him ſome very ſpirited counſel: " Go forth," ſaid he, " put your- " ſelf at the head of the troops you have with " you, or go forth alone; addreſs the two " regiments that are marching againſt you: " Tell them you are their ſovereign, the " grandſon of Peter the Great; aſk them if " they have been aggrieved, and aſſure them " of full redreſs. I will forfeit my hoary " head, if they do not fling down their arms, " and fall proſtrate before you." But Peter was infatuated; would not follow his counſels; and was dethroned.---The preſent Empreſs ſhews every mark of regard and attention to the ſon and grandſons of Munich. Adieu.

LETTER XIV. (EXTRACT.)

Progress of the War.

June 1769.

***** I INFORMED you in my last political letter that we expected daily accounts of the reduction of Chotzim. This event, however, has not taken place. On the contrary, Galitzin has at present relinquished his attempt, and has repassed the Neister. This occasions a good deal of surprize; for people, who know not upon how many minute circumstances military operations very often depend, are ever sanguine in their expectations, and, in the ardour of their wishes, not only desire but expect, that every advantage shall be instantly followed by something still more marvellous and important.

I mentioned to you, that Prince Galitzin's design was to reduce Chotzim by a sudden assault.

ſault. But he was diſappointed by the dexterity of Caraman Pacha, who threw ſo great a part of his army into the place, that it was utterly impoſſible for the Ruſſians to proceed againſt it in the manner they intended; nor were they provided, it is ſaid, with artillery for proſecuting a regular ſiege. Add to this, that the Ruſſian army is by no means ſo numerous as the news-papers report. Beſides, the diſorders in Poland were riſing to ſuch a height, as perhaps made it neceſſary for the great Ruſſian army to give ſome attention to that quarter. That the Poles ſhould be particularly furious at preſent, is not merely to be accounted for by their hope of aſſiſtance from the Sultan, and the removal of ſome of the Ruſſian troops that were ſtationed among them, to the borders of Turkey; but from ſome late meaſures of the Ruſſian court.

The Empreſs, as was already mentioned, is actuated by many conſiderations, not to protract, but to proſecute the war with vigour. This principle appears, and throws itſelf out in a variety of operations: in conſequence of the general determination, it is applied in all caſes; and it is applied in ſome caſes that ought to have been excepted, and where it is not expedient. It is owing to this that the Empreſs iſſued a proclamation, and which produced a ſimilar declaration from Conſtantinople, allowing none of the Poles, in the preſent conteſt, to remain neuter; but to take part, in a decided and active manner, with one or other of the contending powers: and this of itſelf has thrown them into the greateſt ferment.--- From one or all of theſe cauſes, Prince Galitzin has found himſelf under the neceſſity of repaſſing the Neiſter. Nor is it unlikely that his outpoſts, and the detachments ſent from his army, either for proviſions, forage, or to reconnoitre the enemy, may have ſuſtained conſiderable loſſes. The Turks actually contend, that he has been compelled, by force of arms, to abandon the ſiege: and, according to every thing I can learn, the ſuperiority of the Turkiſh cavalry give them a decided advantage in all ſkirmiſhes, and on all occaſions, where the Ruſſian infantry is not engaged. * * * * *

LETTER XV.

Excurſion into Carelia.—State of the Finlanders.

DEAR SIR, July, 1769.

I AM juſt returned from a very agreeable excurſion into the province of Carelia. The appearance of the country at this ſeaſon is remarkably pleaſant. It riſes in little hills, and is a good deal covered with birch, fir, aller, and other trees. In the woods there are a number of hurtleberries, cranberries, and wild ſtrawberries. The ſoil is in general light and ſandy, and the country is diverſified with little green lawns, meadows, and corn-fields. I was ſurprized at the ſize of the graſshoppers; they are at leaſt an inch and a half in length. The houſes in the villages are conſtructed of wood; and the inhabitants of this country are chiefly Fins.

The

The Fins are neither ſo tall, nor ſo handſome as the Ruſſians. Their hair is light-coloured, and their complexions fair; ſo that though their children are very comely, the poorneſs of their diet, and the inclement weather to which they are ſo much expoſed, give them, when grown up to youth and manhood, even a miſerable appearance. Their language is totally different from that of the Ruſſians: being chiefly Lutherans, they are alſo of a different religion; and though all the ſubjects of this empire may be conſidered on an equal footing in regard to freedom, yet having been conquered by the Ruſſians, they are conſidered as their inferiors. They are accordingly treated with the utmoſt inſult and abuſe.

Nothing indeed can be more deplorable than the condition of a people reduced by, and conſtituting a part of another nation, but differing from them in language, cuſtoms and religion. Such differences will expoſe them to contempt; the contempt they meet with will in time make them deſerve it: treated with no reſpect by others who have power over them, they will loſe all ſenſe of character, and have no reſpect for themſelves: thus, not daring to expreſs their reſentment in a reſolute and manly manner, they will harbour ſentiments of latent malice; they will indulge ignominious vices; become mean, inſidious, and deceitful. Perhaps circumſtances of this ſort may account for the character of many modern Jews; and, ſo long as theſe circumſtances continue, they will always be a ſeparate people. ---On the diſperſion of that famous nation, many things concurred to keep them diſtinct from the other nations among whom they dwelt, and to render them even objects of their averſion. This was particularly the caſe in Europe. Among the European ſtates the manners and maxims of chivalry were about to commence: men ſubſiſted by war and agriculture; commerce and manufactures were not held in eſteem. But the Jews were neither proprietors of land, nor retainers on great men: they no longer made uſe of the ſword; and ſubſiſted neither by agriculture nor military depredation. Contemned and deteſted for their origin, their religion, their hatred of Chriſtianity, and their perſecution of its holy Author, they felt that they had no character to loſe, and betook themſelves for ſubſiſtence to ſuch employments as the Europeans deſpiſed. They

carned

earned a livelihood by traffic; and by ſuch occupations as among the Romans, and the northern nations who roſe on the ruins of Rome, were never practiſed but by the dregs of the people. This therefore added to the contempt and hatred of their condition; and contributed, by a correſponding proceſs, to render them really baſe and deſpicable. Perceiving and feeling that they were already hated and deſpiſed, they had not ſufficient fortitude to contend with, and overcome the miſerable influences of ſituation; they ſuffered themſelves to deſerve both contempt and averſion, and not only engaged in employments which were held diſhonourable, but acted diſhonourably in ſuch employments. They not only practiſed commerce, but were guilty of fraud. As Europe became civilized, they found that they were enabled, by their occupations, both to ſubſiſt and become wealthy. Their ſituation, therefore, however deſpiſed by the Gentiles, had conſiderable advantages, which compenſated for the contempt they ſuffered, and reconciled them to their condition. It ought alſo to be remarked, that the opportunity which fraud and deceit gave them of retaliating in ſome meaſure the injuries they underwent, as it it gratified their resentment, tended to darken their understandings, and hindered them from discerning the atrocity of their conduct.—Upon the whole, of this digression it may not be improper to remark, that those who enjoy pre-eminence, and treat their inferiors with contempt, merely on account of difference of situation, trespass against the interests of society, by compelling men to become worthless. It may also be mentioned, that as situations of this sort are of such powerful, as well as of such malignant influence, if there are persons who, in defiance of them, assert the dignity of human nature by the inflexible dignity of their own conduct, they do honour to the species.

In returning from my excursion I saw some very beautiful landskips. Travelling through a thin wood of birch and aller, I had a fine view to the south of the Gulph of Finland, bounded by Æsthonia, which presented the palaces of Peterhoff and Oranibaum, and was diversified by a number of vessels that lay at anchor. Towards the east was a green and bushy wilderness; the numerous islands of the Neva adorned with wood; the river flowing around them in different channels; and the gilded or painted ſpires of the city riſing, as it were, from the midſt of a foreſt. The ſun ſetting bright in the weſt, and pouring a blaze of radiance on the gulph, heightened in a remarkable manner the beauty of the landſkip. I went into a barge at the mouth of the Neva; the courſe of the ſtream was perfectly ſmooth; the banks and borders of the fragrant and green iſlands, as I was rowed along, were for ever changing their appearance; and the bargemen ſtruck their oars according to the cadences of their vocal concert. The moon, ſhining over the whole with temperate but unclouded radiance, rendered the ſcene very ſoft and ſolemn.

Adieu.

LETTER XVI. (EXTRACT.)

Fables translated from the German of LESSING.

**** AMONG those in St. Petersburg who seek amusement in reading, I find that German literature is much in fashion. Indeed many German authors have distinguished themselves of late, not only by their learning and depth of philosophical research, but by elegance of composition, and the graces of fine writing. They seem particularly fond of fables: there is a simplicity in their language which is well suited to that species of composition; and two of their fabulists, Lessing and Gellert, the one in verse, and the other in prose, have risen to very high reputation. With Gellert you are already acquainted; and of Lessing's inventive talents, you will perhaps agree with me, that the following translations of his fifth and fifty-fourth fables are no unfavourable specimens.

JUPITER *and the* HORSE. A Fable.

[Translated from the German of Lessing.]

"Father of men and beasts!" said the Horse, approaching the throne of Jupiter, "it is
"said of me, that I am one of the most beau-
"tiful animals with which thou hast adorned
"the world; and self-love inclines me to be-
"lieve the character just: yet in some par-
"ticulars, my appearance might admit of
"improvement."

"Of what kind? Inform me. I am will-
"ing to receive instruction," said the Father of all, and smiled.

"I would probably run better," replied the Steed, "if my legs were longer, and more
"slender; a neck like a swan would be more
"becoming; a wider chest would improve my
"strength; and, since thou hast ordained me
"to carry thy darling, Man, might I not have
"a natural saddle growing upon my back, in-
"stead

" ſtead of that with which the well-meaning
" rider confines me."

" Have patience," reſumed the God; and with an awful voice, pronounced his creative word *. Life darted into the duſt; inert matter became alive; organized members were formed; they were joined in one conſiſtent body; and, before the throne, aroſe—the hideous Camel! The Horſe ſhuddered, and ſhook with horror.

" See," ſaid Jupiter, " longer and more
" ſlender legs; a neck like that of a ſwan;
" a large cheſt, and a natural ſaddle. Would
" you chuſe to have *ſuch* a ſhape?"---The Horſe quaked with extreme averſion.

" Go," continued the God, " take counſel
" from this event; be henceforth ſatisfied with
" your condition; and, in order to remind you
" of the warning you have now received"---ſo ſaying he caſt on the Camel a † preſerving look, " Live," ſaid he, " new inhabitant of

* Sparch das wort der ſchoepfung.
† Warf cinen erhaltenden blick.

" the world! and may the Horſe never ſee thee
" but with trembling averſion!"

The SHE-GOATS. A FABLE.

[Tranſlated from the German of LESSING.]

The She-goats requeſted Jupiter to give them horns; for in the beginning they had none. But the God deſired them to think better of their requeſt, and to confide in the care he had of them; for that along with horns, they might be obliged, perhaps, to receive ſome diſagreeable appendage. They perſiſted in their demand. They received horns---and a beard; for in the beginning they had none. What vexation they felt for theſe filthy beards! more vexation than joy for their fooliſh horns.

LETTER XVII.

Progreſs of the War.—Retreat of the Ruſſians from Chotzim.

DEAR SIR,

SINCE the laſt accounts I gave you of the war in Moldavia ſeveral events have happened, at firſt favourable, but now unfavourable, to the Ruſſians.

Prince Galitzin, with his army conſiderably ſtrengthened, returned to the Neiſter; croſſed that river on the 13th of July, and fell unexpectedly on a Turkiſh army in the neighbourhood of Chotzim. He gained a complete victory; and of conſequence renewed the ſiege, or blockade, which he had formerly been obliged to relinquiſh. I need not enter into a minute account of the circumſtances of the battle. Suffice it to ſay upon the whole, that in all general engagements, where the ſtreſs of the conflict depends on infantry and artillery, the numbers and impetuous valour of the Turks, their ſabres and horſes, are not a match for the ſteady diſcipline of European armies. Indeed, there ſeems to have been great miſconduct in the Turkiſh officers, in ſuffering themſelves to be ſurpriſed ; and we are told, in confirmation of this, that Caraman Pacha beheaded the Seraſkier who commanded that army.

Meantime the great Turkiſh army, commanded by Meſauge Pacha the Grand Vizir, advanced from the Danube, and took poſt at different places between that river and the Neiſter. The ſlowneſs of this General's operations has occaſioned more uneaſineſs at St. Peterſburg, than if he had advanced with confident and impetuous ardour. He is reported to be a man of comprehenſive and ſteady underſtanding. He is ſenſible that want of diſcipline is the great defect of his army. He therefore protracts his operations, in order that his ſoldiers may be properly trained, and reduced to regular ſubordination. He is alſo ſenſible, that more harm may be done the Ruſſians by haraſſing them, and by attacking the detachments, than by engaging them in a pitched battle. By this Fabian conduct, he has already rendered eſſential ſervice to the Sultan. For although ſome troops were defeated, that attempted in the beginning of Auguſt to throw ſupplies into Chotzim; yet his detachments in other quarters have been ſo ſucceſsful, and the Ruſſian army is ſo much weakened, and ſo much alarmed, that they have again raiſed the ſiege, and repaſſed the Neiſter. But this they were not able to effectuate without conſiderable loſs. Their loſſes, however, have been greatly exaggerated; and if I am not miſinformed, the regular troops in Prince Galitzin's army were not much more than the numbers that, according to ſome accounts, were ſaid to have been ſlain.

Theſe things have flattened our ſpirits. The people are beginning to murmur. Rumours of conſpiracies are ſecretly propagated; ſeveral perſons, I have heard, either guilty or ſuſpected of treaſon, have diſappeared: but theſe things are not noiſed abroad, they are only mentioned in confidential whiſpers. The people are prohibited from ſpeaking or writing about politics. The Empreſs tells them, that as her maternal care for her dear people her ſleepleſs by night, and buſy by day;—and I really believe that her nights are as ſleepleſs as her days are buſy:—they have no occaſion to give themſelves any further trouble about public affairs, than to act implicitly as ſhe directs; and, in order the more effectually to ſave her dear people from unneceſſary labour, ſhe not only exhorts, but actually forbids them to ſpeak, write, or think politics. The ſpies are buſy: the ſuſpected great men are cloſely watched: For,

> Not a Thane of them, but in his houſe
> She has a ſervant fee'd.

Happy king of England! who may go about with as much ſecurity after a defeat, as after a victory; who has no occaſion for a board of ſpies againſt his own ſubjects; and may allow his people to ſpeak, write, and think as they pleaſe.

Among other changes, which, it is ſaid, will take place in the Ruſſian armies, Prince Galitzin is to be recalled, and the chief command given to Count Romanzoff. General Panin, brother to the Prime Miniſter, is to command an army near Bender, and the mouths

mouths of the Danube. Both Panin and Romanzoff have the reputation of great military talents; and the firſt, for I have not ſeen the laſt, has indeed a very bold, blunt, military countenance; very different from the ſmooth ſmiling aſpect of the Prime Miniſter. Theſe changes may be for the public good; yet ſome court-intereſt and intrigue may have helped them forward. Count Romanzoff's mother is much regarded at court; ſo alſo is his ſiſter, the Counteſs Bruce. You will be ſurpriſed at the name. Count Bruce is the deſcendant of a Scots gentleman of that name, who came into Ruſſia after the diſcomfiture of the Scots by Oliver Cromwell; and who, having recommended himſelf to the good graces of the court, married a Ruſſian lady, and was advanced to conſiderable honours. A gentleman, named Hamilton, who came in the ſame ſhip with Bruce, paſſed into Sweden; and, in the laſt war, his deſcendant, Count Hamilton, commanded the Swediſh army in Pomerania.

A fleet of ſeven ſail of the line, and ſome frigates, having with them a conſiderable number of land-forces, and under the command

mand of Admiral Elphinſton, will ſet out, very ſoon, on an expedition into the Mediterranean. The Admiral is a Captain in the Britiſh navy: and, among other important ſervices, conducted the Britiſh fleet through the Straits of Bahama, when the Engliſh, in the laſt war, invaded Cuba. Admiral Spiridoff, with a conſiderable force, ſailed ſome time ago.

LETTER XVIII.

Progress of the War.—A Russian Pasquinade.

"Those whom the gods distinguish by their hate,
"They first confound, and then resign to fate."

October 17, 1769.

I Mentioned to you the prudent conduct of Messauge Pacha, the Grand Vizir; and his plan of wasting the Russian army in small conflicts, rather than of hazarding a general action. I also informed you of his success; and that his adversaries, in a very shattered condition, had again retreated into Poland. But his measures did not meet with the approbation, nor he himself with the recompence, which such ability merited. He was disliked by his army; so little qualified are soldiers to judge of the merits or demerits of a commander. The strictness of his discipline was ill suited to their licentiousness and irregularity. Accordingly, complaints were brought against

againſt him at Conſtantinople, and they were liſtened to with the greater readineſs, that the deliberate ſlowneſs of his operations by no means correſponded with the ſanguine expectations and impetuoſity that reigned in the councils of the Sultan. He was accordingly recalled from Moldavia, and beheaded; and Moldovani Ali Pacha, the new Grand Vizir, was promoted to the chief command.

The meaſures of Moldovani have been violent and precipitate. He has not only put to death Caraman Pacha, but has loſt all the advantages gained by the prudent conduct of his predeceſſor; and has brought ſuch ruin on the Turkiſh army under his command, as may contribute, by its conſequences, to decide the fate of the war.—Prince Galitzin returned again to the banks of the Neiſter. The Grand Vizir, with a prodigious army, was poſted in the neighbourhood of Chotzim. He immediately determined to attack his opponents; but the troops, which he ſent to the other ſide of the river for that purpoſe, at two different times, and who exerted themſelves with obſtinate valour, ſuffered total diſcomfiture. He ſtill perſiſted in his raſh deſign; and laid one large bridge, in place of three, which he had formerly used, across the river. Upon this he sent over twelve thousand men: they were to be followed by the rest of the army; but before the junction could be made, a dreadful tempest arose; the river was swelled to a prodigious height; the bridge was swept away; and the Turks that had crossed the river fell a prey to the Russians. Whether or not any terms of capitulation were offered them, I have not heard; if there were, they were not accepted. The Russians attacked them with unrelenting fury: and thus, in sight of the Vizir and his army, who must have suffered on this occasion the most excruciating torment, as they were unable to give them any assistance; and in sight, I believe, of Chotzim, the finest troops in the Turkish army were cut in pieces. The garrison of Chotzim, and the rest of the Vizir's forces, after the first transports of their rage, gave way to terror and consternation. They deserted the fortress, fled from their encampment, and made the best of their way to the Danube. Thus the Russians are become masters of Moldavia and Walachia; and have finished the campaign with honour.

Still,

Still, however, the nomination of Count Romanzoff to the command of the grand army continues. Prince Galitzin returns to court; and will be received with every mark of diſtinction. Yet that his conduct is not approved of, is abundantly manifeſt, and the following Paſquinade, which has been allowed to circulate, even ſince the reduction of Chotzim, will ſhew you ſufficiently how he ſtands with the public. It will alſo ſhew you with what licentiouſneſs and ſeverity the Ruſſians, if they were allowed, would indulge themſelves in political ſatire.

"Prince Galitzin having been obliged to "retreat from Chotzim, found himſelf much "embarraſſed. One night he was ſo anxious "he could not ſleep. He roſe, dreſſed him- "ſelf, and heard two perſons ſpeaking at the "door of his tent. An old Soldier was tell- "ing his dream to the centinel. I dreamed, "ſaid he, that I was in a battle; that my "head was cut off; conſequently that I died; "and conſequently went to heaven. I knock- "ed at the door. Peter came with a bunch "of keys, and made ſo much noiſe, that he "wakened God, who came in great haſte,

"and

" and enquired what was the matter? Why, " ſays Peter, there is a great war upon earth, " between the Ruſſians and the Turks. And " who, ſaid the Supreme Being, commands " the Ruſſians? Count Munich, replied the " Saint. Then, ſaid God, I may go and ſleep. " I wakened, ſaid the old Soldier; but fell " aſleep, and dreamed again. The circum- " ſtances of the ſecond dream were preciſely " the ſame with thoſe of the firſt, excepting " that the war in which I fancied myſelf en- " gaged, was not that of Count Munich, but " that which we are now waging. According- " ly, when God aſked Peter, who commanded " the Ruſſians? the Saint told him, It was " Prince Galitzin. Then, ſaid God, get me " my boots, for now they need me.—In a " ſhort time after, the Turkiſh bridge over " the Neiſter was ſwept away by a flood."

LETTER XIX. (Extract.)

With ſome Verſes.

*** THE following lines were written during my ſtay in the iſland of Caminioioſtrow. The fine weather, the agreeable ſituation, and the delightful ſcenery around the banks of the Neva, provoked my old propenſity to rhiming. I thought it was at an end; but you know what Horace ſays, about inclinations that are either natural, or by indulgence rendered habitual.

TO A YOUNG LADY*,

With ſome Flowers.

To thee, ſweet ſmiling maid, I bring
The beauteous progeny of ſpring:
In every breathing bloom I find
Some pleaſing emblem of thy mind.

* Now V——ſs of S———t.

The blushes of that opening rose
Thy tender modesty disclose.
These snow-white lilies of the vale
Diffusing fragrance to the gale,
No ostentatious tints assume,
Vain of their exquisite perfume;
Careless, and sweet, and mild, we see
In them a lovely type of thee.
In yonder gay-enamel'd field,
Serene that azure blossom smil'd:
Not changing with the changeful sky,
Its faithless tints inconstant fly;
For, unimpair'd by winds and rain,
I saw th' unalter'd hue remain.
So were thy mild affections prov'd,
Thy heart by Fortune's frown unmov'd,
Pleas'd to administer relief,
In times of woe would solace grief.
These flowers with genuine beauty glow;
The tints from Nature's pencil flow:
What artist could improve their bloom?
Or sweeter make their sweet perfume?
Fruitless the vain attempt. Like these
Thy native truth, thine artless ease,
Fair, unaffected maid, can never fail to please.

LETTER XX.

The Funeral of the Princeſs Kurakin.

DEAR SIR, Nov. 13, 1769.

THERE are, as you apprehend, ſome circumſtances of a very extraordinary nature in the funeral ceremony of the Ruſſians; and I think the beſt method of telling you what they are, is to deſcribe the funeral of the Princeſs Kurakin, of which I was this day a witneſs.

The proceſſion ſet out at ten in the morning from the little Millione, for the burial-place in the Monaſtery of St. Alexander Newſkey, about two miles from St. Peterſburg. All the ſtreets and the road by which it was to paſs, were ſtrewed with green twigs, chiefly of yew. It was preceded by a band of ſinging boys, who ſung hymns, and chanted portions of the funeral ſervice; and who were followed

followed by about twenty inferior priests, attendants on the dignified clergy. The Bishop of St. Petersburg, accompanied with Archimandrites, and other Priests of higher orders, walked immediately before the hearse. They had mitres on their heads, were arrayed in costly dresses, and carried tapers in their hands. The hearse, which was not covered, as in Britain, was drawn by six horses. The coffin was covered with pink-coloured velvet, and adorned with silver ornaments; but had no pall laid over it. The chief mourners walked behind, and other friends and relations followed in mourning coaches. Before they reached the Monastery, the Bishop left the procession, which came on slowly, and got before them into the church. There he put on such pieces of raiment as were customary on such occasions; and performed such parts of the service as were usually performed previous to the arrival of the procession.

When the funeral reached the gate of the Monastery, the Bishop, attended with the Monks and Priests, went out to meet and conduct it to the place of interment. A platform, two steps in height, about six feet in length, and four in breadth, covered with crimſon-velvet fringed with gold, was raiſed in the outward diviſion of the church. Upon this the coffin was placed; and on bringing it into the church, all the ſervants and female attendants of the deceaſed raiſed a moſt dolorous lamentation, wringing their hands, beating their breaſts, tearing their hair, and crying ſo as effectually to drown the voices of the choiriſters. Meantime thoſe who had tapers in their hands, lighted them: and ſix large wax-candles, which ſtood in candleſticks around the dead body, were alſo lighted. The monks were arranged on one ſide of the place before the altar, and the choiriſters on the other. The Biſhop ſat in a chair covered with velvet, in the middle of the church, ſurrounded by deacons and attendants. Others lifted the lid from the coffin, covering the corpſe with a pall of cloth of gold, on which was embroidered a ſilver croſs; and folding it back, diſplayed the dead body lying on a bed of white ſattin. The head, with the face uncovered, and dreſſed in a cloſe coeffure, very richly adorned with lace, lay on a white ſattin pillow. The features were elegant, but the colour was gone; the eyes and lips cloſed;

the

the ſmiles and graces were flown for ever. The body was dreſſed in white ſattin, and the hands, covered with white gloves, were laid acroſs the breaſt.

The Biſhop now performed maſs, with all the uſual ceremonies of ſinging, praying, ſcattering incenſe, carrying about the bread and wine, the goſpels, and the crucifix. This laſted a conſiderable time; and the Biſhop's ſeat being then removed to the head of the coffin, he took his ſtation there, while twelve perſons, in black ſacerdotal habits, with lighted tapers in their hands, arranged themſelves around the dead body. After the burial ſervice, which was indeed very ſolemn, the Biſhop ſtanding up, pronounced a few ſentences in a kind of deep-toned grave recitative. He was anſwered in the ſame manner by a Prieſt on his right, and he by another on the left; and ſo on, by all thoſe that ſtood around the coffin. This part of the ceremony was very ſtriking; and, indeed, very noble. When this was ended, a Prieſt (the Princeſs's confeſſor, as I was told) delivered a ſcroll of paper to the Biſhop, who read it aloud, and returned it to the confeſſor, who, with ſilent and reverential demeanour, put it into the right hand of the deceased. The priests and monks returned to their former position; and then all the friends and relations, both male and female, but chiefly the last, with loud howling, weeping, and lamentation, gathered around the dead body, kissed the hands and forehead, and with a sorrow expressed with too much violence to produce sympathy, took leave of their departed friend. This part of the ceremony, including the preceding hymn, chanted by the Priests, is termed the Aspasmus, or Last Embrace.

When this was over, which was not suddenly, the coffin was lifted up, the platform removed from beneath, and a vault discovered under it, into which the body was let down. The Bishop then advanced, pronounced a short prayer, and threw some earth into the vault. It was then closed: the mourners withdrew, and thus the ceremony was concluded.——I need not add, that the parade was excessive; and the lamentation so loud, as totally to destroy the pleasing melancholy, and the disposition to solemn thought, which such ceremonies ought to produce. I was,

was, however, ſo much pleaſed with the hymn pronounced at the laſt embrace, that I ſhall endeavour to havé it tranſlated, and if ſo, I ſhall tranſmit you a copy. I am,

Yours, &c.

LETTER XXI.

The Hymn chanted at the Aſpaſmus, or Laſt Embrace.

DEAR SIR,

AGREEABLY to my promiſe I ſend you a tranſlation of the Hymn recited by the Prieſts or Monks, for I don't juſt recollect which they were, who, according to the cuſtom of the Greek church in the burial of the dead, ſtand around the coffin previous to the Laſt Embrace. I have been informed that it was written originally in Greek, by the famous Joannes Damaſcenus; and was tranſlated from him, for the uſe of the Ruſſian church, into the Sclavonian, the dialect uſed in this country in acts of religious worſhip. It is divided into ſtanzas ſuited to the method of recitation.

I.

Come hither, brethren, let us worſhip God, and pay our laſt duty to the deceaſed.

No longer mindful of vanity, or the cares of the flesh, he hath forsaken his kindred, and approacheth the grave. Where are kindred and friends! We are now separated from one another—May the Lord grant him repose!

II.

O brethren! what painful separation, what lamentation and wailing accompany this mournful hour! Approach.—Embrace him who was lately one of ourselves. Delivered up to the grave; covered with a stone, he must dwell in darkness, and be buried among the dead. Now, friends and kindred! we are separated from him! May the Lord grant him repose!

III.

Every wicked connection with life and vanity is dissolved. The spirit hath forsaken her cottage. The clay is disfigured: the vessel broke. We carry a motionless, insensible corps to the grave, intreating the Lord to grant him eternal rest.

IV.

Oh what is life! a blossom! a vapour! or dew of the morning! Approach therefore,

fore, and with attention contemplate the grave. Where now is the graceful form! Where is youth! Where are the organs of ſight! And where the beauty of complexion! They are withered like ſtubble. Approach, and weeping worſhip God.

V.

What lamentation and wailing, and mourning, and ſtruggling, when the ſoul is ſeparated from the body! Hades and perdition are then diſcloſed. Human life ſeems altogether vanity; a tranſient ſhadow; the ſleep of error; the unavailing labour of imagined exiſtence. Let us therefore fly from every corruption of the world, that we may inherit the kingdom of heaven.

VI.

Looking upon the deceaſed, let us meditate on our latter end. Like a thin vapour riſing from the earth, he vaniſhed: like a flower, he decayed: like graſs he was cut down; arrayed in periſhing apparel, he is laid in the duſt. Intreat Chriſt to grant repoſe unto him whom ye are now leaving, and ſhall no longer behold.

VII. Come

VII.

Come hither, O deſcendants of Adam! and ſee humbled in the ground a man reſembling ourſelves; diveſted of all comelineſs, ſoon to be conſumed in the grave; to periſh in darkneſs, and crumble into duſt. Intreat Chriſt to grant repoſe unto him whom ye are now leaving, and ſhall no longer behold.

VIII.

When the ſpirit is raviſhed from the body by awful angels, kindred and acquaintance are all forgot; the future judgment engageth our attention; for the vain purſuits and fruitleſs labour of the fleſh are then at an end. Supplicating the Judge, let us beſeech him to forgive the ſins of the deceaſed.

IX.

Come hither, brethren, let us view the duſt and aſhes of which ye are moulded. Whither are we going; and what ſhall we become? Who is poor; or who is rich? Who is the maſter; or who is free? Are not all

aſhes?

ashes? The beauty of the countenance hath faded, for death blasts the blossom of youth.

X.

All the pleasures and dignities of life are vain and perishing: We are all decaying, and shall die. Kings and princes, judges and potentates, the rich and the poor, all are mortal. Those formerly numbered among the living, lie lifeless in their graves. To whom may Jesus accord repose!

XI.

All the members of the body are now rendered motionless: very lately they were active and full of vigour: now they are rendered weak. The eyes are closed; the feet are bound; the hands at rest; the sense of hearing extinct; and the tongue locked up in silence. All are delivered up to the grave: All human things are vain.

XII.

Thou Mother of the Sun that never sets, Parent of God, we beseech thee intercede with thy divine offspring, that he who hath departed ed hence, may enjoy repoſe with the ſouls of the juſt. Unblemiſhed Virgin, may he enjoy the eternal inheritance of heaven in the abodes of the righteous.——Doxology.

Words ſuppoſed to expreſs the ſentiments of the deceaſed, ſpoken by the Chief Prieſt:

"Brethren, friends, kinſmen, and acquaintance! View me now, and lament. It was but yeſterday that we converſed together; for the fearful hour of death hath ſurpriſed me. Come here all who tenderly loved or eſteemed me, and with a laſt embrace pronounce the laſt farewell. No longer ſhall I ſojourn among you: No longer bear a part in your diſcourſe: I go to the Judge who hath no reſpect of perſons. The maſter and the ſervant, the ſovereign and the ſubject, the rich and the poor, are here upon a level: for according to their deeds ſhall they be glorified or put to ſhame. Therefore let me entreat and beſeech you all, intercede with Jeſus who is God, that I may not receive the puniſhment due to my guilt, but that he may eſtabliſh me in the light of life."

The

The following additional Stanzas are uſed at the burial of a Prieſt; they appear to me more ſtriking and more pathetic than the former.

I.

Be ſtill! be ſtill! let the departed reſt in peace. Meditate this awful myſtery. 'Tis an hour of terror! be ſtill! Let the ſpirit depart in peace. It begins the tremendous trial, and with much trembling deprecates the Almighty.

II.

Whether have the ſpirits of the deceaſed departed? Or what is their lot? How I long to learn their condition. But 'tis a myſtery which none can reveal. Like mortals do they remember their friends? Are they for ever unmindful of the mourners? of thoſe who bewail their departure, and celebrate their obſequies with ſorrow?

III.

The ſlaves of ungoverned paſſions enjoy no repoſe in the grave: formidable accuſers are

are there, and there the books are opened. Where wilt thou look for ſuccour, O man, or who will maintain thy cauſe; unleſs thy conduct in life was upright, unleſs thy bounty relieved the poor.

IV.

Haſt thou pitied the afflicted, O man? in death thou ſhalt be pitied. Haſt thou conſoled the orphan? the orphan will deliver thee. Haſt thou clothed the naked? The naked will procure thee protection.

I could ſend you tranſlations of ſome other parts of the funeral ceremony. But you will probably be ſatisfied with what you have.

I mentioned that the funeral ceremony of the Princeſs Kurakin was performed in the Monaſtery of St. Alexander Newſkey. This Saint was formerly a Sovereign of the Ruſſias, and was canonized, not ſo much for his Chriſtian virtues, as for his military atchievements. His exploits, indeed, were in defence of his country againſt the Swedes or Finns, and are engraved on a magnificent ſilver ſhrine within the monaſtery. In the neighbourhood of

5

of St. Peterſburg, at leaſt, he is ſo highly re-vered, as to have become a formidable rival to St. Nicholas. Perhaps, it is becauſe his greateſt actions were performed upon the banks of the Neva; and that the church and monaſtery, conſecrated to him, are very mag-nificent, and happen to be placed in a conſpi-cuous ſituation. The adjoining walks, woods, and garden, are extremely pleaſant, and even romantic.

P. S. I mentioned to you, that, after recit-ing the Hymn previous to the Laſt Embrace, a Prieſt put a ſcroll of paper into the right hand of the deceaſed. This has ſometimes been ludi-crouſly repreſented as a paſſport to be deliver-ed to St. Peter. The following, however, has been given me * as an exact tranſlation of the ſcroll above mentioned, and ſhews the in-juſtice of that account.

The Prayer, Hope, and Declaration of a Chriſtian Soul in the Faith.

" Every God-glorifying, orthodox chriſt-ian, having lived and honoured this hope, de-clares the following: and when he is dead,

* By the Reverend Dr. King, author of a learned account of the Rites and Ceremonies of the Greek Church.

whoever

whoever is willing, may piously put this declaration into the hand of the deceased when in the coffin.

All-creative, Omnipotent God the Father, God the Son, and God the Holy Ghost, in Three Persons, but one Godhead, substance, and essence: incessantly praised by all creatures, who, by thy holy will, foreknowledge, immeasurable goodness, and inexpressible wisdom, didst create all things visible in the world; thou didst create also me thy servant, to glorify thee, O Lord my God! to sing thy holy name; gratefully to thank thee for all thy mercy, and to endeavour, by all virtues, to attain thy everlasting kingdom. But, O, Divine Trinity! I have sinned against thee; have offended thy holiness; have broken thy commandments; and have not preserved, as I ought, thy image and likeness existing within me. I have defiled my soul and body by all manner of sins; and by wicked actions have moved thee to wrath. But though I have been dazzled with the vanities of the world, yet, O Lord! I have not cast myself wholly from thee, my Creator, my life, my joy, my salvation, and hope. And now, my life limited

mited by thy power, I willingly resign. My soul separates itself from my corruptible body; goes into immortality; and if it seem good unto thee, shall with this body arise again; which I hope for from thy goodness and mercy, according to the faith of our holy religion, and because thou didst suffer for our salvation. Yet I am terrified with fear, lest the torments of the wicked be inflicted upon me, for the sins which I have committed against thee. Wherefore, O Immortal King, and my God! with this my last breath I pray unto thee, that thou wouldst forgive all the sins I have committed from my youth up to this time; for thou art my God and my Creator; I believe in thee; I hope in thee; by thy righteous judgment save me, O Lord! and vouchsafe unto me thy kingdom. Thou who for us men became Jesus Christ, to deliver us from sin; by thy power I was born, and brought up in the wisdom of the only holy Eastern Church. And I pray thee, O Lord! consider not my sins; but grant me absolution in presence of the immaculate Virgin Mary, the Mother of God. Free from doubt, I come unto thee, O God! and at the sepa-

ſeparation of my ſoul into all ſpace from the body, receive, O Lord! my ſpirit into thy hands, and according to thy mercy, revive me in the evangelic beatitude, for ever and ever. Amen!

LETTER XXII. (Extract.)

The Library belonging to the Academy.—Reliques of Peter the Great.

* * * * THE Library belonging to the Academy is a large building, containing ſeveral rooms and galleries. It is furniſhed with about thirty thouſand volumes. The books are in bad order; nor are they very valuable. The collection, however, of Ruſs tranſlations of French, Engliſh, and German authors is conſiderable.— Among ſome books in the Engliſh language I found ſeveral political tracts, maintaining the abſolute and indefeaſible right of Kings.—— They had been brought to Ruſſia by Dr. Areſkine.

In one gallery is depoſited a numerous collection of Chineſe dreſſes, coins, and utenſils; together with a number of Chineſe and Tartarian

tarian manuſcripts. I was alſo ſhewn a number of Kamſhatkadale curioſities; and, among others, two waxen figures, as large as the life, repreſenting two Kamſhatkadale ſorcerers. They were accoutred as in the exerciſe of their profeſſion; and had hanging around them a number of iron rings. They had in their hands a ſort of muſical inſtrument reſembling a drum.

In another gallery are a number of reliques of Peter the Great; his walking-ſtick, models of ſhips executed with his own hands; and indeed ſuch a variety of different things, as leſſen their value as reliques. What pleaſed me moſt was a waxen figure of that great man, as large as the life, and made to reſemble him as much as poſſible. He is repreſented ſitting, dreſſed in regimentals, and having on his head an old hat without lace. In one of the cocks of his hat is a large hole, ſaid to have been made by a bullet at the battle of Pultowa. His countenance is ſtrangely expreſſive of thoughtful, but fierce, dignity.

The remains of Peter lie in a church within the caſtle. They are contained in a marble cheſt, inſcribed with his name, and covered with green velvet embroidered with gold. Near them are the remains of ſome other ſovereigns; and near them alſo are ſome of the horſetails and ſtandards taken from the Turks in the laſt campaign. The caſtle is ſituated in a ſmall iſland, oppoſite to the winter palace, and ſurrounded by the greateſt branch of the Neva. * * *

LETTER XXIII.

Tranſlation of a German Poem.

DEAR SIR,

I Mentioned to you, I believe, in a former letter, that German literature was faſhionable in Ruſſia. Indeed the Germans have of late beſtowed conſiderable attention on thoſe kinds of compoſition which are intended to amuſe: and the ſucceſs of their poets, in particular, has, in many inſtances, been very conſpicuous. An elegiac poem, by a young Luſatian, was lately put into my hands: and pleaſed me ſo much, that I have endeavoured to preſerve its beauties in an Engliſh tranſlation. Judge of it: yet I am ſenſible of my doing a bold thing in offering it to *your* peruſal. I have alſo prefixed the author's prefatory note, becauſe it throws ſome light both on the deſign of the poem and the mind of the poet. It ſeems to me as if the firſt part of the performance were dictated by feeling; and the ſecond by a ſenſe of duty. But concerning a work with which I have taken ſo much pains, I am as little entitled, or even qualified, to ſpeak, as the author himſelf. The meaſure in the tranſlation is the ſame as in the original. * * * * * *

ABIRAN;

OR, THE

VICTIM OF FANCIED WOE.

(*N. B.* That "man is born to ſorrow, as the ſparks fly upward," is proved by daily obſervation, and too often by daily experience. The *real* miſeries of human life are numerous: but as if theſe were not enough, men *create* miſeries to themſelves. They ſuffer their fancies to afflict them, when fortune and outward circumſtances, according to the uſual eſtimate of human enjoyments, are not unfavourable. It is ſtrange they ſhould not oppoſe a propenſity ſo adverſe to their happineſs, and apparently ſo unreaſonable; yet ſuch is too often the condition of many an amiable and excellent character. It may indeed happen, that perſons incapable of enormous vice, and having never ſuffered very heavy calamity, may, however, have met with *ſome* affliction, and

may

may *not* have endured it with ſuitable firmneſs. But this is not ſufficient to account for the appearance. Together with, or independent of ſuch ſituation, their feelings are occaſioned chiefly by their having taſtes too refined for the objects in which they are converſant; and in their having deſires for a certain elevated ſpecies of happineſs, which, though it may ſeem paradoxical to ſay ſo, they do not fully conceive. They are even ſenſible of the agreeable circumſtances in which they may happen to be placed; yet wiſhing for ſomething ſtill finer and more perfect, their enjoyments are incomplete. Nay, they loſe all reliſh for the good things in their power. They muſt therefore complain: What elſe can they do? or cheriſh their griefs in ſecret. They can do more. They can have recourſe to religion: in compliance with its dictates, they may do all the good they can in the meanwhile: they may thus look forward to a future period, when pleaſures, more exquiſite than they now feel or imagine, ſhall be annexed to every virtuous exertion; and may thus aſſure themſelves of that happineſs, which, by a wonderful anticipation, in their preſent ſtate not knowing,

they

they yet desire. Though this should be termed delusion, very barbarous is he who would deprive the poor sufferer of its soft consolation.

The following verses are intended as a representation of such imaginary, though the author confesses himself loth to call it unreal, suffering: the cause may be *imaginary*; but the suffering is *real:* and as the great object of poetical imitation is human nature, perhaps there may be some readers to whom this particular aspect of the human mind may not be uninteresting This however depends on the execution of the thing designed, no less than on the design itself; and concerning neither of these has the author any right or any power to determine.)

"WHENCE this oppressive load of woe?
" Th' involuntary sigh?
" And th' oozing tear about to flow
" From my dejected eye?

" O, Melancholy! how thy power
" Against my peace conspires!
" Still will thy leaden aspect lour,
" And quench my genial fires.

" O why

" O why is my deſponding mind
" Become thy very ſlave?
" And may I not—alas! not find
" A refuge in the grave?

" The grave will give ſecure repoſe
" From perſecuting grief;
" For there alone, from heavy woes,
" The weary have relief.

" Alas! in early life to leave
" This world ſo good and fair!
" Not ſo to me, who pine and grieve,
" The victim of deſpair.

" And yet how bright thoſe ſhining ſkies!
" How lovely Nature's face!
" The groves and hills around me riſe,
" Robed with celeſtial grace.

" I know them beautiful! I ſee
" How beautiful they are;
" I feel their beauty! yet, ah me!
" My boſom pines with care.

" In vain to me the vernal gale
" Diſpenſes ſoft perfume,
" While thro' the windings of the vale
" He flies from bloom to bloom.

" Can

" Can wit or gaiety impart
" Enjoyment to my breaſt?
" I ſmile, even laugh; but, in my heart,
" My griefs are ill ſuppreſs'd.

" And what can tuneful numbers do?
" Or the melodious ſtring?——
" They can improve the ſenſe of woe,
" And ſharpen Sorrow's ſting.

" Even when I would be gay, a ſigh
" Betrays my ſecret care——
" Be happy, ye who can, for I
" Muſt ſtruggle with deſpair.

" Nor can I Nature blame; ſhe made
" Me capable of joy:
" She gave me powers: and Fortune ſaid,
" Go, and thy powers employ.

" And I have known Delight; e'erwhile
" Have ſeen her beauty ſhine:
" And bleſs'd with her endearing ſmile,
" Have call'd the bleſſing mine.

" Bear witneſs, every ſoft receſs
" That heard my vocal lay;
" And ſcenes of ſocial happineſs,
" That I was very gay.

" And bring the bliſs of former days,
" O, Memory !---ſhe brings
" The ſportive images : obeys,
" But in obeying ſtings.

" The green-hill and th' enamel'd plain,
" Where blyth I us'd to range,
" How ſoft and lovely they remain !
" But I have ſuff'red change.

" Of early friends untimely reft,
" They are the mould'ring clay !
" They ſleep ; and I, alas ! am left
" More deſolate than they.

" I envy you, ye ſilent dead,
" And your eternal ſleep :
" Ye are from care and ſorrow fled ;
" And I am left to weep.

" My joys are deaden'd ; clouds inveſt,
" And glooms involve my ſkies ;
" And more t' afflict my widow'd breaſt,
" Soft images ariſe.

" I ſee a lovely ſcene with flowers,
" With groves and verdure gay :
" I haſten to the bliſsful bowers,
" Lur'd by the feſtive lay.

" Soft

" Soft melodies around, above,
" Breathe thro' the vocal air ;
" And the long, liquid notes of love
" Soothe and ſubdue deſpair.

" And now I quaff the cup of joy !
" The phantoms fly away !
" Stay, ye tranſporting pleaſures !---why
" Will not the viſion ſtay ?

" Wild waſtes appear, and gloomy ſkies,
" And pealing thunders roll !
" And tempeſts---O what tempeſts riſe
" In my diſtracted ſoul !

" But let me ſearch my ſecret heart ;
" Perhaps ſome latent crime
" Hath planted there a deadly dart,
" And blaſts me in my prime.

" I am not guilty---gracious God !
" I ſay not I am pure :
" And I would kiſs thy chaſt'ning rod,
" And thy rebuke endure :

" But that to guiltier men—O heaven !
" Forgive my froward will—
" To guiltier men than I is given
" Security from ill.——

" Poor

" Poor toiling ſpirit! wilt thou yet
" Thus with thy griefs debate?
" Be ſtill! be ſenſeleſs! and ſubmit
" To thy determin'd fate.

" O then, why am I what I am?
" Why am I made to glow
" With ardour of extatic flame,
" Yet be condemn'd to woe?

" Rage on, ye ſtorms! deſcend, and down
" The ſky with fury roll!
" And let the fiends of horror frown
" On my devoted ſoul."———

Thus flow'd Abiran's ſecret woe,
As thro' a pathleſs glade,
Unſeen, with ſullen pace and ſlow
His wayward footſtep ſtray'd:

And deep into the devious wood
He urg'd his deſperate way,
Where ſavage rocks and groves exclude
The ſun's enliv'ning ray:

And fierce in his diſtemper'd breaſt
The dire ſuggeſtion roſe:
" The grave," he cried, " to the diſtreſs'd,
" The grave will give repoſe."

He

He paus'd ; his cheek grew wan ; his eye
With wild diſtraction glar'd :
He rais'd the gleaming poniard high ;
The frantic boſom bar'd.——

Inſtant, athwart th' incumbent gloom
A flood of light appear'd :
The grove was fill'd with ſoft perfume :
A ſudden voice was heard !

A gentle voice ! gentler than gales
That wave their muſky wings
In Aden's aromatic vales,
Or by Daphnæan ſprings.

" Attend, thou plaintive ſon of earth !
" Yield to the will of heaven :—
" To me, appointed at thy birth,
" The pious charge was given,

" To guard thee from th' inſidious wile
" And craft of vitious care ;
" The Syren ſong that would beguile,
" The ſmile that would enſnare :

" Nor leſs to guide thy reckleſs way
" From thoſe ſequeſter'd bowers,
" Where melancholy would betray,
" And blaſt thy growing powers.

" Spirits of fineſt texture, oft
" Are by her ſighs deceiv'd;
" And by her air and accent ſoft,
" Of inward peace bereav'd.

" Fly then from her receſſes, fly!
" The gales that gently blow,
" In fancied ſympathy reply
" Harmonious to thy woe.

" The turtle cooing in the dale,
" Will with thy grief accord:
" And the deep umbrage of the vale
" Congenial glooms afford.

" Nor ſeek, with fruitleſs toil, to learn,
" Why virtue ſuffers pain.—
" Canſt thou the lightning's path diſcern?
" The lightning's fury rein?

" In earthly frame pent and confin'd,
" How can thy ſoul pretend,
" The conduct of th' Almighty mind
" T' arraign or comprehend?

" If in the Lybian deſart wide,
" To ſlake the Lion's thirſt,
" Even from the rock's reluctant ſide
" He bids the fountain burſt:

"And bids, for wild-birds, lofty trees
"Their ruddy harveſt bear,
"The Father of mankind! he ſees,
"Nor diſregards thy care.

"Nor fruitleſs are the ſtorms of woe
"To the progreſſive mind:
"For they give vigour, and to glow
"With energy refin'd.

"Obſerve how winds, and beating rains,
"Drench and deform the dale;
"And how the huſbandman complains,
"And how the ſhepherds wail.

"But when the rains are blown away,
"Behold! a thouſand dyes,
"And flowers and fruit, and verdure gay,
"In every field ariſe.

"You know not, if with meek regard
"You wait the will of heaven;
"You know not what ſublime reward
"May to your grief be given."

LETTER XXIV.

Journal of the Weather for Fifty-five Days, during the Winter 1769-70.

DEAR SIR, St. Peterſburg, Jan. 24. 1770.

OUR weather is indeed very ſevere. You may judge of its ſeverity by our precautions. We have recourſe to them, not only in our dreſs, but in our houſes.

Our dreſs, within doors, is the ſame as during the winter in England. But when we encounter the external cold, our defenſive raiment is indeed very groteſque. The head is defended by a large fur cap, and the body, by a garment reſembling a night-gown, extending from the neck to the heel, made of whatever ſtuff you pleaſe, but lined throughout with the thickeſt fur. Fur-ſhoes, or conguees, as they are termed, having the hair on the outſide, are tied over the ſhoes we commonly wear. Our arms are ſecured by the long ſleeves of the upper garment, or peliſſe, as it is called; and our hands by large muffs, which are alſo uſed to defend the face. On entering any houſe, ſome of the ſervants immediately untie your fur ſhoes, and diveſt you of your peliſſe: nor is it unamuſing to ſee fine gentlemen, adorned with gold and ſilver, and purple, and precious ſtones, ſtarting forth from their rough external guiſe, like ſo many gaudy butterflies burſting ſuddenly from their winter incruſtation.

In houſes of any diſtinction here, every room is provided with a large ſtove, reaching from the floor to the cieling. It is uſually made of brick; and is often ſo adorned with various colours, and with ornaments of braſs, as to exhibit a very good appearance. From this ſtove, flues and paſſages, for conveying the heat around the room, are ſometimes conſtructed within the walls. After the wood is completely burnt down, ſo that not the ſmalleſt particle of flame or of ſmoke remain, the little iron door by which the fuel was put into its place, but which ſtood open while the wood was burning, is faſtened very cloſe:

and,

and, by another aperture in the ſide of the ſtove, or petchka, as it is called, half way between the floor and the cieling, the paſſage by which the ſmoke enters the chimney is alſo covered. Thus the heat, confined entirely within the room, becomes ſometimes exceſſive, and almoſt inſufferable; nor have I ever felt ſo much warmth in any houſe in London, as in the houſes of St. Peterſburg. For in order ſtill farther to guard againſt the viſitations of Siberian blaſts, and the cold companions they bring along with them, the windows are ſo formed as to admit of double caſements. Of theſe the inner caſement may be removed at pleaſure. It is uſually fixed in its place in October, and remains till the beginning of May. The ſpace between the two may be about ſix or ſeven inches.

In the intermediate ſpace between two of theſe caſements, in an antichamber in my apartment, I have ſuſpended one of Reaumur's thermometers; and, in order to give you a more preciſe idea of our climate, I ſhall ſubjoin a journal of the weather for fifty-five days, beginning with the 1ſt of December laſt, and continued till the date of my letter.

The expoſure is to the ſouth; but the obſervations were uſually made at an early hour. Obſerve, therefore, that by the mark 8 m. in the journal, is meant eight o'clock in the morning. I need not tell you, that by b. fr. is meant below the freezing point.

Dec. 1. 8 m. 9 deg. b. fr. The ſky clear. A little wind N. W. The ground covered with ſnow. At noon the ſpirit of wine fell 7 deg. The ſky cloudy. A fall of ſnow.

Dec. 2. 8 m. 8½ deg. b. fr. Cloudy, with ſome miſt.

Dec. 3. 8 m. 7½ deg. b. fr. Snow. A ſharp wind N. E.

Dec. 4. 8 m. 10¾ deg. b. fr. Clear.

Dec. 5. 8 m. 1¾ deg. above fr. Cloudy.

Dec. 6. 8 m. 2 deg. b. fr. Clear.

Dec. 7. 8 m. 2 deg. above fr. Clear. Wind S. W.

Dec. 8. 8 m. ½ deg. b. fr. Cloudy.

Dec. 9. 8 m. 3½ deg. above fr. Wind S. W.

Dec. 10. 8 m. 3 deg. above fr. At half an hour after eight the ſpirit of wine fell to three degrees b. fr.

Dec. 11. 8 m. 8 deg. b. fr.

Dec. 12. 8 m. 2½ deg. b. fr. Wind W. Some ſnow.

Dec. 13.

Dec. 13. 8 m. 2½ deg. b. fr. Cloudy.

Dec. 14. 8 m. 3 deg. b. fr. Very cloudy. A ſharp wind E.

Dec. 15. 8 m. 3 deg. b. fr. Very cloudy.

Dec. 16. 8 m. 3 deg. b. fr. Snow.

Dec. 17. 8 m. 4 deg. b. fr. Snow. Wind N. E.

Dec. 18. 8 m. 7 deg. b. fr. Cloudy. At nine at night the ſpirit of wine ſtood at 15 deg. b. fr. Wind N. E.

Dec. 19. 8 m. 22 deg. b. fr. Clear. Wind N. E.

Dec. 20. 8 m. 23¾ deg. b. fr. Clear. Wind N. E.

Dec. 21. 8 m. 12 deg. b. fr. Snow.

Dec. 22. 8 m. 17 deg. b. fr. Clear.

Dec. 23. 8 m. 15. deg. b. fr. Cloudy. Snow had fallen in the night.

Dec. 24. 8 m. 14 deg. b. fr. Cloudy. Snow had fallen in the night. Wind N. E.

Dec. 25. 8 m. 11 deg. b. fr. Snow had fallen in the night. Wind N. E.

Dec. 26. 8 m. 9 deg. b. fr. Snow. Wind N. E.

Dec. 27. 8 m. 11 deg. b. fr. Snow. Wind N. E.

Dec. 28. 8 m. 15 deg. b. fr. Clear. Wind N. E.

Dec. 29. 8 m. 17 deg. b. fr. Cloudy. Wind N. E.

Dec. 30. 8 m. 9 deg. b. fr. Cloudy. Wind N. E.

Dec. 31. 8 m. 9. deg. b. fr. Snow.

Jan. 1. 1770. 8 m. 10½ deg. b. fr. Snow.

Jan. 2. 8 m. 8½ deg. b. fr. Cloudy.

Jan. 3. 8 m. 15 deg. b. fr. Cloudy.

Jan. 4. 8 m. 12½ deg. b. fr. Snow. Wind S. W.

Jan. 5. 8 m. 6 deg. b. fr. Cloudy.

Jan. 6. 8 m. 5½ deg. b. fr. Snow.

Jan. 7. 8 m. 6. deg. b. fr. Snow.

Jan. 8. 8 m. 6½ deg. b. fr. Snow.

Jan. 9. 8 m. 8½ deg. b. fr. Snow.

Jan. 10. 8 m. 6 deg. b. fr. Snow.

Jan. 11. 8 m. 5½ deg. b. fr. Snow.

Jan. 12. 8 m. 5 deg. b. fr. Snow. Wind N. E.

Jan. 13. 8 m. 5 deg. b. fr. Snow. Wind N. E.

Jan. 14. 8 m. 1 deg. b. fr. Snow. Wind S. W.

Jan. 15. 8 m. 3 deg. above fr. Snow.

Jan. 16. 8 m. 1 deg. above fr. Snow.

Jan. 17. 8 m. 1½ deg. above fr. Snow.
Jan. 18. 8 m. 4 deg. b. fr. Snow. Wind N. E.
Jan. 19. 8 m. 5 deg. b. fr. Snow. Wind N. E.
Jan. 20. 8 m. 17 deg. b. fr. Mifty.
Jan. 21. 8 m. 15 deg. b. fr. Snow.
Jan. 22. 8 m. 8½ deg. b. fr. Cloudy.
Jan. 23. 8 m. 9 deg. b. fr. Cloudy.
Jan. 24. 8 m. 10 deg. b. fr. Cloudy *.

You will, no doubt, have remarked, in this journal, that our weather is often very dim and cloudy. This, however, is more the cafe in the beginning of winter, before all the fnows have fallen, than afterwards. In the months of February and March, the fky is

* The coldeft weather, during my ftay in Ruffia, was ufually after the fnow fell, in the months of February and March. The fpirit of wine was generally, in thofe months, between ten and fifteen degrees below the freezing point. The coldeft weather known, while I lived in St. Peterfburg, was in the month of March 1771. On the firft, fecond, and third days of that month, the fpirit of wine was at 20 deg. b. fr.; but on the fourth, a little before feven in the morning, it fell to 32 deg. b. fr. According to fome other obfervations, it ftood at 34 deg. b. fr. It did not remain long at 32 deg.; but rofe ucceffively to 10, 8, and 5 deg. b. fr. On the 18th of March it ftood at 2 deg. above freezing.

remarkably

remarkably clear; and the moon-light, in particular, when the firmament is quite ſerene, and the ground covered with ſnow, appears much brighter than I have obſerved it in Britain. Nor in thoſe months, though the colds are more intenſe than at any other period, have we ſo much wind as at preſent. The "Spirantes frigora cauri" ſeem to be the harbingers of the ſevere cold; the dreary attendants of November, December, and January.

Perhaps our hazy and cloudy weather, in the end of autumn, and beginning of winter, is the reaſon that I have never yet ſeen the Ruſſian ſky adorned and enlivened in an evening with an Aurora Borealis. I ſay enlivened, for though once or twice I have ſeen a dull ſullen redneſs in the air, which I was told was an Aurora Borealis; I have never yet ſeen it with ſuch bright colours, rapid motions, and fantaſtic geſtures, as embelliſh the Britiſh autumnal ſky. I have never ſeen any thing like the beautiful and juſt deſcription given us of this object by the bard of external nature:

Oft

Oft in this ſeaſon, ſilent from the north,
A blaze of meteors ſhoots: enſweeping firſt
The lower ſkies, they all at once converge
High to the crown of heaven; and all at once
Relapſing quick, as quickly reaſcend;
And mix, and thwart, extinguiſh, and renew;
All æther courſing in a maze of light.

Though in the line, "and mix and thwart, &c." the Poet employs his verbs in an unuſual manner, the deſcription is juſt and ſtriking. It is more than pictureſque; it is poetic: and by exhibiting a ſwift ſucceſſion of diverſified motions, affords us a fine example of that ſort of repreſentation which ſcorns the powers, great though they are, of painting. On ſuch ſignal occaſions, language is an engine to be uſed as the poet pleaſes. The deſcription is admirably heightened, by his ſuggeſting the effects of ſuch appearances on the ſuperſtitious minds of the vulgar: and by his repreſenting the object as receiving a ſhape and features ſuited to their conſternation.

From look to look, contagious thro' the crowd
The panic runs, and into wond'rous ſhapes
Th' appearance throws: armies in meet array,
Throng'd with aërial ſpears, and ſteeds of fire,

Till

Till the long lines of full-extended war
In bleeding fight commix, the ſanguine flood
Rolls a broad ſlaughter o'er the plains of heaven,
As thus they ſcan the viſionary ſcene.
On all ſides ſwells the ſuperſtitious din
Incontinent; and buſy frenzy talks
Of blood and battle; cities overturn'd, &c.

The deſcription is carried on, and riſes by a fine amplification; till

Nature's ſelf
Is deem'd to totter on the brink of time!

and is then concluded, and finely contraſted, by the following ſerene reflection:

Not ſo the man of philoſophic eye
And inſpect ſage; the waving brightneſs he
Curious ſurveys; inquiſitive to know
The cauſes and materials yet unfix'd
Of this appearance.

Adieu.

LETTER XXV.

Account of a Comet which was ſeen in Ruſſia in the Year 1769.—*Account of ſome other Comets.*

DEAR SIR, St. Peterſburg, Jan. 1770.

YOUR letter, informing me that you were engaged in the ſtudy of aſtronomy, gave me indeed the ſincereſt pleaſure. I congratulate you on the delightful improvement it will afford you. In ſo far as a mere lover of that ſcience may ſpeak concerning it, I will venture to affirm, that no literary purſuit whatever enlarges the mind ſo much, or yields ſuch ſublime enjoyment. I am convinced too, that it influences the heart and manners. At leaſt all thoſe aſtronomers whom I have ever had the happineſs of knowing, have been diſtinguiſhed for their modeſty, condeſcenſion, and candour. Fond as you are of this exalting ſcience, I flatter myſelf, that the following account of the comet that appeared here in the months of Auguſt and September laſt will afford you ſome amuſement.

This brilliant ſtranger, in its progreſs through the planetary regions, made its appearance here on the 28th of Auguſt. I had the pleaſure of ſeeing it early in the morning on the 1ſt of September. Its head was then ſituated almoſt due eaſt, thirteen degrees above the horizon; and made a right-angled triangle, whoſe hypoteneus was ſixteen degrees, with the bright ſtar Aldebaran, and the moſt northern of the Pleiades. September the 1ſt, 2d, and 3d, it advanced with an oblique ſoutherly courſe, ſtraight upon the ſtar Bellatrix in the ſhoulder of Orion. It paſſed that ſtar within leſs than half a degree, on the morning of the 4th. By proceeding in ſuch a tract, and with ſuch accelerated rapidity, towards the Perihelion, it ſeems to have deſcended upon us, through the breaſt of Aries, about the beginning of Auguſt; and to have croſſed the Ecliptic, when near thirty degrees diſtant from the point of the vernal Equinox. At that time it was probably too remote to be diſcerned. From Bellatrix it moved

moved onward to the Solſtitial colure; paſſing that circle with two or three degrees of N. declination; and, before the 10th of September, arrived at the Celeſtial Equator, having a right aſcenſion of an hundred and three degrees. On the 13th, it aroſe along with Sirius at three in the morning, and was then ſeen, for the laſt time, near the tail of Monoceros, diſtant from the Dog-ſtar, as I was informed, twenty-ſix degrees; and from Procyon, or the Star of the Little Dog, fifteen degrees.—In the evenings, about ſix weeks after, it was looked for in its return in the conſtellation Ophiuchus; but I have not heard that it was diſcovered.

During all the nights I had an opportunity of attending to the progreſs of this illuſtrious viſitant, as the atmoſphere was very ſerene, I was much gratified with the fine appearance exhibited by the long train of diverging light which formed the tail. On the morning of the 2d of September, it had increaſed from twelve degrees of length to near thirty, ſtretching from the weſtern arm of Orion, where the head then was, full four degrees beyond the two kappas of the Whale. On the 8th, the diſplay of its radiance was ſtill more majeſtic; for it now occupied a ſpace in the heavens of no leſs than forty-four degrees, reaching acroſs Orion, even beyond the ſtars in Eridanus. All this time it was haſtening towards the Sun's place in the Ecliptic; and by ſuch rapid marches, that it was ſoon afterwards abſorbed from our view by the effulgence of the morning rays.

I need ſcarce obſerve, that all the above motions and diſtances aſcribed to this beauteous and eccentric wanderer, are only apparent. The real track of a body ſo conſiderable, through the orbits of the planets, is another conſideration; and leads to reflections of a very intereſting nature. On this ſubject I have received the following information from an ingenious friend converſant in aſtronomy, who was much occupied in obſerving the places of the comet, and has ſince ſpent ſome time in computing from the data thus obtained. According to him, its neareſt approach to the earth was on the 9th of September, when it paſſed us at about a third part of our mean diſtance from the Sun. Had it arrived at the ſame point of its trajectory twenty-one days

days later, we ſhould have been ſtill three times nearer: though even at this neareſt poſſible approach, as the bulk of the comet was relatively very ſmall, the mutual gravitation would have occaſioned no tendency to diſorder in the motions of our planet. It farther appears, that it paſſed the plane of the orbit of Venus from the north to the ſouth, in the month of Auguſt, and repaſſed it again in October; both times at ſuch a diſtance from that planet, as to produce no ſenſible effects. On the 7th of October it had reached its perihelion, and was ten times nearer the Sun than we are. Mercury was alſo then ſo much out of the way as to eſcape diſturbance.

This comet is thought to be a new one; by which is meant, that it is different from any one marked in the catalogue given us by Dr. Halley, or any additions that ſince his time have been made to it. According to the ſame computations of its real ſituation and diſtance, it follows, that the lucid emanation which formed the tail was elongated from the nucleus, to the amazing extent of thirty-ſix millions of miles. No wonder, therefore, that ſuch unuſual radiance, when contraſted with a dark and ſerene air, ſhould have imparted an awful magnificence to the heavens. Nor could I behold it, for the firſt time, without feeling my ſoul ſhaken with ſolemn terror and veneration. It ſeemed like the banner of Omnipotence, diſplayed by ſome mighty angel, and announcing, not only to the nations upon earth, but to the whole planetary region, from utmoſt Saturn to the Sun himſelf, the power of their great Creator. A voice pealing through the vaſt void of the ſtarry heavens, and proclaiming ſome awful beheſt, or tremendous ſummons, though it might have appalled, would not then have ſurpriſed me.—Reflection, I allow, and ſound philoſophy, excite other emotions. They inſpire confidence in the goodneſs of that Being, whoſe power and wiſdom are manifeſted in the order and harmony ſo conſpicuous in the frame of nature.

These are thy glorious works, Parent of *good!*

You will, no doubt, have already diſcovered, in the courſe of your enquiries and obſervations, that the aſtronomy of con.ets is to be conſidered, even in this age of ſcience, as in its

its infancy. Of the number belonging to the ſyſtem, there is no room even for forming a conjecture: and in regard to their periods, philoſophers are only beginning to know ſomething. The great diſadvantage under which they labour, is the want of ancient obſervations. It was unfortunately the prevailing doctrine of the Ariſtotelians, that comets were but tranſient meteors, compoſed of combuſtible matter, which floated caſually in the atmoſphere; and, on this account, they regarded them with very little attention. It is certain, however, that ſome of the ancients entertained juſter conceptions. Seneca, in particular, reaſons upon this ſubject in a manner ſo juſt and philoſophical, that it is aſtoniſhing the mere authority of the ſchools could have ſo long diverted the attention of enquirers, and prevented them ſo long from beginning really to obſerve. The treatiſe * alluded to, is ſo remarkable for a train of the moſt happy ſuggeſtions, that I cannot help recommending it to your peruſal; and to juſtify what I advance, allow me to lay before you the following quotations:—" Ego noſtris non aſſentior.

* Quæſt. Natur. l. vii.

" Non enim exiſtimo cometen ſubetaneum
" ignem, ſed inter æterna opera naturæ *.—
" Cometes habet ſuam ſedem: et ideo non
" cito expellitur, ſed emittitur ſuum ſpatium:
" non extinguitur, ſed excedit. Si erratica,
" inquit, ſtella eſſet, in ſignifero eſſet. Quis
" unum ſtellis limitem ponit? Quis in an-
" guſtum divina compellit? Nempe hæc ipſa
" ſidera, quæ ſola moveri credis, alios et alios
" circulos habent. Quare ergo non aliqua
" ſint quæ in proprium iter, et ab iſtis re-
" motum ſeceſſerint † ?—Multa ſunt quæ eſſe
" concedimus: qualia ſint, ignoramus.—
" Quid ergo miramur, cometas, tam rarum
" ſpectaculum, non dum teneri legibus certis;
" neque initia illorum, fineſque noteſcere
" quorum ex ingentibus intervallis recurſus
" eſt?"——" With *our* philoſophers I do not
" agree. I cannot believe that a comet is a
" fire ſuddenly kindled, but that it ought to
" be ranked among the everlaſting works of
" nature. A comet has its proper place,
" from which it is not quickly thrown out;
" but goes its courſe: is not extinguiſhed;
" but leaves us. An objector may ſay, if it

* Cap. 22. † Cap. 23, 24, 25.

" were

" were a wandering ſtar, it would keep in " the zodiac. But who can confine the ſtars? " or reſtrain the works of God to a narrow " compaſs? Thoſe very ſtars, believed by " you to be the only bodies of the kind that " have any motion, move in circles very dif- " ferent from one another. Why, therefore, " may not ſome ſtars withdraw into paths of " their own, and diſtinct from the reſt? We " grant that many things exiſt, of whoſe na- " ture we are ignorant. Why then ſhould " we be ſurpriſed, ſince the appearance of " comets is ſo rare, that we know nothing of " the laws by which their motions are go- " verned, nor of the limits within which " they move, nor of the periods in which " they revolve?" To theſe wonderful anti- cipations he ſubjoins the following remark- able prophecy: "Veniet tempus, quo iſta quæ " nunc latent in lucem dies extrahat, et lon- " gioris ævi diligentia. Ad inquiſitionem " tantorum ætas una non ſufficit. Veniet " tempus, quo poſteri noſtri tam aperta nos " neſciſſe mirentur. Erit qui demonſtret " aliquando, in quibus cometæ partibus er- " rent, cur tam seducti a cæteris eant, quanti " qualeſque ſint."——"The time will come,

M 3 " when

" when those things which are now hid " from us, shall, by the diligence and observation of after ages, be fully disclosed. " For one age alone is not sufficient for investigating matters of such importance. " The time will come, when posterity will " wonder that we were ignorant of things so " plain. One will arise, who will demonstrate in what region of space the comets " wander, why they recede so far from the " other planets, how great, and what sort of " bodies they are."

But notwithstanding this bright emanation from a philosophy so pure and refined, it was not till about the year 1300 that comets were observed with any attention. Mention is made, indeed, by authors before that period of no fewer than 415; but from their information, little else, excepting the knowledge that such bodies made their appearance at the time specified, can be derived. The particulars narrated are too general to admit of any certain comparison with comets that have visited us in later times. But since the thirteenth century, or rather since the time of Tycho Brahe, so much has been accomplished, that astronomers

astronomers have now about fifty comets so well ascertained, that they will have no difficulty of knowing, whether any which may hereafter appear be of that number. The period of any one, being in this manner determined, its return in future times may be foretold: and thus, by degrees, the number of all those stars may come to be known, and their courses settled. In the year 1758, astronomers had just cause of triumph, by the actual return of one of those bodies, according to a prediction founded on the principles now mentioned. This was the comet which had appeared before in the year 1682, and which seems to be the Mercury of all the rest, as it is now certain, that it revolves about the Sun in so short a period as seventy-six years. Seventy-five years was its period the time before; but Dr. Halley shewed plainly, from the laws of gravitation, that the action of the planets would necessarily protract its return about one year: and therefore prognosticated, that its return would be towards the end of 1758, or the beginning of 1759. These conclusions were also confirmed by some most elaborate computations made by the members of the French academy, when the time drew near, and when the attention of philoſophers was again directed to a ſubject ſo intereſting. The fact, by a moſt exact agreement, juſtified the principles upon which they had founded their opinion; for, in the evening of the 25th of December 1758, the expected viſitant was diſcovered tending to its perihelion, and continued viſible till the 14th of February 1759, when it was near its conjunction. On the 1ſt of April it again appeared in its receſs from the Sun, in the morning; and was obſerved, by many aſtronomers, in different parts of Europe for a conſiderable time after, with ſuch circumſtances as left no doubt of its being the identical comet that had appeared in 1682.—There is another comet, which, from the correſpondence of period with one formerly obſerved, and other ſtriking circumſtances of agreement, both as to the ſpecies and ſituation of the orbit, is expected to return at a determined time; and that too at no great diſtance. This is the comet which appeared in 1532, and 1661, and which, at an equal interval of 129 years, may be again looked for about the year 1789.

The comet, with whoſe appearance we are next beſt acquainted is, that memorable one which was ſeen ſo long in the year 1680. At that time a concurrence of happy circumſtances contributed to the improvement of this part of aſtronomy. The comet itſelf, of all others, from the extraordinary curvature of its orbit, was moſt ſuited to diſcover to us the laws by which its motions were governed. Its tract in the heavens was carefully and critically marked by Caſini and Flamſtead, in the lately eſtabliſhed obſervatories at Paris and Greenwich. But, above all, Sir ISAAC NEWTON then flouriſhed in the vigour of his genius, and had unfolded the true ſyſtem of the world. He demonſtrated, from many obſervations of this great comet, that, like the planets, it was ſubject to the law of general gravitation; and, like them, reſpected the Sun in its periodical courſe. After this, upon the principles laid down by Sir Iſaac Newton, Dr. Halley determined, by an elaborote computation, what would be the motion of a body carried round the Sun in a certain ellipſis, with a period of 575 years, and found it moſt perfectly to agree with the obſerved places of this very comet. Perceiving this, and remarking that hiſtory makes mention of three very extraordinary comets which ſucceeded one another by the ſame number of years, he concluded, not without the higheſt probability, that all of them were one and the ſame comet, whoſe laſt return to its perihelion was in the year 1680.

The firſt period, according to the information given me by the friend to whom I am indebted for the preceding account, carries us back to the year 1106, when Henry the Firſt was King of England. The comet is recorded in the Saxon Chronicle by one who ſeems to have been an eye witneſs. He tells us, "That on Friday, February 16, a won-" derful comet appeared; and was ſeen a " long time afterwards every evening. The " ſtar itſelf was in the ſouth-eaſt; but the " ray which proceeded from it was very clear " and large, ſhining to the north-weſt."— Alſo, in the conſulate of Lampadius and Oreſtes, in the time of the Emperor Juſtinian, another comet like this appeared; and is mentioned in the following manner by the author of the Antiochean Chronicle:—" A " great and fearful ſtar appeared in the weſt,

" ſending

" sending forth a white beam upwards, " which, as it appeared like the flashes of " lightning, some called it Lampadion. It " was seen for twenty days."—Another period of 575 years brings us to the 44th year before Christ, when, soon after the death of Julius Cæsar, a very remarkable comet appeared, mentioned by many historians; and also by Pliny, who gives us the very words of Augustus Cæsar concerning it:---" In the " very days of my games, a blazing star was " seen in that part of the heavens which is " under the Septemtriones. It arose about " the eleventh hour; and was clearly to be " seen all over the world."---From these accounts it appears, that this comet has been observed thrice since the birth of Christ; and once before that æra. In all four times. But if it performs its revolution regularly and uniformly in the space of 575 years, it must, though unobserved, have returned frequently before that period. If you consult Blair's Chronological Tables upon this subject, you will find, that it must have returned in the year 619, B. C. in the reign of Josiah King of Judah, when Halyattus II. reigned in Lydia, or, according to Alstedius, in the reign of King

King Hezekiah. The next period of its appearance muſt have been in the year 1194, B. C. at the beginning of the Trojan war. Another period of 575 years carries us back to the year 1769, B. C.; and in the year 1764 was the deluge of Ogyges, by which a conſiderable part of Greece was rendered deſolate for 200 years. Other 575 years brings you to the year 2344, B. C. within four years of the univerſal deluge, which happened in the year 1348. Add 575 years, and you come to the year 2919, B. C. the æra of Lamach and Mathuſalem. And by another revolution of our comet, we come at the year 3494, B. C.; ſo that if this account be well founded, it muſt have viſited us ſix times before the birth of Chriſt, excluſive of its appearance in the age of Auguſtus. If you ſuppoſe its revolutions to have gone on in the ſame order before our globe was brought into the ſyſtem, you will have it travelling through our planetary region no later than ſixty-five years before what we call the creation of the world. I leave you to your own reflections on theſe, I had almoſt called them coincidences. If they are not, they are very nearly ſo: and if this be granted, might not great

great allowance be made for inaccuracy of calculations; difficulty of aſcertaining ancient dates; and alſo for variety, produced by unknown cauſes in the period in which the comet itſelf may have performed its revolution? The known anomalies in the motions of other comets, and even of the planets belonging to our ſyſtem, occaſioned by mutual gravitation, or their actions on one another, render this laſt ſuppoſition by no means improbable. But you will ſay, I am launching into the ſea of conjecture.

One thing, however, is certain, that this very comet, of all others yet known, interferes moſt with the path of the planets; and more eſpecially with that of our habitation. Nor is it poſſible to read Dr. Halley's deſcription of the progreſs of a body ſo vaſt and formidable, in its laſt viſit to the Sun, without conſiderable emotion. "Now this comet," ſays he, "in that part of its orbit in which it "deſcended towards the Sun, came ſo near "the path of all the planets, that if by "chance it had happened to meet any one of "them when paſſing by, it muſt have pro- "duced very ſenſible effects; and the mo- "tion

"tion of the comet itſelf would have ſuffered
"the greateſt diſturbance. In ſuch a caſe,
"the plane and ſpecies of its elliptic orbit, and
"its periodic time, would have been greatly
"changed; eſpecially from coming near Ju-
"piter. In the late deſcent, the true path of
"the comet left the orbit of Saturn and Ju-
"piter below itſelf a little towards the ſouth;
"it approached much nearer to the paths of
"Venus and Mercury; and much nearer
"ſtill to that of Mars. But as it was paſſing
"through the plane of the ecliptic to its
"ſouthern node, it came ſo near to the plane
"of the Earth, that, had it arrived thirty
"days later than it did, it would ſcarce have
"left our globe one ſemidiameter of the Sun
"towards the north, and, without doubt, by
"its centripetal force, it would have pro-
"duced ſome change upon the ſituation and
"ſpecies of the Earth's orbit, and upon the
"length of the year. But may the great
"good God avert a ſhock or contact of ſuch
"great bodies, moving with ſuch forces
"(which however, is manifeſtly not impoſ-
"ſible), leſt this beautiful order of things be
"entirely deſtroyed, and reduced into its an-
"cient chaos!"

Allow

Allow me to conclude my letter with repeating my congratulation on your having begun the ſtudy of the ſtars; and to give you joy on the delightful improvement it will afford you. Permit me alſo to ſay, that, in proſecuting this ſtudy, perſons in your ſituation have peculiar advantages.

Dî tibi divitias dederint, artemque fruendi.

I ſee you, in "my mind's eye," ſhaking off the ſlumbers of that light and refreſhing ſleep which only viſits the couch of temperance; anticipating the dawn of morning; aſcending the little eminence in the lawn adjoining to your elegant villa; and there converſing with the hoſt of heaven. You will never repent of ſuch early vigils; but will find thoſe ſilent times, before the buſtle and cares of the day begin, the fitteſt ſeaſon for contemplation. Beholding, with philoſophic attention, thoſe glorious fires that blaze through the regions of boundleſs ſpace, and adminiſter their benign influences to innumerable ſurrounding planets; how your thoughts will aſcend; and your heart glow with ſerene enjoyment! With what tranſport of ſoul will you reflect, that all this exuberance of creation was formed ed by the rule of wiſdom, and is governed by immutable order!---Ye glorious fires! how long have you kept watch in the heavens? Where were ye before your courſes brought time itſelf into being? By what original ſpark were ye kindled? Who ſtored with light your never-failing urns? Is the morning of your exiſtence ſtill remembered, when the Almighty yet held you in the palm of his hand? Know, ye ſtupendous hoſt! though your radiance proclaims an order of things majeſtically great; yet the eye of reaſon is filled with rays of a far purer luſtre. They beam from beyond the veil that ſurrounds you; and with irreſiſtible energy, raiſe our views to that eternal, ſelf-exiſtent Eſſence, the fountain of life, the great Author of univerſal nature.

These are thy glorious works, Parent of good,
Almighty, thine this univerſal frame,
Thus wond'rous fair; thyſelf how wond'rous then!
Unſpeakable! who ſitt'ſt *above theſe heav'ns.*

LETTER XXVI.

An Equeſtrian Statue of Peter the Great.— The Rock intended for the Pedeſtal.

DEAR SIR, St. Peterſburg, 1770.

THE moſt ſkilful and ingenious ſtatuary in Europe, is employed here at preſent in executing an Equeſtrian Statue of Peter the Great. The deſign in this work is partly allegorical. The pedeſtal is to repreſent a rock, and the horſe appears with great ſpirit and exertion in the act of aſcending it. This is to indicate the difficulties ſurmounted by Peter in his great labour of reforming the Ruſſians. An enormous ſnake, by which Envy is typefied, appears, though ſtill lifting its head, to be trampled upon by the hind-feet of the horſe. I confeſs this ſeems to me both a conceit and a common place ornament. Beſides, as benign and complacent emotions are intended to be the general effect produced by the Statue in the beholder, the circumſtance now mentioned conveys too much of a different feeling. For, in works of taſte, unity of feeling is of no ſmall importance.

The ſnake, however, ſerves a more convenient purpoſe; and is very uſeful in ſupporting or in fixing the horſe's tail.

Peter is in the attitude of ſtretching out one of his arms. He is thus intended to expreſs parental affection for his people: and when we are told that this is the artiſt's intention, we are ſatisfied that he has done what he purpoſed. The expreſſion of the countenance is happy and characteriſtic: you ſee in it affection and wiſdom; not, however, without ſome lineaments of that ferocity which ſerved as a foil to Peter's amazing merit. At the ſame time, I could have wiſhed that the work, which, in other reſpects, is really exquiſite, had been leſs allegorical. The graces and beauties of allegory ſubmit not their delicate tints and features either to the pencil or the chiſel. They are challenged by the muſe alone.——The drapery in this ſtatue is, with great judgment, intended to be as ſimple as poſſible. It exhibits the original dreſs of the Ruſſians. The ſtatue, you may be ſure, is a topic of converſation here at preſent; and this laſt circumſtance has given occaſion for ſome good criticiſm on the *Coſtume*.

The

The rock intended for the pedeſtal, is itſelf a curioſity. I went lately into Carelia, where it now lies, that I might ſee it in its natural ſtate. It was then forty feet long, twenty-two in breadth, and twenty-two in height; but before it be brought to St. Peterſburg, it will probably be a good deal curtailed. It is quite detached, lying a little way below the ſurface of the earth, and is altogether unconnected with any ſtratum of ſtone or of rock. In its compoſition it ſeems to contain a great deal of granite and onyx. It admits of an exquiſite poliſh; and diſplays ſome beautiful mixtures of white, black, and grey. In ſome of its veins it ſparkles; and ſome of its ſtreaks exhibit a fine mixture of pale red, or bluſh colour. Ear-rings and ſleeve-buttons, cut out of the fragments of this rock, are at preſent very faſhionable. It is to be conveyed to the ſide of the Neva on a machine drawn by men: it is there to be put on board a large barge, and to be towed by boats to the city.

The artiſt who is engaged in this immortal work, has brought with him to this place a fine marble figure, intended as an allegorical repreſentation of Winter. A very proper ornament, you will ſay, for the metropolis of a northern empire. There is, however, ſomething very particular in the nature of the deſign. Winter is repreſented as a female, very beautiful, and very young. She is arrayed in looſe drapery; her countenance is expreſſive of the moſt tender affection, as ſhe appears gracefully bending over ſome winter flowers, and in the act of protecting them, with a fold of her garment, from the ſeverity of the weather. But how, you will aſk, as I took the liberty of doing, are we to know that this is Winter? By the following—ſhall I venture to ſay, conceit?—Near her, on the pedeſtal, is an earthen vaſe filled with water: the fluid, by expanſion occaſioned by the froſt, had burſt the edge of the veſſel, and the broken fragment is lying beſide it! But my chief objection is againſt the general deſign. Ought not Winter, agreeably to the conduct both of poets and painters, to appear herſelf not inſenſible to the effects of cold? Is not Death, when perſonified, repreſented as a ſkeleton? or ſuch as Milton has repreſented him? And is not Danger, exhibited by Collins, in actual danger?

Danger! whoſe limbs of giant mould,
What mortal eye can fix'd behold?

Who

Who ſtalks his round, an hideous form,
Howling amid the midnight ſtorm;
Or throws him on the ridgy ſteep
Of ſome looſe hanging rock to ſleep.

Fear, by the ſame Poet, appears ſtarting, flying, and in diſorder:

Ah, Fear! ah, frantic Fear!
I ſee, I ſee thee near;
I know thy hurried ſtep, thy haggard eye,
Like thee I ſtart, like thee diſorder'd fly.

Deſpair, too, according to the maſterly delineation of Spenſer, is repreſented as ſuffering the moſt excruciating torment.

"Theſe writers," replies the artiſt, who is alſo an acute critic, "have conducted "themſelves erroneouſly. I follow a plan "more conſiſtent, and more correct. I re-"preſent the Power who preſides over the "ſeaſon; who has the ſole management of "froſts and of tempeſts; and cannot there-"fore be ſuppoſed to ſuffer by their incle-"mency." The thought is ingenious; but I cannot ſubſcribe to the doctrine. The diſcuſſion of this point, however, would involve me in a longer letter than I have leiſure to write at preſent. Adieu.

LETTER XXVII.

Fables imitated from the German of GELLERT.

DEAR SIR, St. Peterſburg, 1770.

THE moſt popular among the living authors in Germany, in ſo far as I may judge from what I can hear of German literature in this place, is the famous Gellert. He is a profeſſor at Leipſig; and is univerſally celebrated, not only as a man of diſtinguiſhed ability, but of great worth. As an author, he is particularly diſtinguiſhed for ſmoothneſs of verſification, propriety of expreſſion, and elegance, rather than ſtrength of invention. His works are of different kinds; Letters, tales, and fables In the apologue, he is conſidered as the Phædrus of Germany. I ſhall therefore conclude the ſpecimens I have already given you of German literature, with the following imitations of ſome of his fables. They are imitations, rather tranſlations: I would

would have rendered them into verſe, if I had felt myſelf in a mood for rhyming; or rather if I had thought myſelf equal to the taſk. Nor can I pretend to any thing elſe in the ſubſequent outlines, than to give you ſome notion of the inventive powers of an author, whom his countrymen have ranked very high among thoſe that excel in elegant compoſition. * * * * *

I.

The NIGHTINGALE *and the* LARK.

A Lesson *to* Poets.

WHILE a Nightingale chanted in the midſt of a foreſt, the neighbouring hills and valleys were delighted with her exquiſite melody. Every wild bird forgot to ſing, liſtening with fond admiration. Aurora tarried behind the hill, attending to her muſical cadences; and Philomel, in honour of the goddeſs, warbled with unuſual ſweetneſs. At length ſhe pauſed, and the Lark took the opportunity of thus addreſſing her: "Your "muſic meets with juſt approbation; the "variety, the clearneſs, and tenderneſs of the

" notes are inimitable: neverthelefs, in one " circumftance I am entitled to a preference. " My melody is uninterrupted; and every " morning is ufhered with my gratulations. " Your fong, on the contrary, is heard but " feldom; and, except during a few weeks " in the fummer, you have no claim to pe- " culiar attention." " You have mention- " ed," replied the Nightingale, " the very " caufe of my fuperior excellence. I attend " to, and obey, the dictates of Nature. I ne- " ver fing but by her incitement, nor ever " yield to importunate, but uninfpired inclina- " tion."

II.

The TRAVELLER.

DURING the violence of a ftorm, a Traveller implored relief from Jupiter, and intreated him to affuage the tempeft. But Jupiter lent a deaf ear to his intreaty. Struggling with the unabating fury of the whirlwind, tired, and far from fhelter, he grew peevifh and difcontented. " It is thus (he faid) " the Gods, to whom our facrifices are offer- " ed daily, heedlefs of our welfare, and

" amufed

" amuſed with our ſufferings, make an oſten-" tatious parade of their omnipotence." At length, approaching the verge of a foreſt, " Here," he cried, " I ſhall find that ſuccour " and protection which Heaven, either unable " or unwilling, hath refuſed." But as he advanced, a robber roſe ſuddenly from a brake; and our Traveller, impelled by inſtant terror, and the proſpect of great danger, betook himſelf to flight, expoſing himſelf to the tempeſt of which he had ſo bitterly complained. His enemy, mean while, fitting an arrow to his bow, took exact aim; but the bow-ſtring being relaxed with the moiſture, the deadly weapon fell ſhort of its mark, and the Traveller eſcaped uninjured. As he continued his journey, a voice iſſued awful from the clouds: " Meditate on the providence as " well as on the power of Heaven. The " ſtorm which you deprecated ſo blaſphe-" mouſly, hath been the means of your pre-" ſervation. Had not the bow-ſtring of your " enemy been rendered uſeleſs by the rain, " you had fallen a prey to his violence!"

III.

A Well-timed REBUKE.

PHILINDA, in the bloom of youth and beauty, ſoon became conſcious of her charms. Like other comely maids, ſhe attired herſelf in gaudy apparel, and was conſtantly conſulting her mirror. Her brother, a grave and formal philoſopher, celebrated for his erudition, declaimed againſt the vanity of the ſex. "Have a care," replied Philinda, with a ſmile, "leſt the charge be retorted. Hourly "I take counſel with my mirror, and hourly "you rehearſe your own compoſitions."

IV.

The TENDER WIFE.

CLARINÉ loved her huſband with ſincere affection; for they had been only ſix weeks married. He conſtituted her ſole felicity; for he was exactly ſuited to her mind. Their deſires and averſions were the ſame. It was Clariné's ſtudy, by diligent attention, to anticipate her huſband's wiſhes. "Such a wife," ſays my male reader, who entertains thoughts of of matrimony, "ſuch a wife would I deſire!" And ſuch a wife mayſt thou enjoy.—Clariné's huſband fell ſick. A dangerous malady. "No hope," ſaid the Phyſician, and ſhook his awful wig. Bitterly wept Clariné: "O Death, might I prefer a petition! "Spare, O ſpare my huſband! Let me be the "victim in his ſtead!" Death heard, appeared; "and what," cried he, "is thy requeſt?" "There," ſaid Clariné, trembling and aſto-"niſhed, "there he lies; pierced with in-"tolerable agony, he implores thy ſpeedy "relief!"

V.

The YELLOW HAMMER *and* NIGHTINGALE.

A Yellow Hammer and a Nightingale were ſuſpended in their cages at the outſide of Damon's window. The Nightingale began to warble, and Damon's child was ſmit with admiration of his melody. "Which of the "birds," ſaid he, "ſings ſo delightfully?" "I will ſhew you them," anſwered the father, "and you may gueſs." The boy fixed his eye on the Yellow Hammer: "This

"This muſt be the ſongſter. How beauti-"fully painted are his feathers! The other, "you may ſee by his plumage, is quite un-"muſical, and good for nothing!" "The "vulgar," ſaid Damon, "judge preciſely af-"ter the ſame manner, and form their opi-"nion of merit merely by external appear-"ance."

VI.

The FOX *and* MAGPIE.

SAID Renard to a Magpie, "May I pre-"ſume to aſk the ſubject of your inceſſant "diſcourſe? Doubtleſs you diſcuſs many cu-"rious and important inquiries." "True," anſwered the Magpie, "I miniſter truth and "inſtruction to the public. From the eagle "even to the bat, all partake of my wiſdom." "May I requeſt a ſpecimen of your know-"ledge?" ſaid the Fox, with a ſubmiſſive tone.—As a quack-doctor mounts the ſtage, extols the virtue of his drugs, draws out a voluminous handkerchief, and coughs, and ſpits, and harangues; ſo the Magpie, ſkipping from bough to bough, whetting his beak, and aſſuming an air of profound ſagacity and importance, addreſſed his diſciple: "My chief

" delight is in communicating and diffusing " knowledge. Attend to the following " theory, proved by inconteſtable facts, and " of ſignal. conſequence to the welfare of " foxes:-- Have you not hitherto imagined, " that it is by four feet alone that you per- " form the operations of running and walk- " ing?" " Certainly," ſaid Renard. " Then " be aſſured," added the inſtructor, " that " you have laboured under a groſs miſappre- " henſion. I will evince, by irrefragable ar- " guments, that you run, walk, and ſkip " upon five feet. When you run, your foot " moves; and when you neither walk nor " run, your foot is at reſt. Again, when you " walk, your tail touches the ground. Theſe " principles are ſimple and ſelf-evident. " Mark the conſequence. When your foot " moves, your tail moves; your foot moves " from one place to another; and ſo does " your tail. And, again, when you run " full ſpeed, your tail touches the ground; " therefore your tail is your fifth foot: " Q. E. D." " Excellent," cried the Fox, " the leſs we know, the readier we are to in- " ſtruct and demonſtrate."

VII.

The PAINTER.

A ſkilful Painter ſhewed a picture of Mars to a Connoiſſeur, and aſked his opinion concerning it. The Connoiſſeur examined it cloſely, and ſpoke his ſentiments without reſerve. He told him he diſliked it; alleging many good reaſons for his diſlike. But the artiſt was of a different mind; and his friend diſputed with him at great length, without being able to convince him. Meantime a Fop entered the room; and caſting a ſuperficial glance at the picture, "Good Heavens!" cried he, in an extaſy of admiration, "what "a maſter-piece of art and invention! what "an elegant foot! and how exactly are the "nails proportioned! Mars lives in the pic"ture! What ingenuity in that ſhield! and "how much ſkill in the execution of the "helmet!" The Painter was covered with utter ſhame and confuſion. "Now," ſaid he, "I am convinced of my miſtake:" And the moment his applauding viſitant withdrew, he expunged the godhead.——The work is bad, if a judge diſapproves; if a fool praiſes, eraze.

VIII.

The HIDDEN TREASURE.

A FATHER, on his death-bed, thus addreſſed his Son: " Providing for your welfare, " I laid up a Treaſure——" Death interrupted him; for, without finiſhing his ſpeech, he died. " A Treaſure!" ſaid the Son; " but " where?"—As ſoon, therefore, as the funeral ceremonies were performed, he gathered his friends and neighbours, and, with ſpades and pick-axes, turned up the adjacent fields. Their ſearch was fruitleſs, and the young man, in deſpair, diſmiſſed them. But looking accidentally into the bed where his Father died, he found the Treaſure. " In like manner," ſays the Moraliſt, " we often neglect the di- " rect and immediate means of diſcovering " the truth, and deſpiſe them becauſe they " are eaſy."

LETTER XXVIII.

The Slavery of the Russian Peasants.

DEAR SIR,

I WILL endeavour, in so far as my own observation extends, and in so far as I may depend on the information I have received from others, to satisfy your enquiries concerning the political situation, and national character, of the Russians. On this subject I shall lay the facts and observations before you in the order in which they occur; and with such occasional incidents or anecdotes, as may tend to illustrate any general remark. Nor will I trouble you with any apology for a method, if it may be termed method, so very desultory. In truth, I want leisure, and, perhaps, many other requisites, for composing a formal treatise. I will therefore console myself, and endeavour to satisfy you, by observing, that, for the purposes of mere amusement, the arrangement I have chosen is perhaps

haps as proper as any other. I have alſo to premiſe, that if any thing ſevere ſhall happen to eſcape me concerning the form of the Ruſſian government, it can only be concerning the *form*, and without any view to the preſent adminiſtration. I believe ſincerely that no deſpot, or, if you like the term better, no abſolute monarch, ever ruled with more prudence, or ſtudied the welfare of his people with more rectitude of intention, than the preſent Empreſs of Ruſſia. Yet it is impoſſible for a native of Britain, giving an account of this country to an Engliſhman, not to expreſs ſuch feelings and reflections, as a compariſon between the Britiſh government, and that of other nations, muſt naturally ſuggeſt.

The peaſants in Ruſſia, that is to ſay, the greateſt part of the ſubjects of this empire, are in a ſtate of abject ſlavery; and are reckoned the property of the nobles to whom they belong, as much as their dogs and horſes. Indeed, the wealth of a great man in Ruſſia is not computed by the extent of land he poſſeſſes, or by the quantity of grain he can bring to market, but by the number of his ſlaves. Thoſe belonging to Prince Sherebatoff, and constituting his fortune, are said to be no less in number than a hundred and twenty-seven thousand.

Every slave pays about a ruble * yearly to his owner; and if he be in the way of making money, the tribute he pays is augmented. In general, every Russian nobleman allots to the peasants that belong to him, a certain portion of land to be cultivated by them, the produce of which, excepting what suffices for their own maintenance, is paid to the proprietor. Sometimes those slaves practise trades, or engage in traffic; and all such persons pay a much greater sum yearly to their owners, than is done by the labourer of the ground. In fact, a Russian peasant has no property; every thing he possesses, even the miserable raiment that shelters him from the cold, may be seized by his master as his own.——A carpenter, being known to have made some money, was commanded by the rapacious steward of a rapacious Knaez, to give two hundred rubles to his owner. The man obeyed, and brought the money in cop-

* Four Shillings.
†
per.

per. "I muſt have it in ſilver," ſaid the ſteward. The ſlave, denying that he had ſo much, was inſtantly ſcourged till he promiſed to fulfil the demand. He brought the ſilver, and the covetous ſuperior retained both the ſilver and copper.——You will eaſily conceive, that men in this ſituation, if they are ever enabled to improve their fortunes, will conceal their wealth, and aſſume an external appearance of indigence and miſery.

The owner has alſo the power of ſelling his ſlave, or of hiring his labour to other perſons; and, it happens ſometimes, that a Knaez, or Boyard, ſhall give a ſlave to a neighbouring Boyard in exchange for a dog or a horſe. The owner may alſo inflict on his ſlaves whatever puniſhment he pleaſes, and for any ſort of offence. It is againſt law, indeed, to put any of them to death; yet it happens, ſometimes, that a poor ſlave dies of the wounds he receives from a paſſionate and unrelenting ſuperior. I have heard, that not long ago a lady at Moſcow, the ſiſter of Mariſchal S———, was convicted of having put to death upwards of ſeventy ſlaves, by ſcourging, and by inflicting upon them other

 barbarous

barbarous punishments. It was a matter of amusement with her to contrive such modes of punishment as were whimsical and unusual. Such enormity, however, notwithstanding her rank, and the great power which the nobility have over their slaves, was not to pass with impunity. She was tried, was found guilty, and condemned to stand in the market-place, with a label on her breast declaring her crime, and to be shut up in a dungeon. But she, who had felt no reluctance in making her fellow-creatures suffer the most inhuman torments, and had even amused herself with the variety of their sufferings, had such a sense of her rank, and such lively feelings of her own disgrace, that pride, shame, and resentment deprived her of her reason. In truth, both the crime and the punishment seem to me strongly marked with the characters of barbarity.

As a Russian peasant has no property, can enjoy none of the fruits of his own labour more than is sufficient to preserve his existence, and can transmit nothing to his children but the inheritance of wretched bondage, he thinks of nothing beyond the present. You are

are not, of consequence, to expect among them much industry and exertion. Exposed to corporal punishment, and put on the footing of irrational animals, how can they possess that spirit and elevation of sentiment which distinguish the natives of a free state? Treated with so much inhumanity, how can they be humane? I am confident, that most of the defects which appear in their national character, are in consequence of the despotism of the Russian government.

I mentioned that the revenue of a Russian nobleman arises from those lands which are cultivated by his slaves; and sometimes in their being employed in other occupations than tillage. They often come from distant provinces, and are either employed as domestic slaves, mechanics, or as day-labourers, at Moscow, Petersburg, and other cities. In these cases they must have certificates and a written permit, specifying their names, owners, and the time they are allowed to be absent. When they come to any great town, with a view of remaining there, and engaging themselves in any work, the person who employs them must lodge their certificates with the maſter of the police in the place where they are about to reſide. After remaining their allotted time, they muſt return to their former owners, and muſt be accountable to them for every thing they have earned.—To theſe practices the Empreſs alludes in the following paſſages, in her inſtructions to the deputies aſſembled for making laws:—" It " ſeems too, that the method of exacting " their revenues, invented by the lords, di" miniſhes both the inhabitants, and the ſpi" rit of agriculture, in Ruſſia. Almoſt all " the villages are heavily taxed. The lords, " who ſeldom or never reſide in their vil" lages, lay an impoſt on every head, of one, " two, and even five rubles, without the leaſt " regard to the means by which their peaſants " may be able to raiſe this money. It is " highly neceſſary that the law ſhould pre" ſcribe a rule to the lords, for a more judi" cious method of raiſing their revenues; " and oblige them to levy ſuch a tax as tends " leaſt to ſeparate the peaſant from his houſe " and family: this would be the means by " which agriculture would become more ex" tenſive, and population more increaſed in " the empire. Even now, ſome huſbandmen

" do

" do not ſee their houſes for fifteen years to-
" gether, and yet pay the tax annually to
" their reſpective lords; which they procure
" in towns at a vaſt diſtance from their fami-
" lies, and wander over the whole empire for
" that purpoſe."

Another hardſhip to which the Ruſſian peaſants are expoſed, is, that they are obliged to marry whatſoever perſons, or at what time their ſuperiors pleaſe. Every ſlave who is a father, pays a certain tax to his owner for each of his children; and the owner is therefore ſolicitous that a new progeny be raiſed as ſoon as poſſible. Marriages of this ſort muſt produce little happineſs; neither huſband nor wife are very ſtudious of conjugal fidelity: hence the lower claſſes are as profligate as can poſſibly be conceived; and, in ſuch circumſtances, we cannot expect that they will have much care of their children.

The condition of thoſe peaſants who are immediate ſlaves of the crown, is reckoned leſs wretched than the condition of thoſe who belong to the nobility; and they are of three kinds: The firſt are thoſe who, having either ſecretly, or by the favour of a humane ſuperior, been able to procure as much money as may enable them to purchaſe their freedom, have alſo the good luck to live under a ſuperior who is equitable enough to free them for the ſum they offer. Such perſons, and their children, are ever after immediate ſlaves of the crown. On the ſame footing are all prieſts and their children; though the dependance of the inferior upon the ſuperior clergy, is ſometimes as grievous as the moſt painful bondage. Soldiers alſo, and their children; and this claſs includes the whole body of the nobility, are immediate ſlaves of the crown.

O fortunatos nimium, ſua ſi bona norint,
Britannos!

Adieu,

LETTER XXIX.

The Perſons—Food—Dreſs—Houſes—and Names of the Ruſſian Peaſants.

THE Ruſſians are tall, robuſt, and well-proportioned; their teeth are remarkably good; their hair is in general black, and their complexions ruddy. I have ſcarcely ſeen any red-haired perſons among them; and thoſe who are fair, are not ſo good-looking as thoſe who are dark-complexioned. Squinting or ſtuttering are ſeldom met with; and you ſee few or none who are either lame or deformed. Perhaps, from the little care the poor people can have of their children, and from the miſery of their enſlaved condition, moſt of thoſe who are feeble and ill-formed die in their infancy. Indeed I have heard another reaſon alleged for the few lame and deformed people that appear in Peterſburg. The Empreſs Elizabeth, it is ſaid, had

had ſo much delicacy, that ſhe could not bear to behold ſuch perſons; and therefore prohibited their appearing in the places where ſhe choſe to reſide. This cauſe, however, now ceaſes to operate; nor have I heard that her preſent majeſty was ever afflicted with ſuch averſions. —The women of all ranks in this country, though very ſprightly and very gay, for ever dancing, and ſinging, and laughing, and talking, have not the ſame pretenſions that the men have to good looks, and the graces of external appearance. They have no delicacy of ſhape; and their complexions are —— what they pleaſe. For thoſe even in the loweſt condition, if they are able to afford it, bedaub their faces with red. Red is the favourite colour here, inſomuch, that the word denoting it in the Ruſſian language, is ſynonymous with beautiful.

The Ruſſian peaſants eat a kind of black bread, made of rye, barley, buck wheat, and other grains of an inferior quality; it is ſour, but not unwholeſome. They alſo eat a great deal of garlic, coarſe oil, and fiſh. They make no cheeſe; and are not much acquainted with the uſes of milk. They drink a bad

kind

kind of mead, and liquors made of wild fruits; but their chief potation, and of which they partake very freely, is extracted from the corns which their country produces.—What Tacitus ſays of the ancient Germans is, in this circumſtance, quite applicable to the Ruſſians: "Potui humor ex hordeo aut fru-"mento, in quondam ſimilitudinem vini cor-"ruptus.—Sine apparatu, ſine blandimentis "expellunt famem: adverſus ſitim, non "eâdem temperantiâ." "Their drink is a "liquor prepared from barley or wheat; "corrupted into a certain reſemblance of "wine.—They ſatisfy hunger without regard "to the elegancies and delicacies of the table. "In quenching their thirſt they are not "equally temperate *."

Though they are in general ſtrong and healthy, they are ſometimes attacked by ſevere diſeaſes. Their fiſh diet in Lent brings upon them violent fluxes. They are alſo ſubject to ſcorbutic diſorders, for which, however, Nature provides an excellent antidote in the berries that grow native in Ruſſia. Theſe

* Aikin:

are

are the maroshki*; a berry in size and shape like a mulberry, but hard, of a reddish or yellowish colour, having a subacid taste, with little flavour, and growing on a small plant about half a foot high; the glukoi, or cranberry; wild strawberries; and hurtleberries.

Their dress, I mean that of the Russian peasants, is very simple, and well suited to their rigorous climate. It consists of skins, coarse woollen cloth, and coarse linen, which they use for shirts or drawers. Their upper garment is a large frock, reaching to their knees, folding over before, and fastened about the middle with a girdle. In the various and glaring colours of the girdle, they sometimes endeavour to display their taste. They have pieces of cloth wrapped in a variety of folds about their legs, and fastened with strings;

* Cloudberry—Rubus chamœmorus folliis simplicibus lobatis, caule inermi unifloro.——The Swedes and Norvegians esteem cloudberries to be an excellent antiscorbutic; they preserve great quantities of them in the autumn, to make tarts and other confections. The Laplanders bruise and eat them, as a delicious food, in the milk of the rein-deer; and to preserve them through the winter, they bury them in snow, and at the return of spring find them as fresh and good, as when at first gathered. LIGHTFOOT.

nor do they ſeem at all ſolicitous of exhibiting in this limb any qualities of ſhape or proportion. Their necks are naked, and expoſed to the weather, and, of conſequence, they reſemble bulls necks. They have long beards and buſhy hair; and have their heads covered with worſted or fur caps, riſing for the moſt part in a conic form. Every Ruſſian, of what rank ſoever, uſually wears upon his breaſt, and hanging by a ribbon or ſtring tied about his neck, a ſmall croſs of gold, ſilver, or lead. They receive theſe croſſes from their God-fathers at their baptiſm; and they never part with them as long as they live.

Their houſes are made of wood, and conſtructed in a very particular manner. A number of large trees are ſtripped of their bark; they are not cut into deals, but are laid cloſe and horizontally upon one another; they are faſtened at the end with wooden pegs; and thus, by fixing the end of one tree into another, they conſtitute the walls. The roof is ſometimes of boards, and ſometimes thatched. I have heard, that houſes of this ſort are frequently placed on wheels, ſo as to be moveable from one place to another. The

Ruſſians,

Russians, in constructing their houses, make use of very few instruments. The hatchet is almost the only one in use among them; it serves them even for a saw; and it is wonderful how straight and regularly they can cut with it. They make use neither of the plane nor of the chisel. I except from this account those who are professed carpenters.

In the country, the Russians generally live in small villages; the ground which they are to labour for their proprietors is in the neighbourhood; and in this case, every man is his own taylor, carpenter, and shoemaker. In every village there are superintendants, petty tyrants!

In so far as I can learn, the Russian peasants have no sirnames. Incapable of holding any property, and having nothing but bondage to transmit to their children, such distinction is useless. Those among them that affect sirnames, generally take the name of their proprietor, additionally to their christian name. The most common christian names that I have heard among them are, Cusma, Gregory, Stephen; Ivan, which they

translate

translate John; Vasili, which they translate William; Demetrius, Alexis, and others, manifestly derived from their neighbours in the south. This circumstance will appear to you the more surprising, that little intercourse subsisted between the Russians and the subjects of the eastern empire. It is owing to their religion. According to the tenets of the Greek church, every day in the year is sacred to some particular saint; and every child is believed to be under the protection of the holy personage who was homaged on his birth-day. Hence, too, unless for some very particular reason, all Russian children are called by the names of saints; and, as many of the saints have Greek names, the Barbarians by the Ladago, or the White Sea, are called by appellations familiar, in later times, in Athens or Byzantium. It follows, of consequence, in a country where the worship of images is practised, that every one has an image of the sainted person who protects him, and who is honoured accordingly. This image is so placed in the corner of his room, as to be the witness of all his actions, and receive humble obeisance as he enters the door. Hence, in every house and shop, you

you ſee an effigy of the tutelary ſaint; and, in days of religious ſolemnity, a wax candle or two are lighted before him. But though the Ruſſians have ſuch ſacred witneſſes of their conduct, they ſoon become ſo familiar with them, as to hazard the performance of any act whatſoever before them; and I have not heard of any but ſome of the fair ſex, who, in caſes of irreſiſtible temptation, have thought of veiling with an apron the face of the bluſhing ſaint.—In regard to ſirnames I already mentioned, that the peaſants, in ſo far as I could learn, have no ſuch appellation. If there are ſeveral of a name, they are diſtinguiſhed from each other by taking the name of their father, compounded with the words, which, in their language, ſignify ſon or daughter, and ſo denoting that particular relation. Thus, Ivan Petrowits, ſignifies Ivan the ſon of Peter; and Anna Ivanowna, ſignifies Anna the daughter of Ivan. Adieu.

LETTER XXX.

The Salutations—Quarrels—and Amuſements of the Ruſſian Peaſants.

DEAR SIR,

IN my laſt, I gave you ſome account of the perſons, food, dreſs, houſes, and names of the Ruſſians. The circumſtances I ſhall now mention, concerning their ſalutations, quarrels, and amuſements, may give you a more particular view of their manners and national character.

Two Ruſſian peaſants, meeting each other, take off their caps, bow moſt profoundly, ſhake hands, wipe their beards, kiſs one another, and, according to their different ages, call one another brother or father, or by ſome appellation that expreſſes affection. Both men and women in their ſalutations bow very low. I was much ſtruck with this circumſtance; and ſoon found, that, in their obeiſance to the great, and in the worſhip of their ſaints, they were early trained to proſtration and pliancy of body. Indeed, the ſervile ſubmiſſion they teſtify to their ſuperiors, can only be equalled by the haughty uſage they meet with in return.

Two Ruſſian peaſants, if they ſhould happen to quarrel, ſeldom proceed to blows; but they deal abuſe with great profuſion; and their abuſive language conſiſts of the baſeſt alluſions, and the moſt ſhocking obſcenity. This can ſcarcely be exemplified in the manners of any other nation. If ever they come to blows, the conflict has a moſt ludicrous appearance; they know nothing of the clenched fiſt of an Engliſhman; but lay about them moſt uncouthly with open hands and extended arms.

I know no circumſtance by which the national character of any people may more eaſily be detected, than their amuſements. When men divert themſelves, they are careleſs, unguarded, and unreſerved: then the heart,

heart, and all its latent tendencies, disguised inclinations, and indulged habits, appear. Nor am I acquainted with any circumstance by which national characters are more diversified. The Romans were a less refined people than the Greeks; their amusements accordingly were coarser and more sanguinary. In like manner the diversions of the French and Spaniards mark the difference of their national character. The pastime of the Spaniards, without doors, is fierce and bloody; nor is the Toros, or bull-fight, of which they are so passionately fond, the amusement of men only, but has its admirers also among the women. Hence Butler has said of them,

That Spanish heroes, with their lances,
At once wound bulls and ladies' fancies:
And he acquires the noblest spouse
That widows greatest herds of cows.

Chess, and the other amusements to which a Spaniard has recourse within doors, are certainly very grave and solemn. How different from the gaiety, sprightliness, good humour, and seeming levity of a Frenchman.

The diverſions of an Engliſhman exhibit ſtrength, agility, and the love of exertion. Thoſe of a Ruſſian exhibit ſloth, inactivity, and the love of pleaſure. The Ruſſians, in their amuſements, are indeed extremely ſocial. They aſſemble in crowds, ſing, drink, ſwing on ſee-ſaws, are drawn up and down and round about in flying chairs fixed upon wheels, ſome with a perpendicular, and ſome with a horizontal motion.

In the winter ſeaſon, they are puſhed down ice-hills and gliſſades. Thoſe ice-hills are raiſed upon the river, and are conſtructed of wooden frames. They are very high; ſo that you aſcend fifty or ſixty ſteps on the ſide behind what is properly called the gliſſade. The ſummit is flat, and encloſed with a rail, in order that thoſe who indulge themſelves in this amuſement, may have room to ſtand and ſuffer no inconvenience in the deſcent. The ſide by which they go down is ſo ſteep, as to be juſt not perpendicular. Upon this ſnow having been piled, and water poured, it becomes a precipice of the ſmootheſt ice. In deſcending, you ſit upon a ſmall wooden ſeat made for the purpoſe, and generally in the lap of a Ruſſian, who ſits behind to direct your courſe, having his legs extended on each ſide of you. In this poſture you are puſhed down the hill, and ſlide with ſuch velocity, that for ſome ſeconds you cannot breathe; and after reaching the bottom, the impulſe you have received carries you forward ſome hundred paces. There are commonly two of theſe gliſſades erected almoſt, but not quite, oppoſite to each other; and at ſuch a diſtance, as that you are carried along the ice from one to another. Thus you may go down the one hill and up the other, alternately, as often as you pleaſe.—Skating is not a common diverſion, becauſe the ice, where it is not ſwept, is uſually covered with ſnow.—The Ruſſians are alſo fond of dancing; yet their dancing does not diſplay ſo much nimbleneſs, agility, and livelineſs, as it expreſſes the ſame tainted imagination, which aſſumes a leſs ſeducing and more boiſterous form in their quarrels and abuſe.

I believe I may reckon their bathing rather an amuſement than a religious practice. In every village, eſpecially in thoſe by the ſide of rivers, where they are generally built, there is a ſteam-bath, conſtructed uſually of wood, to which all the inhabitants, both male and female, repair regularly once a week. The place is ſo inſufferably hot, that a perſon who is not accuſtomed to it, cannot remain in it above a few minutes. But thoſe to whom it is not unuſual, ſit quietly for a long time on the heated bricks, without any covering whatſoever, excepting ſome branches of birch, of which, however, they hardly make any other uſe than to ſcrub themſelves. After they have ſat in this ſituation, till they have perſpired abundantly, they run out, and plunge headlong into the river. They are excellent ſwimmers; but inſtead of ſwimming like frogs, as we do, they imitate rather the motion of dogs. I once ſaw one of thoſe baths catch fire; the weather was dry; it blazed up in a moment, and the whole bevy it contained, ran with the utmoſt conſternation into the water, ſcreaming and plunging, and looking back as if they thought the flames were purſuing them.

You will perhaps imagine, that the practice of uſing the bath, as deſcribed above, contributes to the licentiouſneſs of manners,

ſo

ſo remarkable in the lower claſſes among the Ruſſians. No doubt it does; but ſome other circumſtances, formerly mentioned, have the ſame tendency. The power poſſeſſed by ſuperiors of compelling their ſlaves to marry as they ſhall direct, if ever exerted, muſt be completely deſtructive of domeſtic happineſs and fidelity. The practice ſo common among the nobles, of removing their ſlaves from one place to another, and of keeping them a long time ſeparated from their families, has alſo the ſame effect. You will readily perceive that this muſt be very much the caſe, when they are ſent from the country villages, to earn their wages in Moſcow and St. Peterſburg.

You will have remarked too, in the accounts I have given you, that the lower claſſes here are very ſocial, and much addicted to merriment. They are even infantine in their amuſements. Old, bearded boors divert themſelves with ſuch paſtime and gambols, as in our grave country we ſhould think too trifling for a child. The truth is, that, beyond the preſent moment, they have nothing either to think about, or care for; and, of conſequence, they are perfectly thoughtless and careless. In the country they live chiefly in villages; when they come to the great towns, many of them having no houses of their own, pass most of their time, when they are not employed in labour, in their cabecks*, where they drink, talk, and sing till they fall asleep; and on holidays they assemble together in vacant places in or near the city, for their customary exercises and amusements. Those two circumstances, therefore, namely, their social dispositions, promoted in the manner now mentioned, and their total want of care or concern about the future, give them the appearance of having great sprightliness and good humour, and of possessing no inconsiderable share of enjoyment. Persons of high rank, though their situations must occasion some variety in the circumstances that influence their manners, are subject to the same effects, and exhibit a similar appearance. If you call such enjoyment happiness, or such social dispositions virtuous, you may: I own I cannot agree with you. Russians of all ranks are most ardent in their expressions of

* Public-houses.

friendship;

friendſhip; but I ſuſpect the conſtancy of their attachments is not equal to the fervency of their emotions. They have more ſenſibility than firmneſs; they poſſeſs a temper and diſpoſitions, which, properly improved, and with the encouragements held forth by freedom, might render them a worthy, as, in ſome caſes, they are an amiable, and, in many, an amuſing people.

Conſiſtently with this account, the Ruſſians, though they have great quickneſs in learning the rudiments of art or knowledge, ſeldom make great proficiency. They ſoon arrive at a certain degree of excellence; there they remain; they tire; become liſtleſs; entertain diſguſt; and advance no further. In this particular, alſo, if they enjoyed the incitements afforded by a free government, their national character might improve, and they might be rendered capable of more perſeverance. After the wiſhes of novelty ceaſe, men engaged in arduous purſuits, muſt be carried on by a ſteady regard to their own intereſt and honour. Where their honour and intereſt are not much concerned, how can they perſevere? Adieu.

LETTER XXXI.

Domeſtic Manners of Perſons of Rank in Ruſſia.

DEAR SIR, St. Peterſburg, 1770.

I CANNOT ſay much for the taſte diſplayed by perſons of high rank in Ruſſia, either in their dreſs, houſes, or retinue. They are pompous and tawdry. The equipage of a Ruſſian nobleman deſerves particular notice. The great man lolls in a clumſy gilt coach, drawn by ſix horſes, ſometimes of different colours, and having the traces of hempen ropes inſtead of leather. The coachman and poſtilions are often in the coarſe dreſs of the peaſants, while three or four gorgeous footmen are ſtuck behind. One or two petty officers ride by the ſide of the coach, and theſe are uſually attended by a peaſant, who is alſo on horſeback; and thus princes and noblemen

blemen are dragged to court.——They read plays and novels, and often ſome French philoſophy. They ſometimes write little comedies; and ſometimes repreſent them, both in the French and Ruſſian languages. I was lately preſent at the repreſentation of "Le Philoſope Mari," and "Annette and Lubin," by ſome noblemen and ladies of the higheſt rank. They performed in the theatre in the Winter Palace, and the Empreſs ſeemed much amuſed with the repreſentation.

I mentioned to you formerly, that the inferior orders of men in this country are in a ſtate of abject ſlavery. Nor is it inconſiſtent with this account to ſay, that many perſons of high rank in Ruſſia live on a footing of eaſy familiarity with ſuch of their menials as become favourites, and are capable of amuſing them with their humour and low wit. All domeſtic tyrants, from the days of the Greeks and Romans incluſively, treat thoſe ſlaves who are not favourites with the utmoſt rigour, and thoſe who are, with weak unbecoming indulgence. Perhaps in no other country in Europe could you obtain a juſter idea

idea of the parasitical character, so frequently displayed by the comic and satirical poets of antiquity. The parasites here are in general Frenchmen, whose lively loquacity seems absolutely necessary for the amusement of those great men, to whose tables they have admission.

At the same time, if the following representation, in one of the finest satires that any language can boast of, be founded on observation, the circumstance now mentioned is not peculiar to the Russian Princes.

> All that at home no more can beg or steal,
> Or like a gibbet better than a wheel;
> Hiss'd from the stage, or hooted from the court,
> Their air, their dress, their politics import;
> Obsequious, artful, voluble, and gay,
> On Britain's fond credulity they prey.—
> Studious to please, and ready to submit,
> The supple Gaul was born a parasite:
> Still to his int'rest true, where'er he goes,
> Wit, bravery, worth, his lavish tongue bestows;
> In every face a thousand graces shine,
> From every tongue flows harmony divine.

The description is heightened in the next lines by a characteristical and happy contrast.

These

These arts in vain our rugged natives try,
Strain out with fault'ring diffidence a lie,
And gain a kick for awkward flattery.

The satirist then proceeds in a successful vein of playful irony; and concludes the passage with a serious, and indignant address.

Besides, with justice this discerning age,
Admires their wondrous talents for the stage;
Well may they venture on the mimic's art,
Who play from morn to night a borrow'd part;
Practis'd their master's notions to embrace,
Repeat his maxims and reflect his face;
With ev'ry wild absurdity comply,
And view each object with another's eye;
To shake with laughter, ere the jest they hear,
To pour at will the counterfeited tear;
And as their patron hints the cold or heat,
To shake in dogdays, in December sweat;
How, when competitors like these contend,
Can surly Virtue hope to fix a friend?
Slaves that with serious impudence beguile,
And lie without a blush, without a smile.—
For arts like these, preferr'd, admir'd, caress'd,
They first invade your table, then your breast;
Explore your secrets with insidious art,
Watch the weak hour, and ransack all the heart;
Then soon your ill-plac'd confidence repay,
Commence your lords, and govern or betray.

Besides

Besides parasites, many Russians of high rank retain dwarfs in their families, and persons not without shrewdness, who affect folly, and amuse them in the character of buffoons. They also retain a vast number of other slaves, who are employed by them in all manner of necessary or whimsical services. The Countess W—— has in her family several Calmuck women, who are taught to read German and Russ, who read by her bed-side till she falls asleep; and continue reading or talking, without intermission, all the time she is asleep; for, if they did not, the Countess would awake immediately, not much, I suppose, to the satisfaction of the poor attendants.

I need scarcely tell you, that the Russians are very careless in the education of their children. They do not send them to public schools; but have them taught at home under private tutors. These tutors are generally French or Germans, into whose character they make but little enquiry. If their children learn to dance; and if they can read, speak, and write French, and have a little geography,

geography, they desire no more. I have seen one of those instructors, who has, in the course of his life; appeared in the different shapes of a comedian, valet-de-chambre, and hair-dresser.——Indeed I do not wonder at the conduct of the Russians in this respect. Why educate their children? They are to live and die in thraldom; they may be in glory to-day, and to morrow sent to Siberia. Why should they train their offspring for any expectations beyond those of the present moment? The citizens of free states alone are inexcusable, if they do not improve their minds to the utmost limits of their capacity. Why quicken the sensibilities, or enlarge the mind of a slave? You only teach him to hate himself. If, however, there was any probability, that, by enlightning the minds of the Russians, they should not only be enabled to discern the abasement of their condition; but also to contrive, and execute the means of emancipation, I should heartily regret their present blindness.

The military education of the Russian youth is conducted very differently. They have

have an academy in the Wasiloſtrow, where a very conſiderable number, but none under twelve years old, are admitted. Here they live together; and during the ſummer ſleep in an adjoining field under tents. They are formed into a regiment; and each of them, of what rank ſoever, whether Prince, Count, or Boyard. muſt paſs through every condition, beginning with that of a common ſoldier, and ſubmit to every kind of obedience. They perform their exerciſes with great exactneſs, and are inſtructed in mathematics. From this ſeminary excellent officers may be expected. Like the Perſians, deſcribed by Xenophon, they learn to obey before they are called to command.

After the account I have given you of the taſte and literary education of the Ruſſians, you will not be ſurpriſed if I tell you, that their religious principles are not very correct, nor in ſome of them, perhaps, very deeply rooted. A prieſt came to hear the confeſſion of a great man. "Holy Father," ſays the Count, "have you a good memory." "Yes." "Then you remember what I told you at my "laſt

" laſt confeſſion. Since that time I have had " the ſame temptations from without; the " ſame weakneſs from within; and here is " the ſame number of rubles."—I would not ſay, however, that the Princes of Ruſſia are much inferior, either in religious or moral improvement, to many great men, even in thoſe ſtates of Europe that enjoy the means of ſuperior knowledge. If I am not much miſtaken, there are among them a greater number who affect indifference or diſbelief in religious matters, than who really diſbelieve. Perhaps, in times of ſickneſs, diſgrace, and low-ſpirits, they have more faith in St. Nicholas, than in Voltaire.

The fair ſex in all ages have more ſenſibility, leſs of the pride of reaſon, and I had almoſt ſaid, more good ſenſe than the men; and accordingly you find fewer among them who affect irreligion. Their notions may be erroneous; this is owing to their inſtructors: but their diſpoſitions are pious, and they owe this to themſelves. Indeed, when I ſee Ruſſian Princeſſes, as they ſit down to an entertainment, croſſing themſelves, which they do very gracefully, in teſtimony of religious gratitude, I reſpect both their good ſenſe and their piety. They will excuſe me, therefore, for telling the following ſtory: I do not anſwer for the fact; but that ſuch ſtories are told, and reckoned not improbable, may give you ſome notion of the religious manners of the Ruſſians——A lady of high rank had a child ſuddenly ſeized with a violent illneſs. Full of anxiety, ſhe diſpatched a meſſenger to a neighbouring prieſt, intreating him to ſend a favourite ſaint, who might effectuate the cure. But the prieſt, being a ſenſible man, and unwilling to ſend the hallowed phyſician, without fixing the fee, or for ſome other reaſon, refuſed her requeſt. The lady, in mighty wrath, haſtened to the Empreſs, then ſome miles out of town, and brought a formal complaint againſt the prieſt. The Empreſs ordered him forthwith to comply. Accordingly the ſaint was ſent, but he came a bootleſs errand; for a Scotch phyſician, little deſirous that interlopers ſhould interfere with his trade, had reſtored the child to health, before the arrival of his ghoſtly colleague.

I write

I write to you in a very desultory manner; and I am afraid I may sometimes be guilty of repetition. The truth is, I have not a great deal of leisure, and you have a great deal of indulgence. Adieu.

LETTER XXXII.

Adminiſtration of Juſtice in Ruſſia.

DEAR SIR,

AGREEABLY to your deſire, and to gratify my own curioſity, I have made every enquiry I could concerning the manner of adminiſtring juſtice in Ruſſia. I am ſorry, however, it is not in my power to give you ſuch ſatisfactory information on this ſubject as I wiſhed to have done. Nor can I offer you any other account of the courts of juſtice, the method of conducting a law-ſuit, or the puniſhment of crimes, than the following.

The Judge of loweſt rank in this empire is the Staroſt; and from him, in the firſt inſtance, perſons in the provinces who have ſuffered injury may ſeek redreſs. From his deciſion there lies an appeal to the Governor of the province, and from him to the College of of Juſtice in the capital. For the whole empire is divided into a certain number of governments; to each of theſe a particular college of juſtice is appropriated in St. Peterſburg; and to thoſe colleges cauſes may be appealed. From them too there lies an appeal to the Senate. Nor are the deciſions of that court, though of a name ſo venerable, and though ſaid to have both a legiſlative and judicative authority, conſidered as ultimate; for, as the Sovereign is regarded as the ſource of law and juſtice, there may be an appeal to the Throne, even from the decrees of the Senate. The Sovereign, however, not having leiſure for attending to a multitude of private law-ſuits, delegates this department to Commiſſioners; and their deciſions, or Ucaſes, according to the term uſually given them, are accounted final. All the judges are named by the Sovereign, and hold their places only during her pleaſure.—In general, the adminiſtration of juſtice has been repreſented to me as very tedious, and liable to corruption. I have heard, indeed, that the Empreſs intends to alter the preſent ſyſtem; and if ſo, it will certainly receive improvement. In truth, the Courts of Juſtice now mentioned, bear a greater reſemblance to a Court of Chancery * than to any thing elſe. The deciſions of the judges are neither founded on general principles of equity, nor on eſtabliſhed laws. They are founded chiefly on precedents and former deciſions. This, as you will eaſily conceive, renders the iſſue of a law-ſuit very doubtful; and, indeed, it frequently happens, that precedents and former Ucaſes may be perfectly applicable to the ſame cauſe; and yet in direct oppoſition to one another. In caſes the moſt ſimilar that can be thought of, contradictory decrees of different ſovereigns, and ſometimes even of the ſame ſovereign, may be appealed to. Thus it is obvious, that, on the preſent footing, every thing depends on the will of the Judge.

Thoſe perſons who correſpond to counſel or advocates in Britain, are very little reſpected in Ruſſia. They receive no regular education in the ſtudy of law. And how ſhould they, when there is none to ſtudy? They are uſually ſuch perſons as may have been Judges' ſervants, or have had other opportunities of learning the forms of courts, and

* Blackſtone.

and of being acquainted with precedents or Ucases. Dexterity in the knowledge and application of these constitutes their highest merit. They never plead; but give their advice in the conduct of a law-suit; write the necessary papers; and either in public or private lay the facts before the judges. This last, indeed, may be considered as a species of pleading, since they may represent facts in such colours, as to influence both judgment and inclination. I have heard it surmised, however, by persons, I confess, of acrimony, but not without knowledge, and even experience, that the best service they usually render their clients, is to inform them by what means they may have easiest access to the good-will of the Judges. The most eminent counsel who practises here at present, had been a shop-keeper, and had involved himself in so many law-suits as to become bankrupt. But though he lost his fortune, he gained knowledge; and the same argumentative disposition that had ruined him as a merchant, advanced him at the bar.

Besides the courts above-mentioned, a general Court of Police is established in Russia, of which the principal department remains at St. Petersburg. The chief objects of the Master of Police are, to keep order in the city; to prosecute for robbery and murder; to guard against fires; to keep the streets clean; to prevent or disperse riots; to superintend the Ishvoshicks, who hire sledges or carioles in the streets; and to keep an exact account of the inhabitants. At one time a cause might be carried by appeal from this court to the Senate; at other times, its decisions were determined to be final. All these changes and varieties depend on the will of the Sovereign.

You questioned me in particular about the punishment of crimes in Russia, and seemed to applaud the plan pursued by the late, and continued by the present, Empress, of substituting slavery, hard labour, and corporal punishment, in place of death. The abolition, or suspension of capital punishments, is indeed a very plausible topic; it may soothe our sentiments of humanity, it may please in theory; but in practice it appears very inadequate. Robberies here are frequent and barbarous, and constantly attended with murder. Criminals,

Criminals, I have heard, are profecuted carelefly; and thofe who are punifhed with rigour, are treated with inhumanity. They fuffer the knout; that is, they fuffer dreadful fcourging and diflocation; and though they are not formally put to death, many of them die of the cruel wounds they receive. I faw a crowd lately affembled in an open fpace in the city; I drew near; a fcourge rofe at intervals above the heads of the people; at intervals were heard the repeated ftrokes; and every ftroke was followed by the low fuppreffed groan of extenuated anguifh. After the appointed number of lafhes were given in that place, the poor criminal had a piece of the coarfeft cânvafs thrown over his naked and wounded body; and he was thus led to another quarter of the city, to have his torments not only renewed, but dreadfully encreafed by diflocation.

Thofe who furvive fuch punifhments are very feldom reformed; the difgrace and infamy they fuffer, take away all refpect for themfelves, and regard for the opinion of others. On this fubject I agree entirely with your favourite Greek Tragedian.

" Χρην

"Χρην δε ευθυς ειναι τηνδε τοις πασι δικην
Ὁςτις περα πρασσειν των νομων θελει
Κτεινειν. το γαρ πανεργον εκ αν ην πολυ."

"——— Were all like thee to perish
Who violate the laws, 'twould lessen much
The guilt of mortals, and reform mankind *".

At any rate, the subjects at least of a free state, ought to be much on their guard how they suffer any such punishment to be substituted in place of capital punishment, as may reconcile the imaginations of the people to the possibility of their being happy, or of their enduring life in chains and bondage. They ought always to believe, nor in adopting such a creed, would they suffer any delusion, that slavery is a more miserable condition than death. I have felt less horror in seeing malefactors hanging in gibbets on Bagshot or Hounslow-heath, than in seeing men, beings of my own species, endowed with

* The elegant translator of Sophocles does not appear to me to have translated this striking passage with his usual spirit. Perhaps the Latin version may convey more strongly the Poet's meaning.

"Deceret autem omnes illico has pœnas dare
Quicunque contra leges quidvis agere studet
Ut necaretur. Sic scelera minus crebra forent."

reason

reaſon and a ſenſe of juſtice, doomed to hard labour all the days of their lives, bent down with oppreſſion, having their faces inſcribed with miſery, and their limbs rattling with chains. Crimes are not to be puniſhed by the ſevereſt pains we are capable of inflicting: and I hope the natives of Britain will conſider chains and bondage, in the face of the public, as a puniſhment no leſs barbarous to the mind, than torture to the body. In another view, the effects of ſuch puniſhments on the minds of a free people muſt be pernicious; and I ſhould be afraid leſt their enduring them for any length of time, were a fatal ſymptom that their zeal for liberty was waxing cold. There is much thought and penetration in the following ſentiment, aſcribed by Tacitus to Galgacus, in his celebrated ſpeech before his battle with Agricola:——
"Priores pugnæ, quibus adverſus Romanos
"varia fortuna certatum eſt, ſpem ac ſubſi-
"dium in noſtris manibus habebant; quia
"nobiliſſimi totius Britanniæ, eoque in ipſis
"penetralibus ſiti, nec ſerventium littora
"aſpicientes, *oculos quoque a contactu domina-*
"*tionis inviolatis habebamus.*"——"All the
"the battles, which have yet been fought
"with

" with various ſucceſs againſt the Romans,
" had their reſources of hope and aid in our
" hands; for we, the nobleſt inhabitants of
" Britain, and therefore ſtationed in its
" deepeſt receſſes, far from the view of ſervile
" ſhores, have preſerved even our eyes un-
" polluted by the contact of ſubjection *."

Little proviſion is made in this country for priſoners: and a poor wretch, without friends or money, confined in a Ruſſian jail, runs ſome hazard of ſtarving. I have ſometimes viſited thoſe manſions of miſery: and if famine, chains, nakedneſs, and filth, are ſhocking, the ſcenes I beheld were ſhocking.

On reading over what I have written, it ſeems to me that I might have given you a more complete account of the adminiſtration of juſtice in Ruſſia, by telling you what they have not, inſtead of what they have. Suffice it to ſay then, that they have no trials by jury, and no Habeas Corpus Act. A perſon accuſed of crimes may be kept in priſon for ever; or if he is brought to a trial, he is not tried by his Peers. In other reſpects, cauſes

* Aitkin.

need

need not be numerous and complex. The peaſants who are themſelves ſlaves, will probably have no law-ſuits. The nobility, merchants, and foreigners alone can have any employment for courts of juſtice. Adieu.

P. S. If the Empreſs ſhould really engage, as I believe ſhe intends at preſent, in the laborious work of amending the method of adminiſtring juſtice in Ruſſia, ſeveral paſſages in her inſtructions to the commiſſioners appointed to frame a new code of laws, and the following, in particular, promiſe not only changes, but conſiderable improvements:

" No man ought to be looked upon as " guilty, before he has received his judicial " ſentence; nor can the laws deprive him of " their protection, before it is proved that he " has forfeited all right to it. What right, " therefore, can power give to any to inflict " puniſhment upon a citizen, at a time when " it is yet dubious whether he is innocent or " guilty? Whether the crime be known or " unknown, it is not very difficult to gain a " thorough knowledge of the affair, by duly " weighing all the circumſtances. If the

4 " crime

" be known, the criminal ought not to suffer
" any punishment but what the law ordains;
" consequently the *rack* is quite unnecessary.
" If the crime be not known, the rack ought
" not to be applied to the party accused; for
" this reason, that the innocent ought not to be
" tortured; and, in the eye of the law, every
" person is innocent whose crime is not yet
" proved. It is undoubtedly extremely ne-
" cessary, that no crime, after it has been
" proved, should remain unpunished. The
" party accused on the rack, whilst in the
" agonies of torture, is not master enough of
" himself to be able to declare the truth, &c."

LETTER XXXIII.

Reflections on the Effects of Despotism.

DEAR SIR, St. Petersburg, Oct. 1st, 1770.

YOU say I will have much pleasure in contemplating the manners and political constitution of a people so different from the natives of Britain. I cannot altogether agree with you. No doubt there is some pleasure in what Lucretius says,—" *suave mari magno*, &c." There is some satisfaction in recollecting, that while other nations groan under the yoke of bondage, the natives of our happy islands enjoy more real freedom than any nation that does now, or ever did, exist. In other respects, it is no very pleasing exercise to witness the depression and sufferings of the human race; to contemplate the miseries and manners of slaves! Poor abject slaves! who are not allowed the rights of men—hardly those of irrational creatures! who must toil, undergo hardſhips, and ſuffer the moſt grievous ſuffering, to gratify the deſires, or humour the caprice of ſome oppreſſive maſter! Judge of their condition.—From the hour of their birth they are in the power of a rapacious chief, who may ſell, ſcourge, or employ them in any labour he pleaſes. They have no property—no home—nothing that their proud ſuperior may not ſeize, and claim as his own. The horſe and the bull may chuſe their loves, according to their own inclination; a privilege not allowed to the Ruſſians. They no ſooner arrive at the age of puberty, than they are often compelled to marry whatſoever female their proprietor chuſes, in order, by a continued progeny of ſlaves, to preſerve or augment his revenue. In ſuch families, no conjugal happineſs,—no paternal or filial affection can ever exiſt. Where the huſband and wife hate each other, or are indifferent, there can be little fidelity; the huſband takes little care of the child; the mother is not always affectionate; the poor guiltleſs infant is thus neglected; Nature defeats the purpoſes of avarice, and a great proportion of their children die in their nonage. Thoſe that ſurvive

ſurvive become little better than ſavage. In their early years, no tender affection ſoftened or humanized their hearts; none can grow up in an after period; they receive no prejudices or opinions favourable to mankind; and they enter into life as into a den of tygers. The guile, the baſeneſs, and rugged ferocity attributed to ſlaves, and men overwhelmed with oppreſſion, are chiefly owing to their oppreſſors. Expoſed to the avarice and pride of ſome haughty ſuperior, who is himſelf a ſlave, and who has not in his breaſt one ſentiment of humanity, they have no other defence againſt oppreſſion but deceit; and feel no other emotion from the treatment they receive, but hatred and deep revenge. It is thus, in accuſtoming the mind to vicious habits, more than in merely depriving us of our property, and the ſecurity of our perſons, that deſpotiſm is the bane of ſociety. Thoſe poor unhappy men, who are bought and ſold, who are beaten, loaded with fetters, and valued no higher than a dog, treated with unabating rigour, become inhuman; inſulted with unremitting contempt, become baſe; and for ever afraid of rapacious injuſtice, they grow deceitful.

—— " Chill'd by unkindly blights,
" Their opening virtues languish and decay.
" Their features lose the liberal air of truth
" And open candour. Dark suspicion clouds
" Their low'ring visage; and deceit perverts
" Their fault'ring speech. When pride and avarice warp
" Th' oppressor's heart; bar his relentless ear
" Against the prayer of pity; and eraze
" The sense of merit from his dark'ned soul:
" What shield can weakness to his rav'nous grasp
" Oppose, but dastard guile? Can those who groan
" Beneath th' inhuman task, whose rueful pangs,
" Unpitied, unreliev'd, breed lasting hate,
" And thirst of vengeance in the soul indulge
" Tender emotions, and the glowing heart?
" O ye! who roll the eye of fierce disdain,
" Impute not to the trembling, tortur'd slave,
" Condemn'd by partial fortune to endure
" The stripes of av'rice, and the scorn of pride,
" Impute not guile, or an unfeeling breast.
" Ye teach him feelings! your insatiate rage
" His hate exasperates, and inflames his heart
" With rancour and unusual wrath. 'Twas thus
" Th' Iberian *humaniz'd* the guiltless tribes
" Who roam'd Peruvian forests, and the banks
" Of Orellane, what time, convuls'd and torn
" With agony, the tortur'd sires bequeath'd
" Resentment to their sons! 'Twas then their hearts
" Throbb'd with new horror; with unwonted ire
" The wild eye redden'd, and the virtues fled!
" The gentle virtues! In their stead arose
" Dismay, the counsellor of dastard deeds,

" Revenge

"Revenge and ruthlefs hatred. Then were heard
"Wailing and weeping; howl'd the defart caves;
"And Nature from the roaring torrent figh'd."——

"Facit indignatio verfum." Thofe lines were fuggefted by the fcenes of oppreffion I too often behold. I have introduced them into a fhort poem lately publifhed in Britain; and intended, in fo far as my voice could be heard, to intereft my countrymen in behalf of the Corficans. I fufpect, however, that at prefent, not many of my countrymen feel themfelves much concerned in fuch a caufe.

* * * * * *

LETTER XXXIV.

National Character of the Russians.

DEAR SIR,

IN so far as my own observation reaches, every thing I see, and every thing I hear from such authority as I can trust, confirms me in the opinion I formerly expressed to you concerning the national character of the Russians. They have certainly more sensibility than firmness. They have lively feeelings; but having seldom employed their reason in forming general rules of conduct for the commerce of life, their actions, as flowing from variable and shifting emotions, are desultory, and even inconsistent.

I have heard, for instance, that, in confidential conversation, they sometimes indulge themselves in severe or indignant expressions against the present administration of public affairs.—"That they should always be go-"verned by women, or foreigners, or by fo-"reigners exalted they not how, or by per-"sons

" ſons of no original eminence, men of yeſ-
" terday, and who have ariſen to dignity by
" their guilt or baſe compliances,"—are, on ſuch occaſions, the uſual topics of their diſcontent. They work themſelves into what they conceive virtuous indignation, or patriotic reſentment. They even talk of changes and revolutions: " Things," they will ſay, " that have happened once, may happen " again;" and thus the fervour of their emotion, exhauſted in the expreſſion, abates. Other feelings ariſe, and ſuggeſt other convictions.—" The preſent adminiſtration has " been ſucceſsful; laurels have been obtain- " ed; public meaſures are conducted with " ſpirit and wiſdom; they themſelves enjoy " ſecurity; not only ſo, perhaps they enjoy " fortune and honours; how wrong then " would it be in them to wiſh for change; " how ungrateful! how guilty! even of " treaſon! they deſerve puniſhment! per- " haps it may come upon them! their aſſo- " ciates may think as they do! may feel in- " dignation! or fear for themſelves! the " danger is urgent, and muſt be prevented." Hurried by this new ſet of feelings, they repent, confeſs, and, from the deep ſenſe they

have of their trespass, betray their friends. On account of this extreme sensibility, unsubdued or ungoverned by reason, it is scarcely probable that the Russians themselves, how much soever they may occasionally express resentment, indignation, or love of liberty, as I have heard some of them do with more violence than any liberty-boy of Brentford, unless some dextrous, insinuating, and steady foreigner take advantage of their temporary transports, shall ever accomplish any great revolution. The chief rulers have penetration enough to discern this defect of character; and though they may be often informed of treasonable speeches, they are nevertheless very much at their ease. At the same time, this feature, in the national character of the Russians, shews how necessary it is for their Sovereigns, without incurring the *blame of improper suspicion*, to be watchful over their proceedings, and well acquainted with their secret designs *.

I really believe, that the inconstancy, the deviations from truth, and even perfidy, with which the Russians are sometimes charged,

* See Letter XVII.

are

are not ſo much the effects of determined vice, as of irregular feeling. They may appear wicked, not becauſe they act from perverted principles, but becauſe they have no permanent principles. They never could ſay to themſelves, " *Video meliora proboque, de-" teriora ſequor,*" becauſe whatſoever they do, or even perpetrate, they think they are acting aright; and as they ſeldom look back on the paſt, or anticipate the future, they derive little advantage in the culture of their moral principles from experience. They are bearded children; the creatures of the preſent hour; they will expreſs the moſt ardent affection in the moſt ardent language; they will expreſs the moſt furious rage in the moſt vindictive terms. But as you need not lay great ſtreſs on the advantages to be reaped from their friendſhip, ſo you need not be greatly afraid of their inveterate or latent enmity. In moments of extreme good humour, a Ruſſian will make ample promiſes; he is quite ſincere; his feelings at the time intereſt him in your favour; but thoſe feelings ſubſide; other intereſts engage his heart; he never meant to deceive you; but his promiſes are not fulfilled. If you ſeem anxious about any fact, and if the matter is not exactly as you wish it to be, your Russian friend enters warmly into your wishes; he would not add to your anxiety, but he knows that the fact is not exactly as you conceive; he sees in it, however, some circumstances corresponding to your desire; these he selects; he is loth to tell you a harsh truth; and if he does not tell you a pleasing fiction, he at least lulls your disquietude. Rigid virtue may call this double-dealing; but the Russian neither intends deceit, nor thinks his conduct deceitful. In like manner you may sometimes see persons of the highest rank, even before strangers, engage in violent disputes, particularly if they are playing at cards or billiards; and treat one another at least with impetuosity. Their own language, though they may have been speaking French or German before, becomes, on these occasions, the vehicle of their prayers and wishes; and its habits of phraseology seem better suited, than those of the western languages, for such *pure* and *respectful* intercourse. In a few minutes after they are as calm as if nothing had happened, and seem to love one another the more for this tran-

sient

ſient ebullition, Perſons of ſuch irregular ſenſibility are occaſionally very brave, or very daſtardly; and ſo are the Ruſſians. Sometimes the ſlighteſt danger appalls them; and ſometimes you would imagine that they were incapable of fear, or had no ſenſe of danger. This tendency is corrected in their army by the ſtricteſt diſcipline. It is perfectly conſiſtent with this account, that ſlight enjoyments ſhould raiſe them to the ſummit of happineſs; and that ſlight loſſes, or diſappointments, ſhould caſt them down in deſpair. Accordingly, their happineſs diſplays itſelf in appearances of infantine levity; and their deſpondency often terminates in ſuicide. The immediate view of puniſhment, or the proſpect of evil ſtriking their ſenſes, may reſtrain their emotions; but, removed at a diſtance, or out of ſight, it is of little power. One of their principal dramatic Poets, and he has indeed a great deal of genius, beſides the impetuoſity and eagerneſs entailed upon him by his profeſſion, has alſo to contend with the precipitancy and irregular ſenſibility ſo common among his countrymen. The Governor of Moſcow, where he uſually reſides, ordered

one

one of his tragedies to be represented. The Poet was certainly honoured by this mark of attention; and the Governor really intended to do him honour; nor was there any thing that could reasonably be objected to the representation. But the Poet had been taken in a wayward humour. He opposed the representation with indecent violence, and treated the Governor with rude disrespect. The Empress, whom nothing escapes, was informed of it; but respecting the genius of the Poet, while she rebuked the folly of the Russian, she wrote him with tempered severity, and told him, "That though she was much "pleased with his imitations of passion, she "could not bear the reality."

Persons of the character now mentioned, are often fluent in speech, and eloquent in expression. They are also apt to be influenced by the powers of eloquence. Full of sensibility, they enter easily into the feelings of others. Such are the Russians.—— Walking one day along the Galerinhoff, at a time when, by the removal of a bridge of boats, the communication between that street and an opposite island was interrupted, I saw a Russian a Ruſſian, rather better dreſſed than a common peaſant, putting ſome cows into a boat, intending to have them carried to the other ſide. He had juſt, with much difficulty, and the aſſiſtance of two or three boatmen, got them in, when a petty officer, with ſome ſoldiers, arrived at the place, and ſeemed alſo in great haſte to get acroſs the river. There was no other boat; ſo, with a tone of great authority, he ordered the grazier, or cowherd, or whatever he was, to take out his cattle, and let him have immediate conveyance. The Ruſſian was loth; the officer inſiſted; the Ruſſian argued; the officer grew angry; the Ruſſian ſtill heſitated; and a ſoldier, to gratify the wrath of his ſuperior, jumped into the boat, gave the man a blow, and ſtruck off his cap. The Ruſſian in an inſtant, and you would ſay by involuntary impulſe, put himſelf into one of the fineſt attitudes I ever ſaw. He wore a long garment, faſtened about his body with a girdle; his forehead was high and bald; his hair on the hinder part of his head was ſhort and grey; his beard long; his features well formed; and his aſpect, notwithſtanding the inſult he had met with, did not ſeem diſcompoſed; he lifted

lifted up his hands; he pled with humble ſubmiſſion; he then roſe in remonſtrative tones; he then ſpoke to excite compaſſion; and, at length, poured out a torrent of irreſiſtible vehemence; every change in his addreſs was followed by correſponding changes in the countenance and air of the officer, to whom it was addreſſed. Till, at length, quite ſubdued, he turned to him who had given the blow, and beat him in the moſt furious manner. The orator, in the mean time, lifted his cap, put it on with an air of triumph; and bowing once or twice to the officer, while he was adminiſtering chaſtiſement to the ſoldier, rowed off immediately with his cattle.——That Ruſſians of all ranks are fond of muſic, is no leſs conſiſtent with the foregoing account, than their powers and ſuſceptibility of eloquence.

In a word, the defects in the national character of the Ruſſians, ſeem to me to ariſe chiefly from want of culture. Were they taught to reflect on the paſt, and anticipate the future, they would be led to form maxims and general rules for the direction of their conduct *. Reaſon would then be liſtened to;

* See Letter LIV.

and their moral principles would recover their authority. But they will never either reflect or anticipate, till they are moved to thoſe exercises by ſome prevailing intereſt; nor can they ever have any ſuch intereſt, till they have entire ſecurity for their perſons and poſſeſſions. How is this to be done? It is an important problem; and great and immortal would be the glory of that ſovereign who would really deſire to underſtand the ſolution. Immortal would be the glory of that ſovereign who would reſtore above twenty millions of men to the rights of intelligent and rational beings. But is this atchievement to be performed by one perſon, and at once? I believe not. It muſt be the work of time; and muſt be carried on by ſucceſſive changes. To give liberty at once to twenty millions of ſlaves, would be to let looſe on mankind ſo many robbers and ſpoilers. Before ſlaves can receive freedom in full poſſeſſion, they muſt be taught to know, reliſh, and uſe its bleſſings. This, however, is to be done gradually; and if it is to be done according to a regular plan, thoſe who have ſuch things in their power, muſt obſerve the growth of freedom in thoſe places where it aroſe ſpontaneous,

neous, and without any previous purpoſe.— Perhaps, if a deſpot intended to lay the foundation of a deſign ſo magnificent, it would be proper to begin with giving great privileges to commercial and manufacturing towns. It would alſo be proper to reſtore their rights to ſuch provinces as might formerly have enjoyed ſome freedom; and of which they might ſtill entertain ſome fond recollection. I am the more inclined to expreſs theſe opinions, as ſome of the Ruſſians, and particularly thoſe in the vicinity of Archangel, who, I have heard, enjoy greater privileges than their brethren, are uſually repreſented as honeſt, able and induſtrious, and, indeed, of a character very different from the reſt.

But I quit ſuch Utopian ſpeculations; and will only expreſs my wiſhes, that the ſmall portion of the human race who enjoy real freedom, may preſerve and make a proper uſe of it. Adieu.

LETTER XXXV.

With ſome Verſes.

DEAR SIR, Oct. 10th, 177—.

THE Banks of the Neva are indeed very fine, the iſlands delightful, and the woods fragrant; but they are ſilent. Not a thruſh, linnet, or goldfinch have I ſeen in Ruſſia. People tell me, however, that the fault is my own; and that if I were in the country early enough in the ſeaſon, I might both ſee and hear them. They even pretend that they have nightingales. One nightingale indeed I ſaw, heard, and admired. But it came from Aſtracan. It belonged to a lady; and, unable to endure the approach of winter, ſome weeks ago it died. "Alas!" you will ſay, "Poor Nightingale!" And you have more reaſon to regret its death than you are perhaps aware of; for, inſtead of getting a letter full of news about Turks and Ruſſians, and of hearing how the Ottoman empire is ſhaken to the very centre, you are to have a poem on the death of a bird. In blank verſe too! It cannot be helped; and all you can have, by way of compenſation, is to amuſe yourſelf with remarking, how whimſically we may be affected by the various events and incidents that happen under the ſun. A ſmall bird, hatched near the Caſpian, and buried in an iſle in the Neva, ſhall almoſt diſpoſe you, who are ſitting in a neat parlour, in a trim manſion on the border of Windſor foreſt, to frown!

Verſes on the Death of a Nightingale, written in the Iſle of Caminioſtrow.

MELODIOUS warbler! Lucia lov'd thee, charm'd
With thine enchanting wild note: and I ween
Her gentle manners, that in every breaſt
Kindle affection and eſteem, in thee
Kindled affection; and the ſtrong deſire
To imitate, to ſeize, and to transfuſe
Into thy ſong-like ſweetneſs. And thy voice
Obey'd thee; tuneful in thy native groves,
Where Volga rolls his mighty flood, and laves
The realm of Aſtraean; more tuneful now,

Even

Even in a northern clime, and in the isles
Of Ingrian Neva. Not the mournful plaint
Of that Hesperian Nightingale, that charm'd
The soul of Maro, when his raptur'd muse
Beheld the Thracian Poet, by the stream
Of Hebrus, wailing, with incessant woe,
His lost Eurydice: Nor even the song,
That fill'd with extasy th' impassion'd mind
Of Milton, when, beneath the moonlight pale,
All by the margin of his native Thames,
He held high converse with th' inspiring Powers
That dealt him minstrelsy divine—could e'er
Thy melody surpass. The gentle gales
Children of Summer, born in Tempé, heard
Thy songs expressive; and, with fond delay,
Linger'd amid the northern sky, beyond
The time allow'd them, shedding fragrant flowers,
And mildness unpermitted.—
Boreas beheld, as on a snowy cliff,
Shining with thousands of reflected rays,
Azure, and green, and crimson, he reclin'd,
Wrap'd in a robe rough with effulgent frost,
Viewing his vast domain, from Zembla south
To the chaff'd billows of the Caspian main.
Boreas beheld! "And shall these wanton gales

"Longer insult me? Shall a warbling note,
"Or the weak native of a southern clime,
"Even by my throne, with arrogant delay,
"Detain them? He shall perish." sternly fierce
He spake; and instant sent a rapid blast,
Arm'd with an icy shaft, and in a shower
Of snow envelop'd. Howling how he flew
Across the dark'ning Ladago! The flowers
Wither'd before him: and at evening hour,
He gain'd the border of our isle. O then
Thy melting voice, sweet Nightingale! was lost:
Thy Lucia mourn'd; the muses mourn'd; the gales
Of summer fled reluctant; on thy grave
Sighing full sore, and scatt'ring as they flew
Decaying blooms, sad relics of their woe.

LETTER XXXVI.

Account of Goods exported from St. Peterſburg in 1769.

St. Peterſburg, Nov. 7th, 1770.

* * * * * * THE iron in Siberia is wrought at little expence: the places where it is found are by the ſides of large rivers. Proviſions are cheap: a ſheep may be bought for thirty copics *, and the rivers are ſtored with excellent fiſh. Wood for working the iron is found every where in the greateſt abundance. Not only ſo, but the ſoil in the ſouthern and eaſtern parts of Ruſſia is very fertile. The Ukraine alone, with no other labour than that of plowing, could ſupply the whole of European Ruſſia with corn. The empire, beſides its vicinity to the Caſpian, Euxine, Baltic, and Northern Seas, is interſperſed with lakes, and interſected by

* 1 s. 3 d.

navigable rivers; theſe might eaſily, by means of canals, be made to communicate with one another. Nor is even land-carriage interrupted, or rendered difficult here, as in many other places, by fens and mountains. The natural advantages of Ruſſia, therefore, might render it one of the richeſt countries in Europe.

Accordingly, even in its preſent infant ſtate of improvement, the balance of trade has been, of late years, more unfavourable to Britain than formerly. Many ſuch manufactures as were imported by Engliſh traders, ſome time ago, and ſold here with large profits, are now wrought in the country. Formerly the coarſe cloth, with which the army is clothed, was brought from England; it is now wrought in Ruſſia. Pewter alſo was a profitable commodity; but pewter diſhes, with earthern ware, and even china, may be had here very good, and manufactured in the country. The ſilk manufacture at Moſcow is in a thriving condition; and Ruſſian linen and diaper are ſold in Britain.

You will receive, however, a more diſtinct notion of the commerce of this empire from the following

Account of Goods exported from St. Peterſburg in 1769, by 326 Engliſh Ships, and 247 of other Nations.

Quality of Goods.	Quantity.		First Coſt.	
Iron	Pood	2,409 587	Rubles	1,686,710 : 90
Clean Hemp		1,229 400		1,548,220
Outſhot Ditto		168,691		185,560 : 10
Half clean Ditto		92,258		92,258
Hemp Codille		113,332		45,332 : 80
Flax, 12 headed		104 497		195,931 : 87
Ditto, 9 ditto		39 894		62,833 : 5
Ditto, 6 ditto		10,205		13,011 : 37
Ditto Codille		14,765		66,44 : 25
Hides		144,612		838,749 : 60
Briſtles, 1ſt and 2d ſort		13,761		82,566
Iſinglaſs		4,114		82,798
Soap and Candle Tallow		262,640		630,336
Soap		12,801		19,201 : 5
Hemp Oil		92,403		110 883 : 60
Train Oil		9 388		11,265 : 60
Lintſeed Oil		1,243		2,113 : 10
Wax		814		8,750 : 50
Horſe Hair		3,188		5,738 : 40
Horſe Tails		30,547		3,054 : 80
Cow Hair		180		900
Tallow Candles		9,096		30,016 : 80
Caviar		5,484		13 710
Wax Candles		41		541 : 20
Cordage		6,688		14,703 : 60
Hops		467		1,214 : 20
Tobacco		4,581		4,122 : 90
Soal Leather		6,334		31,670
Copper		4,020		29 145
Pitch		8,392		10,070 : 40
Tar		1,658		1,989 : 60
Roſin		1,475		1,475
Carraway Seed		162		194 : 40
Aniſe Seed		3		3 : 30
Broad Diaper	Arſheen	431,616		36,687 : 36
Narrow Ditto		458,070		22 903 : 50
Broad Linen		262,977		22,353 : 5
Narrow Linen		1,695,668		76,305 : 6
Sundry ſorts Linen		135,534		9,487 : 38
Craſh		873,776		26,213 : 28
Drills	Pieces	61,583		193,749
Flems		12,601		75,606
Raven Duck		43,406		173,624
Sail Cloth		33,335		200,010

Account of Goods, &c. continued.

Quality of Goods.	Quantity.		First Cost.
Hare Skins —	Pieces	297,318	Rubles 47,600
Squirrel Skins —		47,500	3,562 : 50
Bear Skins —		483	2,173 : 50
Fox Skins — —		428	513 : 60
Lynx Skins — —		28	224
Ermine — —	Tun	15	210
Feathers — —	Pood	375	1,420
Down — — —		132	1,348
Gunpowder — —		60	360
Rhubarb — —		1	65
Masts — —	Pieces	62	6,200
Deals — — —	Dozen	85,375	123,319 : 44
Matts — —	Pieces	4,600	184
Wheat — —	Chetwerts	29,100	116,400
Ox Bones — —	Pieces	27,000	300
Old Iron — —	Pood	2,450	1,470
			Rubles 6,964,504 : 6

N. B. 1 Bergeuitz is 10 Pood.

1 Pood is 40 Pound,—run equal to 35½ Pound English.

1 Arsheen is 28 Inches English.

7½ Chetwerts, corn measure, make a Tun.

LETTER XXXVII.

With an Account of the Abdication of Victor Amadeus, King of Sardinia, in the Year 1730.

DEAR SIR, St. Peterſburg, 1770.

I FLATTER myſelf that the incloſed account of the Abdication of Victor Amadeus, King of Sardinia, who reſigned his ſceptre in the year 1730, will afford you ſome amuſement. He is not the only Prince recorded in hiſtory, who exchanged the pomp and cares of royalty for the obſcurity or the peace of retirment. But though ſeveral, before the preſent century, have preſented this curious ſpectacle to mankind, we cannot boaſt of being fully acquainted with their motives or expectations. A crown has ſo many charms, that the ſtate of mind which could induce a Sovereign Prince to reſign his dignity, and his ſubſequent conduct or deportment, are, to thoſe who would obſerve human nature, objects of great curiosity. The following account pretends to give a full view of the motives that urged his Sardinian Majesty in *his* abdication, and of his conduct in his retirement. Nor would I have offered it to your perusal, if I did not believe the intelligence it conveys authentic. It was written originally in Italian, and as I know not of its having been ever published in Britain *, either in the original, or in any other language, I hope the perusal of the following English † translation will afford you some entertainment.

You will recollect, that Pope Paul III. created his natural son, Peter Lewis Farnese, Duke of Parma,—that the sovereignty of the Parmesan remained in the Farnese family till the year 1731,—that as the failure of the the male line seemed inevitable, it had been agreed upon that Don Carlos, son to the Queen of Spain, who was descended of the Farnese family, should succeed to that dukedom; but not without receiving it from Charles Emperor of Germany as a fief of the Empire,—that this settlement was determined

* Yet a French translation of this little tract may be met with in many places on the Continent.

† By an ingenious friend.

by

by a treaty between the Courts of Vienna and Madrid, ratified at Vienna in the year 1725, —that by the treaty of Seville, ratified in the year 1729, Great Britain engaged to aſſiſt the Spaniards in bringing ſix thouſand Spaniſh troops into Tuſcany and Parma,—and, laſtly, that the Emperor, jealous or apprehenſive of the power of Spain, notwithſtanding the treaty of Vienna, was determined to oppoſe the entry of thoſe troops into Italy. Keeping thoſe previous events in view, you will enter eaſily into the following detail.

THE EMPEROR OF GERMANY having formed the reſolution of oppoſing, by the moſt vigorous exertions, the entry of ſix thouſand Spaniards into Italy; having, for that purpoſe, ſent a conſiderable army into Tuſcany and the Parmeſan; and having engaged the Grand Duke of Florence on his ſide, was ſenſible it would be of the greateſt advantage to his affairs, alſo to engage in his intereſts the King of Sardinia. With this view he ſignified to that Prince, by the Governor of Milan, that if he would unite with him, he would furniſh him, in caſe of neceſſity, with an army of 12,000 men, conſiſting of 8,000 foot

foot and 4,000 horſe, to act in concert with the Germans; that he would appoint him Governor of the Milaneſe for life; and to enable him to hold his troops in readineſs to march on the ſhorteſt notice, that he would pay down to him immediately 300,000 philips. Amadeus accepted of theſe conditions; and the Emperor ordered the money to be paid, providing that he ſhould refund it, if he had no occaſion for the 12,000 men. This treaty was concluded and ſigned at Milan by the Ambaſſadors of the Emperor and thoſe of his Sardinian Majeſty, in the month of June, A. D. 1730.

Some time after this the Spaniſh Ambaſſador, then at Genoa, viſited the Court of Turin *incognito*; and, in a private audience with the King of Sardinia, offered him, on the part of the King his maſter, the cities of Novare and Pavia, together with ſeveral adjacent territories beyond the Teſſin, which now conſtitute a part of the Dukedom of Milan, and belong to the Emperor, on condition that he would join him to expel the Imperialiſts out of Italy, unleſs they would allow Don Carlos the unmoleſted poſſeſſion of the Parmeſan. Victor

tor not only regarded theſe offers of Spain as much more advantageous than thoſe of the Imperial court, but alſo believed that England and France had entered into a reſolution to co-operate with the Spaniards in driving the forces of the Emperor out of Italy. He therefore willingly accepted of them, and promiſed to aſſiſt Don Carlos with his army againſt the Germans.

Notwithſtanding the great precautions which he had uſed to conceal this new and perfidious alliance into which he had entered, the Emperor's emiſſaries entertained ſome ſuſpicions of the truth; they communicated them to their maſter; and he, of conſequence, gave immediate orders to the Governor of Milan, to threaten Victor with the heavieſt effects of his vengeance. That Prince excuſed himſelf as well as he could, by denying the charge. But when he was afterwards informed, by his Ambaſſador at Vienna, that the Aulic Council ſeemed diſpoſed to enter into the meaſures of the Allies of Seville, he was filled with terror and conſternation, from the apprehenſion that thoſe two powers would undoubtedly take ſuch ſignal vengeance on his perfidy, as would prove equally ruinous to his interests, and disgraceful to himself.

Victor, thus agitated by a thousand different emotions, and at a loss how to recover the false step he had taken, resolved at length to divest himself of the sovereignty, till his affairs should assume a more favourable aspect. He hoped that he might thus shelter himself from the storm which was ready to burst over his head, and that a pretended abdication of the Crown, by extricating him from those embarrassing engagements, would tend to silence the clamour that might be raised against him. This measure, indeed, was not agreeable to the maxims of Machiavel, whom this Prince had hitherto followed with scrupulous exactness. He flattered himself, however, with hopes of success; and trusted to the implicit submission of his son, together with the affectionate attachment of his subjects. But we shall see, in the sequel, how widely he was mistaken.

Previous to the excution of his scheme, he judged it proper, by communicating some part of his designs to the Prince of Piedmont, to
prepare

prepare him for this important event. With this view, for two months before his abdication of the crown, he retired with him daily into a private apartment, and addreſſed him in ſuch terms as theſe:——" My dear Son,
" I am not yet ſo much ſunk under the in-
" firmities incident to old age, as I am op-
" preſſed by the anxious cares that attend on
" ſovereignty. I am therefore diſpoſed to
" retire for ſome time from public affairs, in
" order to unbend my mind, and to commit
" the reins of government to your hands.
" The burthen, my Son, is indeed heavy,
" and my fears are great, leſt, at ſuch an age,
" you ſhould prove unequal to its weight.
" Your experience in affairs of ſtate is
" ſmall; for you know that I have hitherto
" avoided to initiate you in the myſteries of
" politics, or to truſt to any one the manage-
" ment of the ſtate. I have hitherto govern-
" ed my ſubjects without the aid of any mi-
" niſter. But this is an art to be attained
" only by long experience. It is therefore
" abſolutely neceſſary, my dear Son, that you
" ſhould, in the beginning of your reign,
" have ſome ſage Mentor, to direct your pro-
" ceedings, and enable you to maintain, or
" even

"even increase that authority with which I "am now about to invest you. But as it is "very dangerous for a Prince, in early life, "to repose unlimited confidence in any indi- "vidual of his subjects, I have resolved, un- "til you are qualified to govern alone, that I "myself shall discharge the duty of your di- "rector. On these terms, my Son, I have "resolved to surrender to you my crown; "consider them, and inform me whether "they be suited to your inclinations."

The Prince of Piedmont replied with the most profound respect, "That his Majesty "might do what seemed to him meet; and "that while he enjoyed that life which "he derived from him, he might remain "assured of his submission and fidelity; that, "whether his Majesty chose to divest him- "self of his royal authority or not, he would "ever esteem it his indispensible duty to "yield the most entire obedience to his will. "In one word, he promised that, whatever "events should take place, he should always "respect him as his Father and his Sove- "reign." This declaration, often repeated by a young Prince, hitherto a stranger to the

the arts of dissimulation, gave the most entire satisfaction to the King; and he resolved to delay no longer the execution of a scheme from which he expected, at the same time, to derive both tranquillity and honour.

He therefore issued an order on the second of September 1730, to the Princes of the Blood, the Knights of the Order of the Annunciation, the Ministers and Secretaries of State, the Archbishop of Turin, the Grand Chancellor, the first Presidents, the Generals of the army, and all those who held the chief offices at court, to assemble on the morrow, at three o'clock in the afternoon, at the Castle of Rivole. There, after having summoned a Council of State, he declared, that he made a general abdication of his kingdom, and of all his dominions, in favour of his son Charles Emmanuel, Prince of Piedmont. Then, having ordered all those who had come from Turin, in obedience to his commands, to be admitted, the Marquis del Borgo, Secretary of State, read the Act of Abdication with a loud voice, after which his Majesty addressed the assembly in a very pathetic discourse, to the following purpose:

" The

“ The innumerable troubles and toils “ which I have undergone, without inter- “ miſſion, during a reign of fifty years, “ without mentioning the infirmities to which “ all men are liable, and the age to which I “ have attained, would have been more than “ enough to render the burthen of govern- “ ment heavy and intolerable to me. Be- “ ſides, as my end is now drawing nigh, and “ as I begin to regard death as the common “ lot of ſovereigns and of their ſubjects, I “ conſider myſelf as bound, by the moſt ſa- “ cred obligations, to interpoſe ſome ſpace “ between the throne and the grave. Theſe “ motives have been powerful enough to lead “ me to that meaſure which I have this day “ adopted; and, eſpecially, as Providence “ ſeems to favour my intentions, by beſtow- “ ing upon me a ſon worthy of ſucceeding “ me, and of governing my people; a ſon “ endowed with all thoſe qualities that adorn “ a deſerving Prince. I have therefore re- “ ſolved, without heſitation, to transfer to “ him, by a ſolemn act, ſigned this day with “ my own hand, the ſupreme authority over “ all my dominions, and am reſolved to paſs “ the remainder of my days at a diſtance

“ from

"from affairs of ſtate. I exhort you, there-"fore, to ſerve the King, my well-beloved "ſon, with the ſame inviolable fidelity which "ye have ever demonſtrated towards my-"ſelf; aſſuring you, at the ſame time, that I "have earneſtly recommended you to his "royal favour."

King Amadeus, upon his abdication, had recommended it to his ſon to cauſe all the eſtates of his nobility and gentry to be ſurveyed, and to proportion their taxes to the extent of their poſſeſſions. Had this meaſure been carried into execution, it would indeed have augmented the revenues of the crown, but it would have ruined the nobility. When Charles aſcended the throne, he found it improper to adopt it. This gave great offence to the abdicated Monarch; he wrote his ſon on the ſubject, more in the ſtyle of a maſter than of a father; and when he found that his ſon ſtill perſiſted in neglecting his remonſtrances, he formed the reſolution of reſuming the ſovereignty.

Amadeus had reſerved for himſelf a yearly penſion of 50,000 crowns, and retained only a few domeſtics about his perſon. He had made choice of the caſtle of Chamberry for the place of his reſidence; to which he repaired a few days after his abdication, being then in the ſixty-fourth year of his age, and a widower ſince the 26th of Auguſt 1728. He had left a miſtreſs in Piedmont, who was known by the title of the Counteſs of St. Sebaſtian; and as this lady performs a very conſpicuous part in the ſequel of this ſtory, it will not be foreign to our purpoſe to mention, in this place, the outlines of her life and character.

Her maiden name was Madamoiſelle de Cumiane. While yet only fifteen years of age, ſhe was a maid of honour to the Queen Dowager, the mother of Amadeus. This Prince, who was then only in his thirtieth year, took more delight in the gay converſation of the ladies of his mother's court, than in canvaſſing with his miniſters the difficult affairs of ſtate; and ſuch amuſement was the more agreeable to him, that the Queen *, who

* She had been educated at the Court of France, being the daughter of the Duke de Nemours, who was killed in a duel by the Duke de Beaufort, which was the occaſion of Lewis XIV. prohibiting duels on pain of death.

who was no leſs addicted to gaiety than himſelf, admitted thoſe only into her train who were remarkable for their beauty. Thus the Prince, and the young lords of his court, enjoying the pleaſures of variety, never experienced diſguſt. At length, however, Amadeus, fixing his affections on Madamoiſelle de Cumiane, loaded her with extraordinary favours, ſo that, in a ſhort time, ſhe became diſtinguiſhed from all her fair companions, by an unſeemly change in her ſhape. In order to remove this deformity, the Queen Dowager, who was a faithful confident to her ſon, as well as an affectionate mother, gave her immediately in marriage to the Count de St. Sebaſtian, her *Premier Ecuyer*, who eſteemed himſelf highly honoured in being admitted into ſuch an intimate connection with his Sovereign. The Counteſs his wife was made one of the Queen's *Dames d'Honneur*; and notwithſtanding her marriage, was often honoured by the aſſiduities of the King. Sometimes, however, when any new intrigue intervened, theſe attentions were interrupted. But even when the Counteſs no longer poſſeſſed the King's affections, ſhe had the addreſs ſo effectually to ſecure his friendſhip and esteem, that she still maintained her influence over him; and when she was left a widow in A. D. 1723, the King undertook the care of her children, and attended to them as particularly as if they had been his own. He at the same time appointed her an apartment in the palace, which communicated with his own, and enabled him to visit her as familiarly as he desired, without observation or scandal. He afterwards named her one of the ladies in the train of the Princess of Piedmont.

Such had been the fortunes of the Countess de St. Sebastian, till the abdication of Amadeus. As soon as she received information of this event, being naturally ambitious, and well versed in intrigue, she immediately went in quest of Father Audormiglia, Abbot of a Monastery of Feuillants, and Confessor in Ordinary to King Amadeus, and of Dr. Boggio, Curate of St. John's, his Spiritual Director. She suggested to them, that the King, in order to make reparation for the injury which he had done her and her family, had, since the death of the Queen, frequently promised to conclude with her a private marriage; and that, now having abdicated the throne,

throne, he ought not any longer to delay the performance of his promiſe; for, having thus deſcended to a level with private perſons, he could, with leſs difficulty, fulfil the duty of a Chriſtian, and of a man of honour. She then promiſed thoſe two eccleſiaſtics, that if, by their means, ſhe became the wife of that Prince, ſhe would employ all her intereſt with her huſband, in order to promote them to the chief dignities of the church. Engaged by theſe promiſes, as well as by the pleaſing and inſinuating addreſs of the Counteſs, thoſe eccleſiaſtics did every thing in their power to promote her deſigns, and they found little difficulty in rendering their endeavours effectual; for the King was very well pleaſed to have ſuch a companion in his ſolitude as this lady, to whom, as to another ſelf, he might confide the moſt ſecret ſentiments of his heart. In ſhort, he ſent for her, and married her publicly; he thereupon demanded 100,000 crowns of the King his ſon, which were immediately granted him; this ſum he preſented to his wife, that ſhe might purchaſe with it an eſtate for the children of her former marriage; and, with this view, ſhe purchaſed the Marquiſate of Spigna, of which ſhe henceforth aſſumed the title.

Amadeus, during the firſt four months, appeared to be ſufficiently happy in his retirement; and the Marchioneſs his wife, who ſtudied aſſiduouſly to ſuit herſelf to his humour, alſo aſſumed the appearance of happineſs. At the ſame time, obſerving that the King was diſſatisfied with his houſe, and that he frequently propoſed to repair it, ſhe exerted herſelf ſtrenuouſly to diſſuade him from his purpoſe, by repreſenting to him, that it was not worth his while to repair an old caſtle, which was every where falling into ruin; that he could never render it either agreeable or commodious, but by pulling it down and erecting a new one in its ſtead; and for this ſhe ſaw no neceſſity, ſince his Majeſty had many fine palaces in Piedmont, amongſt which he might chuſe the place of his reſidence; to all which ſhe added, that the climate of that country would be more favourable to his health than that of Savoy.

By ſuch arguments as theſe, the Marchioneſs endeavoured to give her huſband a diſguſt

guſt at his reſidence at Chamberry, and to perſuade him to return into Piedmont. But they only ſerved to agitate him, without perſuading him, as he had firmly reſolved to remain for ſome time at a diſtance from the court, in order the more effectually to conceal his deſigns. The Marchioneſs indeed had other reaſons beſides the health of the King, for being ſo eager to perſuade him to exchange his preſent reſidence for that of Piedmont; but theſe ſhe took care not to diſcover, until ſhe knew how they might correſpond with the inclinations of her huſband.

In the mean time, ſhe ſtudied to inſinuate herſelf more and more, by flattery, and an affected fondneſs, into his good graces; and ſo ſucceſsful was ſhe in her endeavours, that the King one day requeſted of her to check her impatience only for a little; and that, in a ſhort time, ſhe would obtain that for which ſhe moſt earneſtly wiſhed; for that it never had been his intention, notwithſtanding what he had made his ſon believe, on his abdication of the crown, to paſs the remainder of his days at Chamberry.

After this mark of confidence, the Marchioneſs was convinced that it would be eaſy to penetrate into the ſecret motives of his abdication, to which ſhe had hitherto remained a ſtranger. From this period, with great art and penetration, ſhe ſtudied to diſcover his ſecret ſentiments. She knew, by long experience, thoſe ſoft and favourable moments of acceſs, in which a wife can obtain any boon from a huſband; ſhe ſeized the propitious inſtant; and learned that his intention was to reſume the crown in leſs than two years. "Two years!" exclaimed the Marchioneſs, in a tranſport of joy; "and why will you "defer it to ſo diſtant a period?" The King then communicated to her the ſecret motives of his abdication, with the reaſons which hindered him from reſuming the crown, until the differences between the Emperor and the King of Spain, with regard to the Parmeſan and Tuſcany, ſhould be terminated either by a peace or war; previous to which event, he could not extricate himſelf from his engagements, conſiſtently with his honour or intereſts; for, on the one hand, ſhould he join the allies of the treaty of Seville, in the expectation of their ſending a powerful army to ſupport

ſupport him in Italy, he might be very eaſily overpowered by the Germans:—or ſhould he, on the other hand, declare in favour of the Emperor, the allies would not fail to take the ſevereſt vengeance on him if they ever gained the ſuperiority, which in all probability would happen, as the Emperor and he would never be able to make oppoſition againſt four powers ſo formidable as England, France, Holland, and Spain. As he had then been ſo unfortunate as to enter into engagements with the Emperor and the King of Spain at the ſame time, he had been able to find no other expedient by which he could repair his fault, than by abdicating the throne in favour of his ſon, recommending it to him to maintain a neutrality with regard to the contending powers, until their diſputes ſhould be brought to an iſſue.

The Marchioneſs approved of her huſband's conduct; and they agreed to remain at Chamberry, where they might watch for a time and an opportunity favourable to their deſigns.

During their reſidence in Savoy, this haughty woman ſuggeſted to her huſband, that

that it would be proper to exercise, at times, that sovereign authority which he still retained over his son and his ministers, that it might not insensibly be lost. Amadeus entered readily into her views, and put her advice in practice. He ordered the King his son to visit him at Chamberry, to receive his instructions with regard to some important affairs; and that Prince obeyed him, as if he had been still his subject. In the same manner, he ordered the ministers of state, and several of the chief officers of the court, to attend his person; and he was obeyed, as if he had been still *their* Sovereign.

In the beginning of August 1731, Amadeus, having been informed that the Emperor had at length consented to permit Don Carlos, with his 6000 Spaniards, to enter into Italy, communicated the intelligence to his wife. This gave extreme pleasure to the Marchioness, because she saw herself now in a condition to execute the scheme which she had so long meditated. For this purpose, she withdrew with her husband into her closet; where she observed to him, "That it was "now time to return into Piedmont, and to "resume

" resume the crown, whilst his son and his
" subjects yet retained for him sentiments of
" respect and obedience; that any delay, at
" that period, might prove fatal to him;
" especially should the Emperor and Don
" Carlos recognise his son as King of Sar-
" dinia; that the young King, by being any
" longer accustomed to the charms of sove-
" reignty, might begin to feel their influences
" too powerfully, to be willing to renounce
" them, and to descend to the rank of a sub-
" ject." These insinuations of the Marchioness left a deep impression on the mind of Amadeus, who had now become more jealous than ever of his authority, though he had, in appearance, surrendered it to his son. He therefore resolved, without delay, to return into Piedmont; and having signified his resolution to his son, the castle of Montcalier was, by his orders, immediately prepared for his reception. In the end of August, Amadeus left Chamberry, with his wife, and fixed his residence in that place.

The King his son, with the principal persons of the court, immediately attended him, with congratulations on his safe return.

The

The Archbiſhop of Turin, and the Magiſtrates of the city, paid him the ſame marks of their reſpect. The Queen herſelf, accompanied by ſeveral ladies of her court, viſited the Marchioneſs de Spigno; and ſhewed her the ſtrongeſt marks of eſteem and affection. In ſhort, Amadeus and his wife, ſince their return into Piedmont, appeared to be the real Sovereigns of that country. In frequent converſations which that Prince had with the Miniſters of State, and with the Governors of Turin and of the Citadel, he artfully endeavoured to ſound their inclinations; and as thoſe officers had always profeſſed great ſubmiſſion, and a warm attachment to his perſon, he was perſuaded that he might, at that time, reaſcend the throne, without meeting with any oppoſition, either on the part of his ſon, or of his miniſtry. He even relied on the attachment of the ſoldiery: he knew that he poſſeſſed their eſteem, and he flattered himſelf that he alſo had their affection: as the greateſt part of the officers were his creatures, he did not doubt but that they would pay reſpect to his inclinations; and he even hoped, that they would readily concur in promoting his deſigns. But the

ſequel

ſequal of this great event will ſhew how much he was deceived in his expectations.

He wrote to Marêchal Rebhinder in very general, though flattering and inſinuating terms. But that General, who was Commander in Chief of the forces, was immediately ſenſible of how much conſequence it was, to deſtroy every expectation in Amadeus of ever reaſcending the throne. He replied accordingly,—That he acknowledged himſelf his debtor in all that he poſſeſſed,—his eſtate, his honours, and his dignities. " Your Majeſty," ſaid the Marêchal, " has made me what I am. I owe " nothing to King Charles; and all my ex- " preſſions of obligation are due only to your " Majeſty. But of all the favours with " which you have loaded me, I have always " held the honour of your eſteem to be the " moſt precious. Permit me then, Sire, to " preſerve this honour inviolated; which, I " will take the liberty to ſay, I have acquired " at the expence of that blood which I have " ſhed in your ſervice. But I would forfeit " it, Sire, were I unfortunate enough to prove " diſloyal to that King whom you have ſet " over me, and to whom you have bound "me to yield obedience. I will maintain the "ſame fidelity to him that I have done to your "Majeſty; and I will loſe the laſt drop of "my blood in the ſupport of his throne. "At the ſame time, Sire, I ſhall be, at all "times, ready to give your Majeſty the moſt "unequivocal marks of my reſpectful at- "tachment; fully ſenſible that you will ne- "ver impoſe upon me any commands, that "may be inconſiſtent with that juſtice and "honour which have ever accompanied all "my actions."

On the 28th of September, 1731, about ſix o'clock in the afternoon, Amadeus, being then alone with his wife at Montcalier, diſpatched a meſſage to the Marquis del Borgo, with orders to attend him immediately. That miniſter, without entertaining the ſlighteſt ſuſpicion of the buſineſs on account of which his preſence was required, inſtantly obeyed the ſummons, as he had been wont to do on former occaſions. Immediately on his entering the apartment, the King ſaid to him, "Del Borgo, I have ſent for you to ſup with "my wife and me, that you might endeavour, "by your good humour, to remove a head-ach

" with which ſhe is afflicted; and after ſupper " I will impart to you an affair which will give " you pleaſure." The Marquis, with the utmoſt reſpect, acknowledged the honour which his Majeſty had done him, and took his ſeat at table. The King was in high ſpirits during the time of ſupper, and entertained the Marquis with a flow of humour and gaiety. When ſupper was over, and the domeſtics retired, the King addreſſed Del Borgo in the following terms: " It hath " given me great pleaſure to obſerve, that the " King, my ſon, has retained in his ſervice " the ſame perſons whom I had employed " myſelf; ſince, without doubt, he could " not have choſen any that were equal to you " in fidelity, or in abilities, or in experience. " I doubt not, at the ſame time, that you " know ſufficiently, that it was I who ex- " preſsly charged my ſon to employ the ſame " miniſters, on whom I myſelf, during my " reign, had fixed my choice; and I hope " that, as well out of duty as out of gratitude, " you are ſtill firmly attached to him who " has been the author of your fortunes." The Marquis replied, " That his Majeſty " might always rely on his obedience, as

" well

"well as on the affection of all the ministers "and officers of the King his son, in the "same manner as if he were still their Sove- "reign; and that, with regard to himself, he "would, on all occasions, embrace every op- "portunity of demonstrating to him the "most sincere and inviolable attachment."

The King then resuming that haughty and authoritative tone, in which he had been wont to address his Ministers, replied, "We "are so fully convinced, Del Borgo, that you "are entirely devoted to our service, that we "have ever distinguished you above all our "ministers, by our particular regard; we "have always selected you from amongst the "rest, in order to entrust to you our most "important affairs; and we have now made "choice of you to be the depositor of our most "secret resolutions. It is now about a year "since we have abdicated the throne in fa- "vour of our well-beloved son Charles Em- "manuel, from the motives which we set "forth at Rivole on the day of our abdica- "tion; to which it may be added, that we "had also in our view to try how that Prince "would demean himself in the character of a

"Sovereign,

" Sovereign, that we might, in our lifetime, " aſſiſt him with our advice, and be able to " leave you, after our deceaſe, a Prince " worthy of filling our Throne. And though " we have been entirely ſatisfied with his " adminiſtration, yet the intereſt of our ſtate " lays us under an indiſpenſible obligation to " reſume the reins of Government imme- " diately, as we are now upon the eve of ſee- " ing very important revolutions in Italy, " which might prove deſtructive to our Son, " and to his ſubjects, were the adminiſtration " then veſted in a young Prince, yet inexpe- " rienced in thoſe wiles and myſteries of po- " litical art, which a Sovereign, who would " maintain his power, is under a neceſſity of " employing. For theſe reaſons, Marquis, " we command you to deliver up to us the " Act of our Abdication; and then to ſignify " our intentions to our Son, and to his Mi- " niſters, in order that we may be inveſted " to-morrow, without delay, with the Sove- " reignty: for ſuch is our will and plea- " ſure."

A declaration ſo unexpected threw the Marquis into the utmoſt conſternation; and he was at the greateſt loſs how to extricate himſelf from an affair of ſuch delicacy and danger. For, on the one hand, had he given a poſitive refuſal to this high-ſpirited and impetuous Prince, who had never met with a refuſal in his life, he ran the riſque of throwing him into a tranſport of fury, to which he himſelf might have fallen a victim; and, on the other hand, had the Marquis yielded to his demands, he would have proclaimed himſelf a rebel againſt his juſt and lawful Sovereign, and have incurred the penalty of high treaſon.

In this embarraſſing ſituation, that artful miniſter, hoping to eſcape the ſtorm which threatened him by an excuſe full of ſubmiſſion and flattery, replied to the King, requeſting of him, with the utmoſt humility, to reflect, that it was not in his power to reſtore the Act of Abdication, until he had firſt obtained permiſſion of the King of Sardinia, to whom, as his Majeſty knew, he had ſworn fealty. The King, chafed and enraged, interrupted him in theſe words:—"Del Borgo, "do you acknowledge any other Sovereign "than me? To whom did you firſt ſwear "the oath of fealty? To me, or to my Son? "Are you not a traitor, both ungrateful and "disloyal towards the person who hath raised "you to that eminence which you possess, "and to whom you have this moment pro- "fessed perpetual obedience? But I will "easily find means to bring you back to your "duty, should you fail to obey me instantly."

The Marquis, in the utmost trepidation, proceeded in the following terms:—"Sire, if "you will do me the favour to listen to me a "moment, you shall be convinced that I am "not such a man as you imagine me to be. "It is true, that, by your orders, I have en- "tered into a new allegiance to the King your "Son; but, notwithstanding this, I have "ever regarded you as my just and lawful "Sovereign; and in order to convince you, "Sire, of my entire respect and obedience, I "will bring you the Act of Abdication to- "morrow morning, without mentioning the "affair to any person whatsoever; and the "only favour that I will request in return is, "that you should justify my proceeding to "the King your Son." This answer pacified Amadeus, who, after having obliged the

Marquis to promiſe repeatedly that he would religiouſly keep his word, left him at liberty to retire.

The Marquis had ſcarce departed, than this Prince, reflecting on what had paſſed, began to epent of having diſcovered his intentions. He began to entertain a diſtruſt of all his Son's miniſters; he was apprehenſive that they would oppoſe his deſigns; and his mind was agitated by turns with the emotions of ambition and of revenge. At one inſtant, he flattered himſelf with the hopes of ſucceſs from the docile and yielding diſpoſitions of his Son; at another, he was tortured by the moſt agonizing apprehenſions, leſt that Prince, after having once taſted the pleaſures of unbounded liberty, and of abſolute power, ſhould refuſe to ſubmit again to the authority of a Father ſo ſtern and rigid as himſelf, and ſo averſe to the purſuits of pleaſure. Such reflections as theſe ſunk his ſpirit into the loweſt deſpondency; nor did he know of any reſource to which he could apply; but, ſtripped of his power, and abandoned by his friends, he ſaw himſelf devoted to the rigour of his fate. The Marchioneſs, who had hitherto been

been wont to enliven his ſolitary hours, and to baniſh his cares by her gaiety, and tender officiouſneſs, now durſt not open her lips, leſt ſhe might irritate his reſentment, and draw on herſelf the effects of his diſpleaſure. In this ſtate of penſive melancholy, fetching deep ſighs, and at times giving way to tranſports of outrageous fury, which diſcovered the agitations that he inwardly underwent, he walked about his chamber till midnight, when addreſſing himſelf to the Marchioneſs abruptly, as if juſt awaking from a diſmal dream, he exclaimed, "My reſolution is "formed;—order my horſe to be got ready "for me without delay!" She obeyed, with much reluctance, unable to gueſs the motive of ſo ſudden a reſolution, and not daring to make any enquiry. He mounted his horſe, attended by one valet-de-chambre, and preſented himſelf at the gate of the citadel of Turin, demanding immediate admittance.—One of the officers of the citadel immediately acquainted the Baron de St. Remis with the arrival of King Amadeus. The Baron was aſtoniſhed, and could ſcarce be made to believe that he could viſit him at ſo unſeaſonable an hour: he went himſelf, without delay to examine into the truth; and actually found Amadeus on the ſpot, extremely impatient to obtain admittance. The Governor begged to be informed what was his pleaſure with him. "Open the gate this inſtant," replied he, "and I will ſatisfy you." The Baron anſwered, that if he had any orders to give him, he might deliver them from the place in which he ſtood, or ſend them to him in writing, for that he could by no means open the gate at ſuch an hour, without being wanting to his duty, which he was reſolved ſhould never be the caſe.

The King, after this repulſe, returned to Montcalier filled with confuſion, with apprehenſions, and with rage. He had expected that the Baron would have received him into the citadel without ſcruple, becauſe he owed the place which he then held to his good offices; and he had flattered himſelf with the hopes, that were he once admitted, he might be able, by means of the Governor, to ſet himſelf at the head of the troops ſtationed in that place; and thus to compel his Son to reſtore the crown, if he ſhould not be diſpoſed to ſurrender it voluntarily. But now

now all his ſchemes were fruſtrated, becauſe he found nobody inclined to aſſiſt in promoting his deſigns. Overwhelmed by the keeneſt agony, he threw himſelf down on a couch, without ſaying a word to the Marchioneſs, who was ſtanding by, filled with diſtreſs, at obſerving the affliction which her huſband endured, whilſt ſhe was ignorant of the immediate cauſe of his ſufferings.

No ſooner had the Marquis del Borgo got back to Turin, than he haſtened to court, and, with the ſtrongeſt marks of conſternation, demanded an audience of the King. Upon this one of the Ladies of the Bedchamber inſtantly aroſe, and went to awake his Majeſty, informing him, with much trepidation, that it was by the orders of the Marquis del Borgo, who was then expecting him in an antichamber, to confer with him concerning affairs of the higheſt moment. The King aroſe immediately, and entered his cloſet, after having given orders to admit nobody but the Marquis only. He was then informed by that Miniſter, that the King his Father intended, the next day, to reſume the Crown; and that he had commanded him to reſtore into his hands the Act of Abdication, and, at the ſame time, to announce his reſolution to his Majeſty and his Miniſters. The King immediately replied to the Marquis, without any emotion, "That ſince he had aſcended "the Throne by his Father's command, and "with the univerſal approbation of the peo- "ple, he held it to be a duty which he owed "them, to conſult their ſentiments before he "reſigned his ſovereignty." And as the ſhortneſs of the time required deciſive meaſures, he immediately commanded the attendance of the Miniſters of State, the Archbiſhop of Turin, the two Firſt Preſidents, and the other general Officers of the Crown, in order to deliberate, in full council, on an affair of ſuch delicacy and importance, on which depended the happineſs and tranquillity of the realm. Thoſe Miniſters having aſſembled with all poſſible diſpatch, the King communicated to them the intentions of Amadeus, informing them, at the ſame time, that, for his own part, in order to convince his Father of his filial obedience, and of his entire reſignation to his will, he was ready to ſurrender to him his Crown; but that this was a ſtep which he could not reſolve to take, with-

out

out previously consulting their inclinations and opinions. Upon this all the members of that illustrious assembly arose, and after testifying their deep sense of the deference which his Majesty had paid to them, by a low bow, the Archbishop, in the name of the rest, spoke to the following effect: "That since his Majesty had permitted them to declare their sentiments upon the subject which was the occasion of their meeting at that time, it appeared to him, that Amadeus having, more than a year ago, voluntarily surrendered the Crown in the most solemn manner that could be devised, and for the reasons set forth by himself, in his speech on on that occasion (which was inserted in the Act of Abdication), it appeared to him, he said, that the King could not possibly have any just or reasonable motive at that time to resume the Crown; since he must have been fully satisfied with his Majesty's administration, which had been equally agreeable to his subjects, and calculated to promote the ease of King Amadeus, who enjoyed the submission and respect due to a Sovereign, without being subjected to the "troubles

" troubles and cares which attend that exalt-
" ed ſtation : that for theſe reaſons, though
" that Prince had ſo ſoon retracted what
" he had ſolemnly ſworn to obſerve in-
" violably, he did not appear to be influenced
" by juſt and reaſonable motives ; and that
" he ſtrongly ſuſpected that he was inſtigated
" in this affair only by the boundleſs vanity
" of the Marchioneſs his wife, who had often,
" ſince her marriage, betrayed an eager de-
" ſire to be declared Queen : That as they
" had every reaſon to believe this to be the
" caſe, his Majeſty was in honour and duty
" bound to preſerve the Crown, and to pre-
" vent his ſubjects from falling a prey to the
" inſatiable ambition of a miſchievous woman ;
" That he could not help admiring and ap-
" plauding that dutiful ſubmiſſion which his
" Majeſty profeſſed to the will of his Father ;
" but that, in this inſtance, his obedience, in-
" ſtead of meriting applauſe, would become
" the ſubject of cenſure, as it would prove
" ruinous to his own intereſts, and to thoſe of
" his people : That the intereſt of the public
" ſhould ever regulate the actions of a Sove-
" reign ; and that he ought to reject, with-
" out

" out a ſcruple, every meaſure that tended to
" obſtruct this general view."

All the other members of the Council unanimouſly concurred with this Prelate in opinion, and approved of the dutiful remonſtrances which he had offered to his Majeſty. As they were deliberating concerning thoſe meaſures which it would be proper to embrace, in order to ward off the calamities which threatened the ſtate, they were interrupted by a ſudden knocking at the door of the hall, in which they ſat: The Marquis del Borgo, by his Majeſty's command, went to examine what was the matter, and found that it was an officer diſpatched from the citadel by the Baron de St. Remis, with a letter to the King, containing an account of the late ſtep which Amadeus had taken there, in order to promote his deſigns. The King and all the Council were ſo much alarmed by this information, that they agreed, with one voice, on the neceſſity of immediately ſeizing the perſons of King Amadeus, and of the Marchioneſs his wife, in order to ſecure the tranquillity of his Majeſty, and that of the ſtate, which they threatened to diſturb.

The

The young King exclaimed repeatedly againſt this meaſure: "What! make my "Father be ſeized! No," ſaid he, "it is im-"poſſible that I ſhould ever conſent to it." It was a long while before he could be prevailed upon to agree to this meaſure; and it was only in compliance with the preſſing intreaties of his council, that he was at length brought to give his conſent. When he ſigned the order, his hand trembled ſo violently, that the Secretary of State was obliged to guide his pen.

They committed the execution of this bold enterprize to the care of twenty officers, of the moſt intrepid reſolution, accompanied by a detachment of dragoons and infantry; and the Count de la Perouſe, Lieutenant-General of the forces, was charged with the office of ſeizing the King, with the aſſiſtance of a large detachment of troops, entruſted to him for that purpoſe. Theſe troops had been drawn out from Turin, and the places adjacent; they ſallied forth at the ſame inſtant from their ſtations, and, without knowing the place of their deſtination, marching in profound ſilence, without beat of drum, or ſound of trumpet,

trumpet, they appeared before the caſtle of Montcàlier, the ſtation appointed them; and it was immediately ſurrounded by dragoons. The Count de la Perouſe, attended by the Chevalier de Solave, Lieutenant-Colonel of the guards, at the head of a detachment of grenadiers with mounted bayonets, aſcended the ſtaircaſe which led to the King's apartment; and the Marquis D'Ormea, Secretary of State, who carried the order ſigned by King Charles, with another detachment of grenadiers, took poſſeſſion of the back-ſtairs. De la Perouſe, finding the door of the apartment locked, gave orders that it ſhould be forced open; and there he ſeized a page, who being then in waiting, lay in the anti-chamber. In the ſame manner he advanced forward, forcing all the doors, till he reached the bed-chamber, where the King lay with the Marchioneſs his wife. That Lady, hearing the noiſe, as it approached, aroſe ſuddenly; and having only time to throw a night-gown around her, ſhe ruſhed towards the door. On ſeeing ſo many armed men advancing, ſhe exclaimed, "Sire, "we are betrayed!" They did not allow her time to ſay any more. Two officers immediately conducted her into an adjacent apartment, where they ordered her to dreſs; and they afterwards conveyed her to the caſtle of Ceve, in Piedmont.

Neither the cries of Madame de St. Sebaſtian, nor the noiſe which the officers made, had diſturbed Amadeus, who ſtill continued ſunk in the profoundeſt ſleep. The Chevalier de Solave took poſſeſſion of the King's ſword, which he obſerved lying upon the table, and M. de la Perouſe advanced and drew the curtain. The King, upon this, ſtarting out of his ſleep, demanded what was the matter? "I have an order from the "King," ſaid Perouſe, "to ſeize your per-"ſon." "And who is your King," returned Amadeus: "I am your King and your "maſter; nor ought you to acknowledge "any other as ſuch." "Your Majeſty has "been my King," replied the Count, "but "you are ſo no longer; and ſince you have "thought proper to give us Charles for our "Sovereign, and to command us to obey "him, I hope you will yourſelf be diſpoſed "to ſet us the example of loyalty."

The

The King was quite transported with rage; he menaced the officers, and refused to get out of his bed. He gave the Chevalier de Solave, who advanced too near him, a blow on the breast, and angrily commanded him to retire. As he obstinately refused to rise, the officers found themselves under a necessity of raising him, and dressing him by force. He declared that he wished to fill the throne again only for two hours, that he might have it in his power to hang the miscreants who had seduced his Son; and among this number he reckoned the principal persons at court.

When he was dressed, the officers surrounded him, and conducted him by the great staircase towards his chariot, which waited for him in the court. He appeared confounded when he saw the anti-chamber full of armed men; and the soldiers, who were as yet in the dark with regard to the business, were astonished when they found that it was their old King whom they were carrying a prisoner. "What! 'tis our King!" they whispered among themselves:" "What has "he done? What are we about?" The

Count

Count de la Perouſe, apprehenſive of a mutiny, cried out to the ſoldiers, "By the "King's authority I command ſilence, on "pain of immediate death."

The King found in the court a regiment of dragoons which he had always diſtinguiſhed above the reſt of his troops. Their preſence ſeemed greatly to affect him, and he made an attempt to addreſs them particularly; they did not however allow him leiſure for this, but hurried him precipitately into his chariot. The Count de la Perouſe, and the Chevalier de Solave, begged his permiſſion to take their ſeats by him; but he replied, that this was what he would by no means allow. Mounting therefore on horſeback, they took their ſtations on each ſide of the chariot, which was at the ſame time ſurrounded by the troops; and in this manner the King was conducted to Rivole. I had omitted to obſerve, that when departing from Montcalier, he demanded three things, his wife, his papers, and his ſnuff box: of all theſe he obtained only the laſt. The garriſon of the citadel was reinforced that night with two regiments, and that of Turin was conſiderably augmented.

Early

Early in the morning the officers and dragoons that guarded Amadeus at Rivole were relieved by a body of 600 foot; and ſtrict orders were given to the commanding officer to keep that Prince always in ſight. For after the refuſal of the Baron de St. Remis to admit him into the citadel, he had ſunk into a kind of liſtleſs inſenſibility; his ſpirits having been exhauſted, by ruminating on the affront which he thought had been offered to him on that occaſion, and on the means of revenging it. But when he found himſelf ſeized by his own officers, and abandoned by all thoſe who had hitherto profeſſed the greateſt reſpect and attachment to his perſon, he became outrageous and ungovernable. They were therefore under the neceſſity of confining him in a room, of ſecuring the windows with iron bars, and of watching his actions narrowly, leſt he ſhould deſtroy himſelf, or commit any other outrage. When the King obſerved the glazier buſy about the windows of his apartment, he demanded what he meant? "I "mean," replied he, "to furniſh you with "a double caſement, leſt you ſhould catch "cold during the winter." "What! vil-

" lain," ſaid the King, " do you imagine " that I ſhall paſs the whole winter here?" " Ay, faith," replied the glazier, " this, and " many more."

He was ſerved in his confinement with all the attention and reſpect due to his rank. The Chevalier de Solare, with two Captains of the guards, had the charge of attending him; and he ſometimes amuſed himſelf in playing with them at billiards. They had orders to treat him with every mark of reſpect; but never to return any anſwer to the complaints which he might be diſpoſed to utter in their preſence.

The Council of State iſſued orders, on the ſame day, to arreſt the Confeſſor of that Prince, together with near fifty perſons of diſtinction, who had entered into the cabal with the Marchioneſs de Spigno, for the purpoſe of dethroning the reigning Prince.— An expreſs was diſpatched to the Governor, to the Intendant-General of Chamberry, and to the Count de St. George, his brother, who was firſt Preſident of that city, with orders

ders for them to repair immediately to Turin, to receive new inſtructions. The Count de St. George, who was ſuſpected to have engaged in the affair more deeply than the reſt, he being a near relation of the Marchioneſs de Spigno, was ſent to the citadel of Turin, to be privately examined. The Count de Cumiane, her brother, obtained his pardon, by diſcovering all the ſecrets with which his ſiſter had entruſted him. What may be reckoned ſingularly fortunate for King Charles in this affair is, that none of his ſubjects were found deficient in loyalty towards him; and that he was not laid under a neceſſity of tarniſhing the glory of his reign by ſhedding the blood of any of his ſubjects. Madame de St. Sebaſtian ſunk into the loweſt dejection of ſpirits, and took no other ſuſtenance than broth, which ſhe herſelf prepared. After her diſgrace, her ſon, then an Enſign in the guards, withdrew from Court. The young King took notice of his abſence, and very generouſly gave him to underſtand, that he might again appear at Court, and continue in his employment; ſignifying to him, at the ſame time, that however guilty

Madame de St. Sebaſtian had been, the conſequences would not be extended to him; and aſſuring him that he himſelf would take the charge of his future fortune.

LETTER XXXVIII. (Extract.)

The Hoſpodar of Wallachia.

St. Peterſb rg, Oct. 12, 1770.

**** THE Hoſpodar, or Prince of Wallachia, arrived ſome months ago at St. Peterſburg. He is a captive. Soon after the reduction of Chotzim he was taken priſoner in the capital of his dominions. Captive Princes are objects of curioſity. They are like ſtars ſhorn of their radiance, and caſt down from the firmament. If they conduct themſelves with ſuitable dignity, we regard them, even in their fall with veneration: and according to the fortitude they diſcover, along with a proper ſenſe of their calamity, are our feelings of reſpectful compaſſion. Beſides, in conſidering them as fallen from exalted power, to a ſtate of humble dependence, our ſentiments are finely ſhaded by obſerving the fleeting weakneſs of human grandeur.

Even circumſtances of no very important nature give a certain energy to thoſe feelings. ſo that not only a graceful deportment, but even a good appearance, and a dreſs ſuited to their character and ſituation, promote and improve them.

Some circumſtances of this ſort concur in the appearance of the Prince of Wallachia. He is tall, robuſt, aged about fifty, of a dark complexion, and of a grave aſpect. He wears on the crown of his head, which ſeems either bald or very cloſely ſhaved, a ſmall round cap of ſcarlet cloth; it is entirely without ornament; does not cover his ears, nor reaches to his neck or forehead. His body is wrapped in a wide peliſe of crimſon cloth, with long ſleeves, lined with ſable, and flowing down to his feet. He wears yellow leather half-boots hanging looſe about his ankles; and has nothing about him very ornamental, excepting that on his little finger he has a ſmall gold ring, ſet with a beautiful turquoiſe, ſurrounded with a row of diamonds.

As he is of Greek origin, his being a man of ſome accompliſhments will not ſurprize you. He is fond of muſic: ſpeaks Latin and Italian,

Italian, and underſtands French. But he ſpeaks little. Indeed he ſeems conſtitutionally grave and taciturn. He appears to have been, at all times, a man of more pride than vanity; and exhibits at preſent a fine picture of ſullen grandeur.

He looks, as doth the tower, whoſe nodding walls
After the conflict of heaven's angry bolts,
Frown with a dignity unmark'd before
Even in its prime of ſtrength.

Alas! in my next ſentence, ſo faithful are our *feelings*, at leaſt, to the intereſts of virtue! I ſhall undo the charm; efface every pleaſing impreſſion I may now have given you; and deſtroy all the prepoſſeſſions you may have entertained for the Hoſpodar of Wallachia. He is ſaid to have proved falſe to the Sultan, and to be inwardly pleaſed that he is a captive. Away then with his princely ſtature, his grave aſpect, his few words, and his flowing robe.—Gregory Giko, for that is his name, wears nothing about his neck; but if he fall into the hands of the Muſſulmen, it will probably be embraced with a bowſtring *.

* If I have not been miſinformed, he was reſtored to his dominions when the peace was concluded between the Turks and Ruſſians, and was ſoon after aſſaſſinated in his palace.

You will ſay, perhaps, that as he was a Greek, his wiſhes were naturally hoſtile to the Turks. But you will alſo remember, that he was protected by, and depended upon, the Sultan. You know that the principalities of Moldavia and Wallachia, as well as the Crimea, are dependents on the Turkiſh empire; and that their Sovereigns, if they may be called ſo, are, in ſome meaſure, nominated at Conſtantinople. In this view therefore he is inexcuſable. You will obſerve, that the great Deſpots of Europe ſeem deſirous of having ſmall Princes, rather than mighty Potentates, on the frontiers of their dominions. Such neighbours are not ſo formidable: in caſe of foreign wars they ſtand in the way of invaſion; and may in time become a part of the neighbouring empire. Perhaps the Sovereigns of Ruſſia would not be ſorry to ſee Finland and Lithuania, no leſs than the provinces of ancient Dacia, erected into what they might be pleaſed to term independent Dukedoms or Principalities. "Why," they will ſay, in the ſuperabundance of their goodneſs, 'ought the Finlanders and the Lithua-
" nians to be ſubject to the Kings of Poland
" and Sweden?'"

It

It is impossible to consider the present state of the districts bordering on the north side of the Danube and the banks of the Neister, without feeling regret. No soil is more fertile; no climate more delightful; and the Euxine, together with the navigable rivers that fall into it, afford the means of intercourse with the rest of the world Yet those fine provinces, which might form of themselves a respectable kingdom, oppressed and ravaged, are almost a desart.

LETTER XXXIX.

Anecdotes of the Battle of Kahul—and of Count Romanzow.

St. Peterſburg.

IT gives me the ſincereſt pleaſure, my dear Sir, that our correſpondence, after a long interruption, is now renewed: and I congratulate you, with all my heart, on the pleaſure you will receive in viſiting France and Italy.
* * * *

Long before this reaches England, you will have heard of a deciſive victory obtained by Count Romanzow at the River Kahul, over the Vizir and the grand Turkiſh army. It will at leaſt determine the fate of Bender, which General Panin has for ſome time paſt been very cloſely beſieging.

Some amuſing circumſtances relating to the battle are mentioned here.—The Sultan having

ing consulted his astrologers, was told, that if the Vizir crossed the Danube on one day, and the Aga of the Janissaries on another, both which days were particularly specified, and if they marched immediately, and began their attack on the Russians, they would prove successful. Accordingly orders were sent to the Vizir to act agreeably to the predictions of the wisemen; and in so far as the Russians permitted them, they were punctually obeyed. For Romanzow, by beginning the attack, has afforded an excuse to the astrologers for the failure of their prophecy; and so perhaps may have saved them their heads.—The Russians, going on the attack, had to march through a field of wheat; and the common soldiers embracing this opportunity of making an addition to their provisions, filled their pockets with the wheaten ears. This circumstance was a better omen to the General, than were the predictions of astrologers to the Sultan: it shewed him that his men had no apprehension either of dying, or of being forced to return.

The Empress has rewarded Romanzow with the rank of Field Marshal; and has given him a present of 5000 slaves, corresponding to the number of slain on the field of battle. You will know the value of this present, by recollecting, that a great man's estate in Russia is not reckoned by the extent of his lands, so much as by the number of boors he possesses. They labour the ground; pay him an annual tax; and, in proportion as their wealth increases, their tax is augmented.

Count Romanzow, by his conduct in this campaign, has justified the high opinion that was generally entertained of him as a soldier. Persons on whose veracity and information I can depend, have given me the following account of him.—He possesses great strength of mind, and is, of consequence, very steady and determined. His eagerness and activity in prosecuting every enterprize he undertakes, are invincible. His ambition is very great; yet, in his temper, its violence may be counteracted by attention to present interest. He is friendly, and even respectful to his equals; condescending to his inferiors; to his superiors haughty and unpliant. This disposition

may

may prove inconvenient to himſelf, and hinder him from enjoying much happineſs in attending on a court; but it marks a high-minded man. In particular, the perſon who reſpects his equals, ſhews that he reſpects himſelf. Perſons of conſcious inferiority alone expreſs a mean opinion of thoſe who are in the ſame condition with themſelves.—Count Romanzow's abilities, as a politician, are ſaid to be no leſs eminent than his military talents; and his negociations may perhaps be no leſs ſucceſsful than his ſword, in putting an end to this cruel war.

The following anecdote of his youth is related and believed.——His earlieſt paſſion was the love of military glory: his ſuperior underſtanding ſoon convinced him, that improvement in his profeſſion could not, at that time, be obtained in Ruſſia; and his eagerneſs determined him to a meaſure which his perſeverance and addreſs enabled him to execute. He left his own country without the knowledge of his friends, and enliſted as a private ſoldier in the army of his Pruſſian Majeſty. Here he continued for ſome time; was

was at length difcovered; received promo tion fuited to his rank; and did not return to Ruffia but in obedience to the commands of his Sovereign. This anecdote receives fome confirmation from an expreffion in a letter from Romanzow to the Britifh Ambaffador, delivered by a Scotch officer who had been recommended to him by his Lordfhip, and who ferved with diftinguifhed honour to himfelf as a volunteer in the Ruffian army. Of that letter *, written originally in French, the following is an extract:——" I confefs " I have always been ambitious of having " the good opinion of your nation. I had " much intercourfe with the natives of your " country in my youth; and I reckon " among them many particular friends. " Befides the obligations I owe to the late " Marefchal Keith, that is to fay, all the " knowledge I have in my profeffion, and " confequently all my fortune, fhall make " me, on all occafions, ardently defire to " render juftice to the merit of Englifhmen. " It is a fort of retribution; and the wor-

* Communicated to me by the gentleman who had been recommended to Count Romanzow.

" thieft

" thieſt incenſe I am capable of offering " to the manes of that great man."——The letter is written with the ſpirit of a ſoldier; with the politeneſs of a gentleman; and, I may add, with the elegance of a fine writer.

I am, yours, &c.

LETTER XL.

To a Lady, who had gone to London from St. Peterſburg, requeſting her Return.

St. Peterſburg, Dec. 23, 1770.

ALLOW me, Madam, to tell you, that by remaining in London, inſtead of returning to Ruſſia, you neither conſult your own intereſt nor ours. I will give the reaſon in a compariſon. You have probably obſerved in a froſty evening, and ſuch evenings are not ſcarce in St. Peterſburg, that there are fewer ſtars in the north-weſt quarter of the ſky than in any other. You will alſo have obſerved, that any bright ſtar that condeſcends to ſhine there, does more good than if it ſhone in the milky way; it ſeems to illuminate thoſe who would otherwiſe have ſat in darkneſs; and, of conſequence, as the reward of ſuch condeſcenſion, it draws much more attention, and is much more admired. The application is obvious. But leſt proſe ſhould not prevail, and that nothing may be left unattempted, let us try alſo what verſe may do.

LESBIA, return—I cannot ſay
To flowery fields, and ſeaſons gay:
The Muſe, deſponding, cannot ſing
Of the ſweet garniture of ſpring;
Of ſunny hills, and verdant vales,
And groves, and ſtreams, and gentle gales;
Theſe, in more hoſpitable climes,
May run mellifluent in my rhymes:
For Winter, hoary and ſevere,
Rules an imperious deſpot here.
In chains the headlong flood he binds,
He rides impetuous on the winds;
Before him awful foreſts bend,
And tempeſts in his train contend.
But what tho' wintry winds prevail,
And Boreas ſends his rattling hail,
Siberian ſnows, and many a blaſt,
Howling along the dreary waſte,
From Samoïda to the ſhores,
Where black with ſtorms the Euxine roars;
Thy blameleſs wit, thy poliſh'd ſenſe,
Can eaſe and gaiety diſpenſe.

Come, then, enchanting Maid, and bring
The kindly influence of Spring;
Come, with thy animating air,
And Nature's weary waſte repair.

LETTER XLI.

Prince Henry of Pruſſia at St. Peterſburg—a ſplendid Maſquerade and Fire-Works.

DEAR SIR, St. Peterſburg, Jan. 4. 1771.

THIS city, ſince the beginning of winter, has exhibited a continued ſcene of feſtivity and amuſement: feaſts, balls, concerts, plays, operas, fireworks, and maſquerades in conſtant ſucceſſion; and all in honour of, and to divert his Royal Highneſs Prince Henry of Pruſſia, the famous brother of the preſent King. Yet his Royal Highneſs does not ſeem much diverted. He looks at them as an old cat looks at the gambols of a young kitten; or as one who had higher ſport going on in his own mind, than the paſtime of fiddling and dancing.

He came here about the beginning of November, on pretence of a friendly viſit to the Empreſs; to have the happineſs of waiting on ſo *magnanimous* a Princeſs; and to ſee with his own eyes the progreſs of thoſe immenſe improvements ſo highly celebrated by Voltaire, and the French writers, who receive gifts from her Majeſty. As the Queen of Sheba had heard of King Solomon's "acts "and wiſdom;" and "came to ſee whether ſhe "had heard a true report of them in her own "land;" ſo alſo this royal Prince hath come to viſit this mighty Princeſs. It may be too, that, like the Queen of Sheba, he is come to prove her Majeſty with "hard queſtions;" if ſo, he may depend upon getting anſwers to all his queſtions; and if he has any deſires which ſhe can grant, ſhe will "grant him his "heart's deſire." I could, with the greateſt eaſe, make out an excellent parallel, in which the precious ſtones, the camels and aſſes brought by the Sheban Potentate to Jeruſalem, would, I aſſure you, make no contemptible figure.

But do you ſeriouſly imagine, that this creature of ſkin and bone ſhould travel through Sweden, whence he is come at preſent, and Finland, and Poland, all for the pleaſure of ſeeing the metropolis and

Empreſs of Ruſſia? Other Princes may purſue ſuch paſtime; but the Princes of the Houſe of Brandenburg fly at a nobler quarry. Or is the King of Pruſſia, as a tame ſpectator, to reap no advantage from the troubles of Poland, and the Turkiſh war? What is the meaning of his late conferences with the Emperor of Germany? Depend upon it, theſe planetary conjunctions are the forerunners of great events. Time, and perhaps a few months, may unfold the ſecret. You will recollect the ſigns, when you ſhall hear after this of changes, uſurpations, and revolutions.

Prince Henry of Pruſſia is one of the moſt celebrated Generals of the preſent age. So great are his military talents, that his brother, who is not apt to pay compliments, ſays of him,—that in commanding an army he was never known to commit a fault. This, however, is but a negative kind of praiſe. He reſerves to himſelf the glory of ſuperior genius, which, though capable of brilliant atchievements, is yet liable to unwary miſtakes; and allows him no other than the praiſe of correctneſs. To judge of him by his appearance, I ſhould form no high eſtimate of his

 abilities.

abilities. But the Scythian ambaſſadors judged in the ſame manner of Alexander the Great. He is under the middle ſize; very thin; he walks firmly enough, or rather ſtruts, as if he wanted to walk firmly; and has little dignity in his air or geſture. He is dark-complexioned; and he wears his hair, which is remarkably thick, clubbed, and dreſſed with a high toupée. His forehead is high; his eyes large, with a little ſquint; and when he ſmiles, his upper lip is drawn up a little in the middle. His look expreſſes ſagacity and obſervation; but nothing very amiable: and his manner is grave and ſtiff rather than affable. He was dreſſed, when I firſt ſaw him, in a light-blue frock, with ſilver frogs; and wore a red waiſtcoat and blue breeches. He is not very popular among the Ruſſians; and accordingly their wits are diſpoſed to amuſe themſelves with his appearance, and particularly with his toupée. They ſay he reſembles Samſon; that all his ſtrength lies in his hair; and that, conſcious of this, and recollecting the fate of the ſon of Manoah, he ſuffers not the nigh approaches of any deceitful Dalilah. They ſay he is like the comet, which, about fifteen months ago,

appeared

appeared ſo formidable in the Ruſſian hemiſphere; and which, exhibiting a ſmall watry body, but a moſt enormous train, diſmayed the Northern and Eaſtern Potentates with "fear of change."

I ſaw him a few nights ago at a maſquerade in the Palace, ſaid to be the moſt magnificent thing of the kind ever ſeen at the Ruſſian Court. Fourteen large rooms and galleries were opened for the accommodation of the maſks; and I was informed that there were preſent ſeveral thouſand people. A great part of the company wore dominos, or capuchin dreſſes. Though, beſides theſe, ſome fanciful appearances afforded a good deal of amuſement. A very tall Coſſack appeared completely arrayed in the "Hauberk's "twiſted mail." He was indeed very grim and martial. Perſons in emblematical dreſſes, repreſenting Apollo and the Seaſons, addreſſed the Empreſs in ſpeeches ſuited to their characters. The Empreſs herſelf, at the time I ſaw her Majeſty, wore a Grecian habit; though I was afterwards told, that ſhe varied her dreſs two or three times during the maſquerade. Prince Henry of Pruſſia wore a white domino. Several persons appeared in the dresses of different nations, Chinese, Turks, Persians, and Arminians. The most humorous and fantastical figure was a Frenchman, who, with wonderful nimbleness and dexterity, represented an overgrown, but very beautiful parrot. He chattered with a great deal of spirit; and his shoulders, covered with green feathers, performed admirably the part of wings. He drew the attention of the Empress; a ring was formed; he was quite happy; fluttered his plumage; made fine speeches in Russ, French, and tolerable English; the ladies were exceedingly diverted; every body laughed but Prince Henry, who stood beside the Empress, and was so grave and so solemn, that he would have performed his part most admirably in the shape of an owl. The parrot observed him; was determined to have revenge; and having said as many good things as he could to her Majesty, he was hopping away; but just as he was going out of the circle, seeming to recollect himself he stopped, looked over his shoulder at the formal Prince, and quite in the parrot tone and French accent, he addressed him most emphatically with *Henri! Henri! Henri!*

and

and then diving into the crowd, disappeared. His Royal Highness was disconcerted; he was forced to smile in his own defence, and the company were not a little amused.

At midnight a spacious hall of a circular form, capable of containing a vast number of people, and illuminated in the most magnificent manner, was suddenly opened. Twelve tables were placed in alcoves around the sides of the room, where the Empress, Prince Henry, and a hundred and fifty of the chief nobility and foreign ministers, sat down to supper. The rest of the company went up by stairs on the outside of the room into the lofty galleries, placed all around on the inside. Such a row of masked visages, many of them with grotesque features and bushy beards, nodding from the side of the wall, appeared very ludicrous to those below. The entertainment was enlivened with a concert of music; and at different intervals persons in various habits entered the hall, and exhibited Cossack, Chinese, Polish, Swedish, and Tartar dances. The whole was so gorgeous, and at the same time so fantastic, that I could not help thinking myself present at some of the magnificent

cent festivals described in the old-fashioned romances:

> the marshal'd feast
> Serv'd up in hall with sewers and seneshals.

The rest of the company, on returning to the rooms adjoining, found prepared for them also a sumptuous banquet. The masquerade began at six in the evening, and continued till five next morning.

Besides the masquerade, and other festivities, in honour of, and to divert Prince Henry, we had lately a most magnificent shew of fireworks. They were exhibited in a wide space before the Winter Palace; and, in truth, "beggared description." They displayed, by a variety of emblematical figures, the reduction of Moldavia, Wallachia, Bessarabia, and the various conquests and victories atchieved since the commencement of the present war. The various colours, the bright green, and the snowy white, exhibited in these fireworks, were truly astonishing For the space of twenty minutes, a tree adorned with the loveliest and most verdant foliage, seemed to be waving as with a gentle breeze. It was entirely of fire; and during the whole of this ſtupendous ſcene, an arch of fire, by the continued throwing of rockets and fire-balls in one direction, formed as it were a ſuitable canopy.

On this occaſion a prodigious multitude of people was aſſembled; and the Empreſs, it was ſurmiſed, ſeemed uneaſy. She was afraid, it was apprehended, leſt any accident, like what happened at Paris at the marriage of the Dauphin, ſhould befal her beloved people. I hope I have amuſed you; and ever am,

Yours, &c.

LETTER XLII.

Account of the Consecration of the Waters:

DEAR SIR, St. Petersburg, Jan. 7. 1771.

ONE of the most magnificent ceremonies in the Greek church, and that which seems chiefly to draw the attention of strangers is, the consecration of the waters. It is performed twice in the year; but the most splendid display of this ceremony is exhibited on the 6th of January, and is performed in commemoration of the baptism of our Saviour. As I was yesterday present at this solemnity, I shall mention to you some of those circumstances in the shew, which seemed to me most remarkable.

A pavilion, supported by eight pillars, under which the chief part of the ceremony was performed, was erected on the Moika, a stream which enters the Neva between the Winter

Winter Palace and the Admiralty. On the top was a gilded figure of St. John: on the ſides were pictures of our Saviour, repreſented in different ſituations; and within, immediately over the hole which was cut through the ice into the water, was ſuſpended the figure of a dove. The pavilion was ſurrounded with a temporary fence of fir-branches; and a broad lane from the palace was defended on each ſide in a ſimilar manner. This paſſage, by which the proceſſion advanced, was covered with red cloth. The banks of the river, and the adjoining ſtreets, were lined with ſoldiers. The Moika, in honour of the event commemorated by this ſolemnity, is always dignified, on the 6th of January, with the name of the river Jordan.

On the preſent occaſion the Archbiſhop of Novogrod preſided; and the firſt part of the ſervice was performed in the Imperial chapel. The proceſſion then advanced, by the paſſage abovementioned, to the Jordan of the day. It conſiſted of muſicians, inferior clergy, and dignified clergy, with all their uſual parade of tapers, banners, lofty mitres, and flowing robes. They ranged themſelves

within

within the pavilion, and were ſoon after joined by another proceſſion of ſuch of the Empreſs's Court and Family as choſe to be preſent at this ſolemnity; for the Empreſs, owing to ſome indiſpoſition, was abſent. No parade of Prieſts and Levites, even in the days of Solomon, and by the banks of Shiloh, could be more magnificent. After the rite was performed with cuſtomary prayers and hymns, all who were preſent had the happineſs of being ſprinkled with the water thus conſecrated and rendered holy. The ſtandards of the army and the artillery received ſimilar conſecration; and the rite was concluded with a triple diſcharge of muſquetry.

The Ruſſians conceive that the water, thus ſanctified, poſſeſſes the moſt ſingular virtues. Accordingly the multitude who were aſſembled on the outſide of the fence, and the guard ſurrounding the pavilion, when the ceremony was over, ruſhed with ungoverned tumult to waſh their hands and their faces in the hallowed orifice. What puſhing and bawling, and ſcolding and ſwearing—to get rid of their ſins! the Prieſts of different churches, and many other perſons, carried home

home with them large quantities of holy water; and believed themſelves in poſſeſſion of a moſt invaluable treaſure. For they apprehend, that it is not only bleſſed with ſpiritual energy, and is efficacious in waſhing away the diſeaſes of the ſoul, but is alſo a ſovereign antidote againſt the malign influences of evil ſpirits; and may be preſcribed with great advantage againſt the pains and maladies of the body.——A Lady, as the ſtory goes, had a child ill of a fever; many medicines were tried, but without effect: ſhe was at length prevailed with to adminiſter holy water: it was many months after the time of conſecration; the water was ſpoilt; but ſhe did not believe it was ſo: for ſuch water is reckoned incapable of ſpoiling. Be that as it may, ſhe adminiſtered a copious draught; and the child died. But having been poiſoned by the waters of Jordan, the mother could not repine.

On the ſame principle, all infants who are baptized with the water of the ſacred orifice, are ſuppoſed to derive from it the moſt peculiar advantages. Parents therefore are very eager, even at the hazard of their childrens'

childrens' lives, to embrace the bleſſed occaſion. I have heard that a prieſt, in immerſing a child, for baptiſm is performed here by the immerſion of the whole body, let it ſlip, through inattention, into the water. The child was drowned; but the holy man ſuffered no conſternation. "Give me another," ſaid he, with the utmoſt compoſure, "for the "Lord hath taken this to himſelf." The Empreſs, however, having other uſes for her ſubjects, and not deſiring that the Lord ſhould have any more in that way at leaſt, gave orders, that all children to be baptized in the Jordan, ſhould henceforth be let down in a baſket. Adieu.

LETTER XLIII. (EXTRACT.)

To the Reverend ——,

Concerning the Effect of pompous religious Rites on the Devotion of the Worshipper.

* * * * I AM more than ever of your opinion, that simplicity ought to reign in the forms of religious worship.— "Piety, and a sense of the Supreme Being," as I have heard you observe, "ought not to "be mere holiday raiment, or a cloke to be "worn only on Sundays. The sentiments "and dispositions produced by true religion "ought to be mingled with, and form a part "of our temper. We ought to entertain "them habitually in our minds, and carry "them with us even to scenes of business and "of amusement. They will render business "agreeable, and heighten the pleasure of the "rural walk." These are your doctrines,

 and

and they are well founded. But if we think it eſſential to the exerciſes of devotion, that our minds be much elevated and tranſported; if we muſt feel violent raptures and ſtrong emotions, we deceive ourſelves. Theſe tranſports are of little ſervice. Extacy ſoon ſubſides: the reſolutions which it occaſions are no leſs tranſient; they vaniſh with the mood that produced them; they are a gaudy ſtructure, but have no foundation. Pompous ceremonies, glaring pictures, and even raviſhing muſic, have, no doubt, very pleaſing effects; but they rather tend to produce wild enthuſiaſm, than meek religion. I had lately a whimſical inſtance. At a very magnificent ceremony of the Greek church, at which I was preſent, every thing was contrived to work on the ſenſes, and inflame the imagination: Solemn proceſſions of mitred Prieſts—a reſpectable and numerous audience—the Empreſs of this great empire, and all her Court—every one with the geſtures and face of devotion—myſterious forms—and ſolemn muſic. I was ſtruck! 'tis a falſe religion, ſaid I to myſelf: but ſtill I was amazed at what I felt; and almoſt joined in worſhipping the glaring Saint.——I was next night at an an exquiſite opera: the muſic rapturous—the ſcenery like enchantment—the theatre lofty—the dreſſes magnificent—and the dancing, which was intermixed, reſembled the light airy geſtures of ſylphs. or præternatural beings. In one part, a Prieſteſs of Diana, accompanied with a chorus, conſiſting of an hundred Prieſts and Nymphs, ſung hymns to the Goddeſs: it was affecting. "It is "ſtrange, thought I; yeſterday I was of the "Greek perſuaſion; and I am this night a "Pagan." * * * *

LETTER XLIV*.

Obſervations on the Puniſhment of Crimes, in Anſwer to the Thirty-ſecond Letter in this Collection, concerning the Adminiſtration of Juſtice in Ruſſia.

DEAR SIR,

THERE are ſeveral circumſtances in your ſituation which muſt afford you a great deal of pleaſure, eſpecially the opportunity which you enjoy, and which I ſee you do not neglect, of comparing the condition of mankind in foreign countries with that which you were acquainted with at home, and of

* The Author of this Volume had no notion, when he wrote the Thirty-ſecond Letter, of the merit it was about to have with his Readers. It produced this Anſwer, which the ingenious Writer has moſt obligingly allowed him to publiſh. If the Editor could have preſented every other Letter in the collection ſo well ſupported as that which has occaſioned this return, the ſolicitude he now feels on coming before the Public, might perhaps have been leſſened.

obſerving

obſerving the varieties which the difference between them produces upon manners and character. It is flattering to our national pride, that you have hitherto met with nothing that tends to weaken your attachment to the liberty and the cuſtoms of your countrymen.

In your enquiries, the various regulations of police deſervedly occupy a part of your attention; and, among theſe, the laws relating to the prevention or puniſhment of crimes certainly occupy a very diſtinguiſhed place. Every good citizen ought earneſtly to wiſh, that the magiſtrate ſhould be enabled to watch over the intereſts of all the individuals belonging to the community, and to reſtrain any perſon whatever from violating their rights. For the ſake of abſolute ſecurity from all injuries to his perſon or property, he might perhaps be diſpoſed to ſacrifice ſeveral other valuable privileges.

There are regulations and eſtabliſhments of police in other countries, which tend more effectually to protect the inhabitants from the fraud and violence of their fellow-citizens, than any proviſions that have been made by our laws. I entirely acquiefce, however, in your judgment, that fimilar plans, for prevention of crimes, would be attended with great and imminent danger, if they were adopted in Britain. It is not to be denied, that, in this ifland, daring attacks have often been made by defperate individuals upon the perfons and properties of men; and, on account of thefe, our unequalled form of government has frequently fuffered reproach among the advocates for arbitrary power in foreign ftates. The reprefentations of this evil that have been given are not entirely groundlefs, though they are fometimes grofsly and induftrioufly exaggerated. But even granting that they are ftrictly true, it will not be found eafy to devife a remedy that will not occafion more fatal confequences than the difeafe. It is better to remain as we are, though fometimes expofed to danger from the feeble attack of a timid and fkulking plunderer, than to arm a protector with irrefiftible powers, that may afterwards be openly employed to rob us of our moft valuable rights.

I have

I have heard of two ſchemes that have been ſeriouſly propoſed, with a view to prevent the frequency of crimes, eſpecially of robberies, in this country. The one of theſe is, to erect a Board of Police in the capital, reſembling that which is eſtabliſhed in France, under the inſpection of a fit perſon, correſponding to the Lieutenant of Police in Paris, who, by means of ſpies and emiſſaries, and by means of information regularly tranſmitted to him from proper officers ſtationed in the country, may have a perfect acquaintance with the reſidence and tranſactions of all perſons whoſe characters are ſuſpicious. The other ſcheme is, to condemn all perſons, guilty of robbery, or of other groſs crimes, to bondage and hard labour. I am not ſatisfied that either of theſe propoſals, if carried into execution, would anſwer the end intended by them; and I am thoroughly convinced that neither of them is adapted to the conſtitution of Britain, and the temper of its inhabitants.

The firſt of theſe ſchemes, by which it is propoſed to form a great eſtabliſhment of police, comprehending many inferior departments, with their proper officers, is recommended by the ſucceſs in preventing or ſpeedily detecting crimes, with which ſimilar plans have been attended on the Continent, eſpecially in France. We muſt not, however, allow this conſideration alone to determine our judgment, for there may be regulations well adapted to the manners and government of other nations, that are inconſiſtent with our ſentiments, and with the ſpirit of our conſtitution.

An obvious objection to this plan ariſes from the great expence with which the execution of it muſt neceſſarily be attended. It would require a vaſt number of ſpies of different ranks, connected with one another by their ſubordination to common ſuperiors.—We can hardly ſuppoſe that theſe ſpies could, at all times, poſſeſs a ſufficient degree of intelligence for the purpoſes of the eſtabliſhment, if they were leſs numerous than the officers of exciſe. As it might be neceſſary, however, that, in appearance at leaſt, they ſhould carry on ſome ordinary buſineſs, with a view to conceal their real employment, they might not entirely depend on the public trea-

ſury

ſury for ſubſiſtence, and might therefore be ſupported for a ſmaller ſum than the ſame number of exciſe officers. At the ſame time, when we reflect, that ſecret ſervices muſt be liberally paid for, and that it might be requiſite to have ſpies who could eaſily obtain admiſſion into faſhionable circles, there is reaſon to believe that the difference of expence upon the whole might not be very conſiderable. Though the exciſe be a very productive tax, the nation has always complained of the heavy charges paid for collecting it. If a burthen equally grievous were laid upon a free people, without any pretence of defending their country, or of annoying their enemies, it would be altogether unſupportable. The French indeed do not murmur; but the French do not tax themſelves, and they claim no right to enquire into the expenditure of public money.

There is another objection to this propoſal of much more weight than that which I have already mentioned, ariſing from the nature of our civil conſtitution. A free people will never ſubmit, for the ſake of the moſt perfect ſecurity from the injurious attacks of individuals,

duals, to the reſtraint of acting always under the inſpection of ſpies. They will not allow their houſes to be examined by officers of police, without legal warrants from the magiſtrate; nor will they bear with patience to ſee their fellow-ſubjects carried away to priſon, unleſs they know the grounds upon which they are ſuſpected, and are alſo aſſured that they ſhall ſoon be brought to a fair and open trial. Men who love civil liberty, would rather chuſe that their goods and perſons ſhould be expoſed to ſome ſmall degree of danger, than purchaſe a complete ſecurity from ſuch injuries, by ſuffering thoſe who are in power to inſpect every man's buſineſs and converſation. An eſtabliſhment of police, perfectly adapted to anſwer its end, requires that cognizance ſhould be taken of the ſuſpicious as well as of the guilty, and is therefore inconſiſtent with liberty.

It is only in arbitrary governments that ſuch great and regular ſyſtems of police have been carried into execution: and there is reaſon to believe, that they are ſupported at great expence, and with unremitting attention, much more from reaſons of ſtate than from

from any regard to the ſecurity of the ſubject, or the good order of the community. The end which they have in view does not appear to be ſo much the puniſhment or the prevention of crimes, as the ſafety of the Prince's perſon, and the maintenance of his authority. A deſpot is at all times jealous and ſuſpicious. He dreads every whiſper, as if it were the voice of a conſpirator; and his throne ſhakes below him whenever there is the ſmalleſt commotion among his ſubjects. Spies are neceſſary to bring him information of every thing that has the appearance of deſign or of exertion, that he may be enabled to preſerve, through all his dominions, the ſtillneſs of night. But he endeavours to conceal his own fears under the plauſible pretence, that all his anxieties are produced by his unceaſing attention to the ſafety and ſecurity of his ſubjects. The Sovereign of a free ſtate is agitated by no ſimilar fears, for he reigns agreeably to the declared inclinations of his people; he poſſeſſes their confidence, and can depend upon their affections. As long as the Sovereign of a free country is diſpoſed to rule agreeably to the principles of the conſtitution, he will endeavour to be directed by the general

ral wiſhes of his people; and whenever he begins to ſuppreſs the open declarations of their fears and diſguſts, and to obtain ſecret and indirect information concerning their ſentiments, he certainly means to increaſe his own power, and to leſſen their influence. He diſtruſts them, becauſe he knows that he himſelf deſerves not to be truſted.

A ſyſtem of police, for the purpoſe of detecting crimes by means of Spies, has, for a conſiderable time, been carried on in London, under the inſpection of Sir John Fielding; but it is not extenſive, nor is it ſubſervient to any thing but the adminiſtration of juſtice. It muſt be conducted in ſome way that is very different from its preſent form, before any ſuſpicion can reaſonably ariſe, that it may, at laſt, be made uſe of to ſerve purpoſes of ſtate. The beſt of rulers, however, are naturally deſirous of increaſing their power; and men who have privileges to loſe, ought for ever to be on their guard. The conduct of the ſuſpicious muſt ſometimes be enquired into; but let the nature and grounds of the ſuſpicion under which they lie always be made publicly known; and let the enquiry be open, im-

partial,

partial, and not unneceſſarily delayed. Notwithſtanding every precaution that can be taken, the innocent may ſometimes be injuſtly ſuſpected, and may become ſufferers by confinement before the truth can be inveſtigated; but let them never ſuffer, unleſs ſtrong preſumptions lie againſt them, and let it be underſtood, that ſuffering is very different in its nature from puniſhment, for though it may be ſevere, it is not ignominious.

The other ſcheme, by which it is propoſed to condemn certain claſſes of criminals to hard labour, as well as the former, ſeems liable to ſtrong objections. Puniſhments of various kinds may be deviſed, and many kinds of them have been inflicted in different countries, ſome of them with better and ſome with worſe effects. All thoſe which are accompanied with torture are happily laid aſide in our own iſland; and, in the opinion of the wiſeſt men, ſhould be aboliſhed every where. Why ſhould the delicate, the ſenſible, and the compaſſionate, be wantonly ſubjected to that anguiſh which they muſt neceſſarily feel, when they are forced to ſee, or to hear of ſufferings that are ſhocking to humanity? Is it even prudent to expoſe atrocious guilt in thoſe particular circumſtances, in which its baſeneſs is concealed, or palliated, by emotions of pity excited in favour of the criminal? Such puniſhments are inconſiſtent with the natural principles of man, and with the ends of penal ſanctions.

The puniſhments that are ſhocking to humanity ought never to be inflicted; yet there are crimes that juſtify great ſeverity. Juſtice may reaſonably demand, that a man who has been guilty ſhould ſuffer in his fortune; though, at the ſame time, rigour, in this reſpect, ſhould always be avoided, when the future welfare of his family is connected with the forfeiture. A man may alſo deſerve to be baniſhed from his country, and to be legally diveſted of all thoſe privileges which he formerly enjoyed as a citizen. He may even be guilty of ſuch atrocious acts, that the indignation of mankind cannot be ſatisfied, if his life be ſpared. Baniſhment and death are puniſhments, by which future danger from the attempts of a perſon, who, by the perpetration of groſs crimes, has diſcovered an inclination and capacity to injure ſociety in its moſt eſ-

ſential

ſential intereſts, may be effectually prevented; and they do not ſeem improper under any form of government.

Deprivation of liberty is a kind of puniſhment that may alſo, in ſome forms of it, be adopted in any civil community. Impriſonment for a limited time, if it be regarded as a ſevere and not as a ſhameful puniſhment, may often be very reaſonable and proper. Even perpetual impriſonment is a ſort of puniſhment that is not inconſiſtent with the principles of free government; but in any ſtate, whether free or deſpotical, to retain a perſon who is never to be of any ſervice to the community, and who might perhaps be uſeful elſewhere, ſeems to be a meaſure unneceſſary and inexpedient. If there be a man, whom it is dangerous to preſerve in the community, the obvious dictate of common ſenſe ſeems to be, that he ought to be thrown out of it.

Inſtead of preſerving an uſeleſs life in a ſtate of long impriſonment, it has been thought a wiſe expedient in ſome nations to condemn to ſlavery thoſe criminals, whoſe guilt is not considered as heinous enough to deserve death, though their vicious inclinations are so well known that it would be dangerous to entrust them with liberty. It has been imagined, that while their labour was a punishment to themselves, it might be productive of some benefit to the state. This is the mode of treating certain classes of felons; which some are desirous of seeing established in Britain.

There are several lights in which the tendency of this sort of punishment may be examined. If we look upon it as an engine of police, merely intended to prevent men who are ill-disposed from the commission of crimes, it appears to be very well contrived. While persons, from whom danger might be apprehended, are kept under the immediate inspection of proper officers, while their tasks are regularly demanded from them, and the rod of correction is continually suspended over their heads, they can hardly find any opportunity to injure the properties of others.

It cannot, however, be reasonably expected, that this mode of punishment will produce

any

any ſuch good effect, unleſs the criminal be condemned to ſlavery for life. There are ſome, indeed, who are inclined to believe, that hard labour, continued for a limited courſe of years, may be ſufficient to anſwer the purpoſe. They found their belief upon the perſuaſion, that a happy alteration in the manners and characters of the ſufferers may gradually be produced. I am rather of opinion, that every ſucceſſive year the morals of perſons in ſuch circumſtances will become more and more corrupt. Slavery muſt be followed with conſequences entirely ſimilar to thoſe which attend other puniſhments of an ignominious nature; all of which ſeem very ill adapted to make any deſirable alteration in the offender. A man who is ſubjected to public infamy immediately loſes all ſenſe of ſhame, and becomes from that time bolder in guilt than ever he was before. This evil is common to all ignominious puniſhments when the criminal is permitted to ſurvive them, and to continue in the ſame ſociety to which he formerly belonged. But there are alſo other evils which are peculiar to that mode of infamous puniſhment which we are conſidering. If it ſhould become common to condemn felons to hard labour, it will be impoſſible to keep them under proper diſcipline, unleſs a number of them be collected together; and if they be permitted to live in ſociety with one another, each of them will become more corrupted than he was before: and perſons thus trained up in the ſchool of vice, whenever their period of ſervitude expires, will become the moſt daring of villains. The contagion of bad principles that infects every manufactory where labourers are collected together, cannot fail of ſpreading with great rapidity among men who are ſtigmatized for their villany, and legally deprived of reputation. The lot of ſlavery alone is ſufficient to debaſe the minds even of the ingenuous, and muſt render thoſe who are already corrupted totally abandoned. If, therefore, it be at all proper to make ſlavery the puniſhment of crimes, it ought to be perpetual; for in no other way can it effectually prevent the diſturbance to which Society might afterwards be expoſed from the ſame perſons who had formerly violated its laws.

The matter may be examined in another view. One important end of puniſhment is to prevent the future commiſſion of crimes ſimilar to that for which the penalty is inflicted. Condemnation to hard labour does not ſeem to be an expedient well adapted for anſwering this valuable purpoſe. Its effects indeed extend to the guilty perſons who ſuffer; it reſtrains from injurious acts ſome of the worſt members of the Society; but it does not ſufficiently deter other perſons of abandoned principles from committing the ſame crimes for which they are ſuffering. No puniſhment can be very effectual, unleſs it ſtrike the imagination of the ſpectator; and for this purpoſe, it is not enough that it be ſevere, it is further requiſite that it ſhould rarely occur. Slavery in itſelf is undoubtedly very ſevere, even more ſevere than death; but it ſeldom appears to an indifferent ſpectator in this light. The generality of men thoughtleſsly eſtimate the lot of a ſlave as not much harder than that of the labouring poor. They look only to his external appearance, without entering into the diſtreſsful thoughts that are inſeparable from his wretched ſtation. Where ſlavery is eſtabliſhed, the evils attending it are frequently expoſed to view, and the impreſſion which they make upon the mind, even of the compaſſionate, is ſcarcely felt. A puniſhment that is continually exhibited cannot be very ſtriking. We ceaſe to be moved with the moſt ſhocking ſpectacles when we are accuſtomed to ſee them every day; and a villain will not feel much uneaſineſs from the dread of thoſe ſufferings which long obſervation has rendered familiar to him.

It may be added, that condemnation to hard labour is the moſt unequal of all puniſhments that can be inflicted. Death and exile are equally ſevere upon the generality of men; but the evils of ſlavery fill men with different degrees of diſtreſs, according to the diverſity of their circumſtances. A man who, during the greater part of his life, has been accuſtomed to work with his hands, and whoſe expectations ſcarce ever roſe beyond proviſion for a ſcanty maintenance, could not ſuffer nearly ſo much from being obliged to labour in a way ſimilar to his ordinary employment, as the man who has been brought up in luxury and refinement. The ſpendthrift clerk of a grocer may be guilty of the ſame crime with a coal-heaver; but it would be moſt unmerciful to condemn the former

to

‡

to undergo the ſame bodily labour with the latter. One of them wants entirely thoſe habits which the other has ſpent his days in acquiring. Caſes might eaſily be ſuppoſed, in which puniſhments of this ſort would be more ſevère than any thing which the ingenuity and cruelty of men have been able to deviſe. A judge might indeed be allowed to diſcriminate among a number of criminals, and allot to each of them the degree of puniſhment which he thought proper, and adequate to his offence, his conſtitution and his habits; but in a free ſtate, every diſcrimination of ſuch a nature is looked upon as groſsly iniquitous.

A law, then, condemning criminals of a certain deſcription to hard labour, though it might be attended with ſeveral advantages as a regulation of police, appears at the ſame time to be inſeparable from various diſadvantages that are more than ſufficient to counterbalance all its ſalutary effects. The inconveniences, however, that have been mentioned, are not the whole, nor are they the moſt alarming of thoſe that might be mentioned. It is to be apprehended, that ſuch a law, if it were executed with rigour, might indirectly produce consequences of a public and most important kind. I am fully satisfied that slavery, limited to a certain term of years, will not answer the intention of preventing crimes. In order, therefore, to render a law, by which felons are condemned to hard labour, effectual in bringing about its end, it will be necessary to make the penalty perpetual. If the condemnation of felons to a state of bondage, which is to terminate only with their lives, were established by statute, and if the law were rigorously executed through every part of the kingdom, it is manifest that the number of bondmen would soon become very great. The expence necessary for supporting the institution would, in a short time, become enormous and intolerable to the nation; for the labour of slaves, employed in public works, and placed under the direction of an overseer who has no interest in them, will produce nothing by which the charge of maintaining them may be defrayed. The expences might indeed be lessened, by employing them in the ordinary occupations of civil life; but if this were the case, the distinction between them

and

and other classes of citizens would be too slightly marked to render their punishment examplary; while, at the same time, the honest labourer would suffer degradation in his own fancy and that of others, from the reflection, that he earned his bread by manual acts so mean and so severe, that condemnation to the performance of them was thought a proper punishment for those who are the disgrace of our species. The following seems to be the only remaining expedient for preventing these evils, if this sort of penalty be insisted upon, to wit, That those who may be condemned to hard labour shall be made the private property of individuals, who being bound to maintain them, will have an interest in obliging them to perform the tasks assigned them. But still this expedient would bring along with it new inconveniencies. It is greatly for the interest of the community, that persons of notoriously abandoned characters should be kept by themselves; but, according to this scheme, they would again be dispersed and mingled with the great body of the people, whom they would have an opportunity to corrupt. Their punishment might be abundantly and even excessively severe; but being endured in private, it could not be exemplary; and there is reaſon to fear, that it would very frequently be capriciouſly and iniquitouſly inflicted. It muſt be added, that, from the inſtant when ſuch a regulation took effect, domeſtic ſlavery would be introduced, and ſupported by the authority of law.

If domeſtic ſlavery, in any conſiderable extent, were tolerated, and a legal method of acquiring ſlaves inſtituted, the horrors of that deplorable ſtate would appear to the imagination in colours much leſs lively than they do at preſent, and would ſoon ceaſe to be ſhocking. Cuſtom and familiarity would reconcile the minds of men to the view of miſery, and in proceſs of time it would probably not be thought cruel to deprive men of their liberty for very ſmall offences. The conſequences might at laſt become worſe than at firſt might be ſuſpected, or indeed can be eaſily conceived. In ſuch circumſtances, would an ambitious ſtateſman heſitate to court the favour of the rich, by freeing them from the burthen of poor's-rates, which might be eaſily done, if the minds of men were reconciled to

domeſtic

domeſtic ſlavery, by adopting the plan for maintaining the poor, which was propoſed and recommended, about the beginning of this century, by Mr. Fletcher of Saltoun? Would he think it hard, to make thoſe who could not ſupport themſelves and their families, together with their wives and children, the legal property of their rich and powerful neighbour, who might be willing to ſupply with food the feeble and the infant, from the proſpect of acquiring a ſufficient recompence by their future labour? As one ſtep naturally and inſenſibly leads to another, we might reaſonably expect, that a ſcheme of this nature would be embraced, as ſoon as the minds of men could be brought to bear it. The ancient Romans allowed the perſon of a man who could not pay his debts to be ſold. If we were accuſtomed, as they were, to the deprivation of liberty, domeſtic ſlavery would ſoon become univerſal.

A ſtate in which domeſtic ſlavery prevails may be great and vigorous, and may enjoy very extenſive political liberty; but its freedom muſt be the freedom of an ariſtocracy, under which inauſpicious form of government,

ment, whatever bleſſings may be enjoyed by a few, the great body of the people muſt be in a condition of bondage and ignorance, very little ſuperior to the condition of beaſts of burthen.

I have given you my ſentiments with reſpect to theſe two expedients for preventing and puniſhing crimes. Both of them muſt, in my opinion, be inadequate, as long as they are managed conſiſtently with the principles of free government. I think it would be highly dangerous to this country to carry them into execution in any degree whatever; becauſe it is not improbable, that, at ſome future period, a miniſter inclined, as miniſters often are, to increaſe the power of the crown, might avail himſelf of them to promote purpoſes that were not intended by thoſe who at firſt propoſed them. A free country can never be enſlaved till the cuſtoms and the feelings of men be altered; but this is a ſort of change that may, by ſlow and inſenſible degrees, be at laſt effected. In a ſtate where the conduct of none of the citizens has ever been watched over by ſpies, the miniſter who employs ſuch emiſſaries, for his own ends,

ends, will be univerſally deteſted. But if an eſtabliſhment of this jealous nature be already founded in one department, and the minds of men reconciled to it, ſomething of the ſame kind may, with leſs difficulty, be introduced into another. Free men abhor ſlavery; but if they can be induced by motives of conveniency to tolerate it in one inſtance, they may gradually be brought to bear it with patience in more. If they can behold a felon reduced to ſlavery, without any emotions of indignation, they may be brought, by degrees, to behold thoſe whom they deſpiſe, or in whoſe welfare they have no intereſt, reduced to the ſame condition, without feeling much for their miſery. It is the duty of a free people to watch over their liberties with a jealous eye, and to look even upon ſmall circumſtances, by which they are infringed or endangered, as matters of great importance.

LETTER XLV.

Concerning the Progreſs of the Feudal Syſtem in Ruſſia.

DEAR SIR,

FROM all the enquiries I have been able to make, I do not find that the Feudal Syſtem was ever ſo fully eſtabliſhed in Ruſſia as in the other countries of Europe.

The Sovereigns of this country, for near a thouſand years, ſeem to have reigned with unlimited power. Nor have I ever found, notwithſtanding the fond aſſertions of ſome patriotic Ruſſians, that in all that period they ever beheld a ſingle glimpſe of freedom.—— You will readily obſerve, from the ſituation of this country, that it was, in early times, much expoſed to the invaſions and ravages of the neighbouring nations. It had been the thorough-fare, in ſome meaſure, by which the Eaſtern tribes had entered into, and taken poſſeſſion

poſſeſſion of Europe. After that period, the nations that remained in it were governed by various independent leaders, or Knezes. Theſe neceſſarily quarrelled, and waged war againſt one another. At length they were all ſubdued by the anceſtors of the Ruſſian Emperors, whoſe territory being in early times limited, they reſided firſt at Wolodomir, but afterwards transferred the ſeat of their dominion to Moſcow.

Not only were the Ruſſians expoſed to the inroads of ſurrounding barbarians, but the whole country may be conſidered as one extenſive plain. It is not defended by ſuch faſtneſſes of rocks, and chains of mountains, as have ſometimes ſerved as a barrier to other nations. In order therefore to be ever ready to repel violence, and protect his ſubjects from the predatory aſſaults of their rapacious neighbours, the Sovereign, or Velike Knez, was provided with a body of armed troops. He gave them regular pay; he kept them in readineſs to obey his commands; and never diſmiſſed them from his ſervice. In this manner he afforded ſuch ample protection to his ſubjects of every denomination from the incurſions

incurſions of foreign enemies, that they became careleſs of their own defence. Every thing was entruſted to the Velikè Knez, known, after the reduction of Caſan, by the name of Czar, and of late by the more faſhionable name of Emperor. His valour and activity, aided by his army, though ſometimes ſeverely tried by his ſurrounding adverſaries, preſerved them, upon the whole, not only from depredation, but inſult.

Another conſequence flowing from the ſame cauſe was, that perſons of great property did not fix their conſtant reſidence on their eſtates in the country, nor lived ſeparately from one another, ſurrounded by their dependants, and in a ſtate of rural magnificence. They left the care of their eſtates to ſuperintendants, and reſorted to the great towns, and particularly to Moſcow. Here they not only enjoyed ſome ſecurity from the ravages of the Tartarian and northern tribes, but ſhared in the intercourſe of ſocial life. This intercourſe, however, though it might be favourable to projects and conſpiracies againſt the power of the Sovereign, never produced any combination ſo ſucceſsful as to

overthrow,

overthrow, or even ſhake his authority. Were they ever ſo much inclined to revolt againſt, or abridge his power, they were deſtitute of the means. They were removed to a diſtance from their dependants; their dependants themſelves had no other connection with them than to render them obedience, or the fruit of their labour *; and were not preſent to partake of the glory, or adopt the reſentment of their ſuperiors. Add to this, that the armed force in the hands of the Czar would immediately cruſh the beginning of a rebellion.

The ſame ſeems to have been the ſituation in the eaſtern monarchies, and particularly in Perſia and Aſſyria. The great men lived together in fenced and walled cities: they were at a diſtance from their vaſſals, and under the immediate view of the Sovereign. Hence thoſe cities of enormous magnitude, that diſtinguiſhed in early times the more improved parts of Aſia. Hence too the name of the capital ſometimes became the name of the country or of the people. The Sovereigns of

* Stuart's View of Society in Europe, p. 2. ch. 1.

Chaldea were often ſtyled Kings of Babylon. In like manner the city of Moſcow had almoſt impoſed the name of Muſcovy on Ruſſia, and of Muſcovites on the Ruſſians. It required a conſiderable effort in the rulers of Ruſſia to recover and preſerve their original name.

In conſequence of the armed force and ſucceſs of the Velikè Knez in defending his ſubjects, he entertained ambitious views, and meditated conqueſt. Accordingly he ſubdued the kingdoms of Caſan and Aſtracan, and extended his dominions towards the Baltic. Theſe conqueſts contributed in a variety of different views to confirm his abſolute power at home. He roſe, accordingly, to the ſtate of an Oriental Deſpot. So totally were all notions of real rights and privileges extinguiſhed in the breaſts of the nobility, that when the line of Ruric, which had reigned 700 years, was extinct, and when a new Sovereign, or Dynaſty of Sovereigns, was to be appointed, the Ruſſians never thought of binding their race of rulers by any ſuch covenant or regulations as would even tend to emancipation. Even of late, when the Em-

preſs

preſs Anna Ivanowna was exalted to the throne, and was in ſuch critical circumſtances as would have induced her to grant any privileges to her ſubjects, thoſe which were demanded had little reſpect to the general freedom of the people, or even of the nobility; and, therefore, that ſhe was not compelled to grant them, need not be regretted. Such abſolute and undiſputed authority has the Sovereign of this empire continually maintained; and ſo little oppoſition has he ever encountered from his great lords or chieftains, that I have not learned of his ever having found it expedient, in order to encumber their ambition, to interpoſe in behalf of their vaſſals, or countenance among them any pretenſions to independence. In the ſame view it is amuſing to remark the nature of the ſuſpicions entertained by the Ruſſians againſt Demetrius, a pretender to the Ruſſian throne, and the charges that were brought againſt him. "His laying aſide the haughty
"ſtate of the former Czars, by appearing in
"public more than they had uſed to do;
"and his ſuffering people to ſpeak to him
"without being commanded, a treatment the
"Ruſſians had not been uſed to, were deem-

"ed derogatory from his dignity, and con-
"strued into proofs of his not being the
"person he pretended."—The manner too, in which some of the Russian Emperors chose their wives, resembles that of the Artaxerxes's and Ahasuerus's, and other Sovereigns of antient Asia. "The finest maidens in the empire were sent for to court; the monarch or saw them either under a borrowed name, without disguise; the wedding day was fixed; and the bridegroom declared his choice, by presenting a wedding garment to the bride. It was thus the Czar Michael Romanzow married Eudoxia, the daughter of Streshneu, who was tilling his ground with his own servants, when a messenger brought him presents from the Emperor, and informed him that his daughter was on the throne."

Although, therefore, you may have remarked some circumstances in the accounts I have given you that resemble feudal manners, yet I cannot think they have their origin in the feudal institutions. No doubt, in so far as feudal principles are common to all men, in a certain state of society, and may be traced among the Greeks and Romans, no less than among

among the anceſtors of the modern European nations, the Ruſſians alſo may have exhibited ſome correſponding appearances. But the chief particulars in their manners, that diſplay any ſuch pretenſion, ariſe from the ſupreme authority of the Emperor over the nobility, and of the nobility over their ſlaves.

The peaſantry were obliged to obey their ſuperiors, either in labouring the ground, or in going out to war; but it does not appear, that the terms on which they were allowed to derive ſubſiſtence to themſelves from tillage were, that they ſhould, on demand, perform military ſervice. If they tranſgreſſed againſt the will of their owner, they might no doubt be driven out of his eſtates. But the maſter was unwilling to inflict this kind of puniſhment; it was like depriving himſelf of a dog or a horſe. The moſt common puniſhment would be the ſeizure of their effects, or corporal ſuffering. In this we ſee nothing like the incident of *eſcheat**. In like manner the incident of *marriage* is not to be looked for in the power of the

* Millar's elegant and ingenious Account of the Origin of the Diſtinction of Ranks.

maſter

maſter to make his ſlave eſpouſe whom, or at what time, he appointed. He did ſomething ſimilar for the propagation of his herds and flocks. Conſidered as having no property but what depended on the good-will of their owners, we need not ſearch among them for *wardſhips*, *non-entries*, or *aids*. Nor does any relation of a feudal nature ſeem to have ſubſiſted between the Sovereign and his nobility. He was as abſolute over them, as they were over the labourers of the ground. If he wanted to recruit or augment his army, he told the rulers of certain diſtricts the number of men he wanted, and they were bound to ſupply them. In caſes of great emergency, no doubt, they muſtered all their vaſſals, and this force has been termed a militia: it is manifeſt, however, that it could only be employed for defence, and that other forces were neceſſary for the wars waged at a diſtance, and the extenſive conqueſts atchieved by the Czars. As we have nothing, therefore, in the early accounts of this country, correſponding to the *military ſervice* in the weſt of Europe, the Ruſſian hiſtory, if I miſtake not, furniſhes few inſtances of the judicial combat, nor of the manners and cuſtoms

flowing

flowing from ſuch practice or inſtitution. Neither have I found any thing in the early ſtate of this country that has the appearance of an aſſembly of chieftains, met together for the purpoſes of enacting laws, adminiſtering juſtice, or of deciding concerning the expediency of peace and war. The Senate as it is termed, ſeems to me to have been originally no other than a certain number of leading men, nominated by the Sovereign, to aſſiſt him in his deliberations. But what clearly ſhews that feudal cuſtoms were never very much known in Ruſſia, is the manner in which a man's family ſucceeded to his eſtate. The right of *primogeniture*, till of late, was never much recognized or regarded. The wife generally ſucceeded to one fourth part of a moveable ſubject, and one-ſeventh, or one-eighth, of immoveables. The huſband, in like manner, ſucceeded to the fortune of his wife; and if ſhe had no children, the remainder of her effects was divided among her relations. In theſe particulars, however, I ſuſpect there is ſome inaccuracy. I ſuſpect the intereſts of the wife, in ſuch a diviſion, would be little attended to. But, as Herodotus ſays, with regard to circumſtances in his narrative, which ſeemed to himſelf rather ſtrange, I tell you what I was told. Each of the daughters in a family ſucceeded to a portion equal to half what the widow received; and all the reſt was divided equally among the ſons. If this was the caſe in early times, you will obſerve that it tended directly to deſtroy an hereditary nobility; and ſo contributed in the moſt obvious manner to increaſe the power of the Sovereign.

There is ſo great a difference, according to the views now ſuggeſted, between the manners, cuſtoms, and political conſtitutions of the Ruſſians, and other nations of Chriſtendom, that I mention them with the utmoſt diffidence. I believe I am founded in the account I have given you; I have no theory to ſerve by the things now mentioned; yet you may ſet them down, if you pleaſe, under the head of conjecture. Two particulars, however, I muſt ſubjoin; the one in favour of what I have ſuggeſted, and the other rather inimical.

1. I am apt to think, that the full completion of the feudal ſyſtem, as it aroſe in the weſt

of

of Europe, is a ſingularity in the hiſtory of mankind; and particularly in the hiſtory of thoſe nations that have any pretenſions to improvement. The great empires of Aſſyria, Chaldea, and Perſia, if we make due allowances for difference of climate, preſent nearly the ſame appearance with the ſovereignty of the Czar, or Velike Knez. Their Emperors commanded great armies, which enabled them not only to make extenſive conqueſts, but to extend their authority at home; and their nobility reſided either in the metropolis, in Nineveh, Babylon, or Suſa; or in the fenced cities of the provinces. The government of the provinces was altogether military. I am inclined therefore to view the Ruſſian ſtate as a great oriental empire: and if I may truſt certain ſymptoms in the character of the nation and its rulers, notwithſtanding the efforts made by Peter the Great and the preſent Empreſs, to give it ſome reſemblance to other European ſtates, for they are the only Potentates who have really made the attempt, it will again return, I will not ſay relapſe, into its former oriental condition.

 2. The

2. The other circumſtance to be mentioned is, that feudal cuſtoms are aſſerted by grave authority to prevail not only in the neighbourhood of Ruſſia, but even in ſome diſtricts that are now provinces of the Ruſſian empire. An ingenious French Writer, the author of an Eſſay on Public Happineſs, expreſſes himſelf in the following manner:——" We have " ſtill in the Ukraine a ſtriking example of " the feudal government in all its purity, " and ſuch as it muſt have been in the be- " ginning. The Czars gave this province " to the Coſſacks, on condition that they " ſhould improve it, and be ready to " render them what ſervices they ſhould re- " quire. Military forms and regulations " were in place of every other rule or inſti- " tution. The province is divided into ſeve- " ral regiments, which form ſo many diſ- " tricts. One company makes a village, " ſubject to a Captain, who is under the Co- " lonel, who reſides in the city. The Het- " man reſides in a ſort of capital, which is " no other than a camp, where he always " keeps in his pay a certain number of in- " fantry and of cavalry. The reſt labour " and cultivate the ground, on no other con-

‡ " dition

" dition than that, whenever there is any
" need for them, they ſhall appear in arms."

According to this account, no doubt, there is in the Ukraine an appearance of feudal inſtitutions. But, as was hinted above, the principles, ſo to ſay, of feudality may be found in all nations; among the Romans, in the relation of Patrons and Clients; among the Greeks, at the ſiege of Troy; in Mexico, when that country was ſubdued by Cortes; in Otaheite, and the South Sea Iſlands. Nor has the above quoted Author aſſerted that the particular incidents of the feudal ſyſtem, and which give it its peculiar character, are to be met with among the Coſſacks. I confeſs, though the outlines of the ſyſtem may be traced among them, I doubt much whether they ever had it in its full completion.

At preſent the Ukraine may be conſidered as in all reſpects a Ruſſian province. It has no pretenſions to independence. The title of Hetman is in ſome meaſure aboliſhed. Count Roſamouſky, the preſent Hetman, is more commonly known by the title of Mariſchal than of Hetman. He was raiſed

to

to his office by the Sovereign of Ruſſia, and may be removed at the Empreſs's pleaſure. He reſides in a ſplendid palace at St. Peterſburg, and exhibits all the indolent magnificence and gorgeous luxury of a Magabazus, or Artabazus, or any other Perſian Satrap in the reigns of Darius or Artaxerxes. I have been informed that the peaſants in the Ukraine, who were not, as in Ruſſia, attached to the lands they laboured, the ſole property of their maſters, and to be bought and ſold at their pleaſure, but might hire their ſervices on any eſtate, or to whom they choſe, have lately undergone a deplorable change, and have been reduced, by an edict of the preſent Empreſs, to the condition of her other Ruſſian ſubjects.

You will perhaps infer from the foregoing account, that Ruſſia was, in early times, in a more improved ſtate than the Tartar and other nations in its vicinity. You will be apt too, to aſk the reaſon. I am afraid, however, I can give you no farther ſatisfaction on this ſubject, than to ſay, that the difference muſt have ariſen from difference of ſoil and climate. The ſouthern and eaſtern parts of Ruſſia, eſpecially

eſpecially about the banks and mouths of the many great rivers by which this empire is ſo abundantly watered, are exceedingly fertile, and capable of the higheſt improvement. This, therefore, along with ſome other circumſtances, determined the inhabitants of this country to ſow corn and build towns, while their Scythian, Laponian, and Tartarean neighbours led a wandering and fugitive life. In like manner, thoſe who lived in former ages by the banks of the Tigris and Euphrates, cultivated the ground, and were expoſed to the depredations of thoſe ſavages who iſſued from the wilds of Arabia, the faſtneſſes of Mount Taurus, or the deſerts of Caucaſus.

LETTER XLVI.

Concerning the Causes that Duelling and Single Combat have not been so usual in Russia as in other Countries in Europe.

DEAR SIR,

THE Russians are not addicted to duelling. Persons of fashion, in so far as I can learn, do not appeal to the sword, either to revenge an affront, or to vindicate their honour In this respect also, the manners of the Russians differ from those of other nations in Christendom. The circumstance is indeed so singular, that you will be inclined to ask how it happens.

It occurs immediately, in considering this subject, that we hear of no duels among the Romans, Greeks, Jews, Persians, or any people of antiquity; nor even among the moderns, if we except the Europeans and their descendants. That contests between two persons,

ſons, even bloody conteſts, and terminating in death, have not exiſted in all times and places ſince the days of Cain and Abel, is not aſſerted. I only aſſert, that we have no evidence that the judicial combat ever exiſted, or gave riſe to the modern duel, but among European nations. By no other people, in ſo far as I have heard, was ever perſonal valour made the teſt of truth; or a matter of fact proved by the ſword; or the will of heaven ſuppoſed to be revealed by the death or victory of a combatant in ſingle combat. But among our eaſtern and northern progenitors, even in very early times, conflicts, having ſuch ſingular importance annexed to them, were not unuſual. Frothon, a very ancient Scandinavian Prince, declared by edict, "that it "was better to terminate differences by arms "than by argument; and by blows than by "words." This doctrine was very readily and very generally embraced. Rotharis, King of the Lombards, who was the firſt in his nation that formed a regular ſyſtem, or code of laws, and who borrowed nothing, as we are told, from ſtrangers, but only collected and renewed the unwritten laws of his fathers, enacted, "that if a man, poſſeſſing "lands,

"lands, or any kind of property, were ac-"cused of holding them unjuſtly, he might "aſſert his right by ſingle combat." Such edicts might be expected from the deſcendants of thoſe who, according to the accounts both of Cæſar and Paterculus, determined the moſt ſacred rights, and ſucceſſion to the moſt important offices, by the ſword. About thirty years after Rotharis, Grimoald, his ſucceſſor, boaſted of having reformed his ſyſtem. A King of the Burgundians alſo, at a very early period, enacted, that the ſingle combat might be uſed as lawful evidence. The Goths, and other nations, who ſettled in lands that had been much occupied by the Romans, became, in this reſpect, milder than their brethren of the north. Hence King Theodoric, according to Caſſiodorus, propoſed them as a pattern to be followed by his ſubjects in Hungary, and in the regions along the Danube. "Why," ſays he, "have re-"courſe to ſingle combat, ſince the judges in "my dominions are incapable of being venal. "Meddle not with arms but againſt your "foes; and in this reſpect follow the "Goths."—"Univerſis barbaris, &c. per "Pannoniam conſtitutis. Res parva non vos

"ducat

*

"ducat ad extrema diſcrimina. Acquieſcite
"juſtitia qua mundus lætatur. Cur ad Mo-
"nomachiam recurritis qui venalem judicem
"non habetis. Depoſite ferrum qui non
"habetis inimicum, &c. Quid opus eſt
"homini lingua ſi cauſam manus agat ar-
"mata? Aut unde pax eſſe creditur, ſi ſub
"civilitate pugnetur? Imitamini certè
"Gothos noſtros qui foris prælia, intus no-
"runt exercere modeſtiam."

In explaining the reaſons of a difference ſo remarkable between the manners of the Romans, to whom I ſhall chiefly appeal on the preſent occaſion, and the anceſtors of ſome modern European ſtates, you will probably be able alſo to diſcern the reaſon of the ſimilar difference between them and the Ruſſians. Whence then has it ariſen?—In attending to the ſubject, you will perhaps agree with me, that three circumſtances reſpecting the *dreſs*, *government*, and *ſuperſtition* of the nations, concerning whom we are treating, have, by their joint operation, produced this curious effect. Diſunited, no one of them apart from the reſt could have done it; but by combining their powers, and by exerting

exerting them in the ſame direction, they have given riſe to this ſingular difference. I will endeavour, in this view, to illuſtrate thoſe three particulars; and if in this diſcuſſion I offend your patience, let me crave the indulgence of a friend.

I. We have the teſtimony of ſeveral antient authors, hiſtorians as well as poets and orators, that neither the Romans nor the Greeks, nor indeed any nation of antiquity, unleſs in very rude times, uſed offenſive arms as a part of their dreſs; nor indeed upon any other occaſion than that of actual engagement with an enemy. Our information concerning the Romans, is apprehended to be no leſs appoſite than deciſive. No Roman who was not a ſoldier was allowed to carry arms. Even thoſe who were enrolled in the legion, were not entruſted with offenſive weapons, but in the time or inſtant expectation of battle. The arms of the army, when they were encamped, were carefully depoſited near the Prætorium, and were not to be uſed, nor put into the hands of the ſoldiery, but by the expreſs order or leave of the Commander in Chief. "Accedunt inſuper

" hoſtes

"hoſtes ferocius multo, ut ſtatuiſſe, non pug-
"nare conſules cognitum eſt. Quippe im-
"pune inſultaturos. *Non credi militi ar-*
"*ma* *." When Turnus Herdonius was charged by Tarquin, in a general meeting of the Latins, with a deſign againſt his life, the proof was, that he was poſſeſſed of arms. A ſearch was inſtantly made: arms were found in his cuſtody: they had been conveyed privately to his lodging by the partizans of Tarquin; and he was of conſequence accounted guilty. "Non dubitare ſi vera deferantur
"quin primâ luce, ubi ventum in concilio ſit,
"inſtructus cum conjuratorum manu, *arma-*
"*tuſque* venturus ſit. Eunt, inclinatis qui-
"dem ad credendum animis, tamen niſi gla-
"diis deprehenſis, cætera vana exiſtimatura †."
In times of peace, or during any ceſſation of hoſtilities, the arms, even of thoſe ſoldiers who had been recently engaged, or were about to engage in warfare, were taken from them, and depoſited in the armory ‡. Add to this, that no perſon was allowed to fabricate arms, either in the city or in the pro-

* Liv. l. ii. ca. 45. † Liv. l. i. c. 51.
‡. Petiſcus. Servius

vinces, without the permiſſion or authority of the ſtate*. Virginius, who came directly from the army to ſave his daughter from diſhonour, does not appear to have been armed even with a ſword; but put her to death with a butcher's knife. "Ab lanio cultro "arrepto, hoc te uno quo poſſum, ait, modo, "filia in libertatem vindico. Pectus deinde "Puellæ transfigit†"——The Senators of Great Britain, like their German anceſtors, when they meet in their legiſlative aſſembly, appear in arms; but the Roman Senators, who put Cæſar to death, armed themſelves ſecretly for that particular purpoſe; nor had Cæſar any weapon to defend himſelf with, but an iron pen ſeized ſuddenly from the hand of a clerk‡. It was certainly owing to the regulations, which hindered the Romans in the city from wearing arms, that for many centuries before the time of the Gracchi, notwithſtanding the tumults and violent conteſts between the Patricians and Plebeians, excepting in two or three inſtances, there was little bloodſhed, and no life ever loſt.

* Petiſcus. † Liv. l. 3. c. 48. ‡ Suetonius.

But

But in this respect, the practice of the Germans, according to the accounts given us by Tacitus, was very different. Armour constituted a part of their dress. In all public meetings, and in all deliberative assemblies, even in times of the profoundest peace, they never met but in arms. The consequence was, that in all disputes and dissentions they appealed to the sword, as to a prompt and decisive umpire. Impatient of contradiction, passionate and furious, as men in an early state of society; high minded, courageous, and expert in arms as the progenitors of the French and English, they proceeded to instant conflict. "Tum ad negotia nec "minus sæpe ad convivia procedunt armati crebræ rixæ, raro conviciis, sæpius "cæde et vulneribus transfiguntur."—Not only was this practised by the Germans in the times of Tacitus, Paterculus, and Cæsar, but was continued long after. The posterity of the Germans, when they became a mighty people, and were divided into various states went in armour, not only to their parliaments and public councils, but to their visits and private meetings*. Indeed, no race of men, ſo far advanced in improvement, continued this practice ſo long as the anceſtors of the nations in the weſt and north of Europe. Yet the cuſtom is ſo peculiar, and muſt neceſſarily have been of ſo much influence in the common intercourſe of life, that we need not be ſurpriſed, if it ſhould diſtinguiſh the people, among whom it prevailed, with the moſt peculiar uſages and inſtitutions. Indeed the wonder would be, ſuppoſing ſuch a difference to ſubſiſt between two nations, the Romans, for example, and the deſcendants of the antient Germans, if its conſequences, in a variety of remarkable circumſtances, did not diverſify their manners, and render them diſſimilar. Hence not only the duel and judicial combat, but the jouſts and tournaments, that make ſo great a figure in the hiſtory of modern Europe.

II. It is obvious, that ſuch exceſſes as thoſe mentioned in the paſſage from Tacitus, tended to injure, and even ruin ſuch ſmall communities as German tribes; and called upon

* A View of Society in Europe, by Dr. Gilbert Stuart: a work to be ſtudied by all who would really underſtand Tacitus's Treatiſe of Ancient Germany.

the

the rulers to interpose every means of prevention. The loss which the State sustained by the death of intrepid leaders; the tumults occasioned by such outrageous dissention; and the lasting enmity between different families, disseminated by sudden acts of violence, were in the number of those calamities that arose from furious and irregular strife. The rulers, therefore, were much interested in having them softened, or entirely prevented. But how was this to be done? Not surely by positive and express prohibition. The powers of government were then so weak, that such prohibition, opposed to the furious passions of valiant men, were of little effect. "Nec re-"gibus infinita, aut libera potestas: et duces "exemplo potius, quam imperio, &c. præ-"sunt *." "Their Kings have not an abso-"lute or unlimited power; and their Gene-"rals command less through force of autho-"rity than of example."

In order, therefore, to prevent misfortunes of the kind above-mentioned, the rulers of States betook themselves to other means than direct prohibition. They said to the angry

* Tacitus.

 persons,

persons, who would terminate their dissentions by violence, " Do as you please; fight " if you will; but have respect for the meet- " ing: let not the business of a public deli- " beration be cast into disorder by your disa- " greement: nay, do justice to yourselves: " let no one take advantage of another: go " forth to an open place: use proper wea- " pons: and let each of you carry along with " him an equal number of friends, to assist " you in so far as may be consistent with ho- " nour, and be the faithful witnesses of your " valour."—In all this there was nothing that opposed their passions: nay, their self-importance was in some degree flattered. Meantime delay was obtained: by the good offices of friends their anger might be appeased: at any rate, the mischiefs arising from outrageous discord were lessened; and as the person who fell would seem to have met with sufficient justice, the resentment of his adherents would be asswaged.

The disposition of rulers, in early times, to prevent violence by indirect means, and even by a seeming compliance with the angry passions of those they governed, when their real design

design was to counteract and oppose them, is well illustrated by the methods practised by some Indian nations in punishing murder. They are mentioned particularly by Lafitau; and their chief object seems to have been, to appease the resentment of those who would feel themselves incited to avenge the death of a friend The criminal was obliged to give sixty presents; nine of these were given to the friends of the deceased, and the rest were suspended over the dead body. Some of them were said to be given to make the tomahawk fall from the hand of vengeance; some to wipe the wounds of the dead; and others to console his friends and relations.

III. Another circumstance, which, along with the preceding, tended to produce the judicial combat, and particularly the formalities of that custom among a rude people, so situated as the ancient Germans and their descendants, was their proneness to superstition. Their gods, as they believed, were interested in their fortunes; and, of consequence, were interested in nothing so much concerning them, as what related to their life or death. Hence they regarded the single combat as an appeal to the juſtice of the Beings they worſhipped; or an infallible method to prevail with them to reveal their will to mankind. Thus every ſuch conflict implied a ſort of tacit convention with the præternatural objects of divine adoration; and the appeal to heaven conſtituted a ſtriking feature of this ſingular cuſtom. The diſpoſition to believe that the Gods announced promiſes of protection, and conſequently their opinion concerning the juſtice of any cauſe, by the ſucceſs of a combatant in ſingle combat appeared ſo early as among the nations deſcribed by Tacitus. "Ejus gentis cum qua bellum eſt "captivum quoquo modo interceptum, eum "electo popularium ſuorum, patriis quemque "armis committunt: victoria hujus vel il-"lius pro præjudicio accipitur." "They ob-"lige a priſoner, taken by any means what-"ſoever from the nation with whom they are "at variance, to fight with a picked man of "their own, each with his country arms; "and according as the victory falls, they "preſage ſucceſs to one or the other party."

As the ſingle combat was thus conſidered as a demand on heaven to interpoſe in behalf

half of truth or innocence, it was conducted with religious solemnity. Moreover, as the Gods could not be ſuppoſed to favour falſehood or injuſtice, a perſon's proneneſs in calling the ſword to witneſs, was held a ſymptom of his integrity: his ſucceſs was regarded as inconteſtible evidence in his favour: and thus perſonal valour, ſupported by ſkill in arms, became, in ſome meaſure, the teſt of truth. The propagation of Chriſtianity, by a ſtrange perverſion, contributed to give the cuſtom ſtability. By the doctrines of that benign religion, the Deity was repreſented as inclined to interpoſe, in a very particular manner, in behalf of integrity, and as regarding deviations from truth with peculiar diſpleaſure. From the miſapplication of thoſe opinions, by the groſſeſt and moſt arrogant ſuperſtition, the Supreme Being had a method preſcribed to him for the diſplay of his authority; and was required to manifeſt his juſtice within the liſts of the ſingle combat. The manners of men became gradually more improved: government acquired vigour: offences were reſtrained or puniſhed by poſitive laws: the judicial combat, like the fiery ordeal, was no longer appealed

pealed to; and ſo went into diſuſe. But a connection had been formed between valour and truth: it was cheriſhed by the ardent ſpirits of impetuous men: they wore arms to defend their honour: it was natural they ſhould feel reſentment againſt thoſe who impeached their veracity: and girt with a ſword, it was no leſs natural that the ſword ſhould expreſs their reſentment. Thus, though the judicial combat was diſcontinued, it left us its repreſentative, the modern duel. I am aware of the diſtinction between the ſingle combat, conſidered as an inſtitution of honour, and an inſtitution of civil polity *; nor does it ſeem inconſiſtent with the foregoing obſervations.

Upon the whole, the northern nations wore arms on all occaſions, and in periods of conſiderable improvement; the Romans ſeldom: the powers of government among the northern nations were weak; among the Romans ſtrong: and theſe circumſtances, along with ſuperſtition, a quality of which all men, as well Romans as Huns and Lombards, have always poſſeſſed quantity enough

* Dr. Stuart's View of Society.

for producing ſuch *valuable* inſtitutions as judicial combats and fiery ordeals, explains the difference above ſtated; and apply with propriety enough to the ſingularity in the manners of the Ruſſians, which has impoſed the taſk upon you of reading this tedious Letter. If am not miſinformed, the Ruſſians, excepting the guard of the Veliké Knez, and the ſtanding army, were not accuſtomed to appear in arms No abuſes, therefore, ariſing from the promiſcuous uſe of military accoutrements, called either for the direct or indirect interpoſition of government. The judicial combat, and conſequently the duel of honour, never exiſted among them. But as the faſhions of Europe, and particularly thoſe of France, are making progreſs among the natives of this country, ſome perſons among them who affect patriotiſm, expreſs their expectations, that they will ſoon have the credit of blowing out one another's brains in the eaſieſt and politeſt manner. Adieu.

LETTER XLVII.

English Players in Russia—Prologue on opening an English Theatre at St. Petersburg.

DEAR SIR, St. Petersburg, Feb. 12. 1771.

YOU will be surprised to hear, that we have got at St. Petersburg an English Playhouse. A Company of Players arrived here in the end of autumn. They were advised, you may be sure, to return home without loss of time; they chuse, however, to make their home, at least for one winter, in Russia, and trust to the well known humanity of their countrymen in the Gallerinhoff. Accordingly, with great diligence, and much tinsel, they furbished up an old barn into the likeness of a theatre; and that every thing might be as complete as possible, they had in it, not only a seat for the British Ambassador, but boxes for the Great Duke and her Imperial Majesty of all the Russias. So, on the first

firſt night that the theatre was opened, all their countrymen came to them, to give them charity, and to laugh, as might have been expected, at the Tragedy of Douglas. But inſtead of laughing, they cried. The part of Douglas was performed by a female player with inimitable pathos. The audience were ſurpriſed into the warmeſt applauſes. The fame of this excellent performance was ſpread through the city; and for two or three ſucceſſive evenings the theatre was crowded with Ruſſians and Germans as well as Engliſh. On the fourth night of the repreſentatation, juſt as the play began, the door of the Empreſs's box was unexpectedly opened; and her Majeſty, without having given any previous warning, took poſſeſſion of her ſeat. You may eaſily imagine how much we were pleaſed and flattered with this mark of her Majeſty's confidence and condeſcenſion. This was ſtill more the caſe, when, in anſwer to ſome apology that had been conveyed to her, about the badneſs of the accommodation, ſhe replied, "that, among the Engliſh, ſhe was "quite at eaſe." In order, however, to remedy the real inconveniences of the ſituation,

and

and to teſtify ſtill farther her *preſent* partiality to our nation, ſhe ordered a better theatre to be prepared; and on occaſion of opening it, the player who had drawn ſo much attention, delivered the following Prologue:

WITHOUT the aid of ornament or art,
To ſpeak the language of a grateful heart,
I come reſpectful. Little known to fame,
Thro' ſtormy ſeas to diſtant ſhores we came;
And to us, Britons, in a foreign land,
Britons extended the protecting hand:
Friendleſs we came; but every Britiſh heart
In all our intereſts took a friendly part.
Fair fame attend you! O may due ſucceſs
Reward your merit and your labours bleſs!
Kind as ye are, and generous, may ye ſtill
Enjoy the power, as ye poſſeſs the will!

The Rulers of this land beheld, with joy,
How Britiſh hearts on Britiſh hearts rely:
How Albion's ſons, incapable of change,
Thro' no variety of friendſhips range:
Kind without intereſt, with affection true,
Gen'rous and conſtant where their faith is due.

The Rulers of this land, whoſe hoſts defied
The rage of Infidels, and quell'd their pride;
Made Kahul's ſtreams with ſlaughter'd foes run red;
Heap'd Bender's walls with thouſands of the dead;

Undaunted

Undaunted in the gallant ſtrife of arms,
Even to Byzantium carried dire alarms;
Ting'd the Ægæan wave with Ottoman gore,
And ſhook with terror Aſia's diſtant ſhore;
They ſaw your goodneſs, felt it, and were mov'd
To emulate the worth their ſouls approv'd:
This gen'rous ſympathy their favour drew;
Us they applauded, but they honour'd—You.

With unexampled goodneſs from the Throne
The radiance of th' Imperial bounty ſhone,
Beam'd glory round us, rais'd us from the ground,
And bade us bloom, and bade our fruits abound.
Far thro' the nations may that radiance blaze,
The good to cheriſh, and the meek to raiſe;
To foſter merit, from the haunts of men
To baniſh Diſcord, and her ghaſtly train:
Envy ſhall pine and ſicken at the ſight;
And Turkiſh creſcents mingle with the night.

LETTER XLVIII.

Copy of a Letter from Count Orloff to Rousseau, with the Answer.

DEAR SIR,

I SEND you inclosed what I am persuaded you will consider as a literary curiosity: a letter sent by Count Orloff to the famous Rousseau; and another from that strange citizen of the world in return.

Copie d'une Lettre de Mons. le Comte D'Orloff en Russie, à Mons. J. J. Rousseau en Angleterre.

MONSIEUR, Dec. 1766.

VOUS ne serez point etonné que je vous écrive, car vous savez que les hommes sont inclins aux singularités. Vous avez les vôtres; j'ai les miennes: cela est dans l'ordre: le motif de cette lettre ne l'est pas moins.

Je

Je vous vois depuis long-tems aller, d'un endroit à l'autre. J'en ſais les raiſons par les voies publiques; et peut être, les ſai je mal: parcequ'elles pouvent être fauſſes. Je vous crois en Angleterre chez le Duc de Richmond, et je ſuppoſe que vous y êtes bien: cependant il m'a pris fantaſie de vous dire, que j'ai une terre eloignée de ſoixante verſtes de St. Peterſburg, ce qui fait de dix lieux d'Allemagne, où l'air eſt ſain, l'eau admirable, les coteaux qui entourrent differents lacs, forment de promenades agréables très propres à rever; les habitans n'entendent ni l'Anglois ni la Francoiſe; encore mois la Grec et la Latine. Le curè ne ſait point diſputer ni precher; et les ovailles, en faiſant le ſigne de la croix, croient bonnement que tout eſt dit. Hé bien, Monſieur, ſi jamais ce lieu là eſt à votre gout, vous pouvez y venir de demeurer. Vous auriez la neceſſaire, ſi vous la voulez. Si non, vous auriez de la chaſſe, et de la pêche. Si vous voulez avoir à qui parler pour vous déſengager, vous le pourrez:. mais en tout, et ſur tout, vous n'eſſuyerez aucune gene ſur rien; ni n'auriez aucune obligation à perſonne. De plus, toute publicité ſur ſe ſejour, ſi vous ſauhaitez, pourroit être eviteé: et dans ce dernier cas, vous ferez bien, ſelon moi, ſi vous pouvez ſupporter la mer, de faire le trajet par eau. Auſſi bien les curieux vous importunerent moins ſur ce chemin, que ſur la route de terre.

Voilà, Monſieur, ce que je me ſuis crû endroit de mander, d'après la reconnoiſſance que je vous ai, pour les inſtructions que j'ai priſe dans vos livres, quoique ils ne fuſſent pas écrits pour moi. Je ſuis, Monſieur, avec beaucoup de reſpect, V. S. &c.

LA REPONSE.

Le 23me de Fevrier, à Hatton.

VOUS vous donnez, Monſieur le Comte, pour avoir des ſingularités. En effèt, ce'n eſt preſque une d'être bienfaiſant ſans interet: et c'en eſt une bien plus grande, de l'être de ſi loin, pour quelqu'un qu'on ne connoit pas. Vos obligéantes offres, le ton dont vous me les avez fait, et la deſcription de l'habitation que vous me deſtinez, ſeroient aſſurement très capable de m'y attirer; ſi j'étois moins

moins infirme, plus allant, plus jeune, et que vous fussiez plus près du soleil. Je craindrois d'ailleurs, qu'en voyant celui que vous honorez d'une invitation, vous n'y eussiez quelque regret: vous attendriez à une manière d'homme de lettres, un beau diseur, qui devroit payer en frais d'esprit et de paroles votre genereuse hospitalité; et vous n'auriez qu'un bon homme bien simple, que son goût et ses malheurs ont rendu fort solitaire, et que pour tout amusement herberissant toute la journée, trouve ce commerce avec les plantes, cette paix si douce à son cœur, que lui ont refusè les humains. Je n'irai donc pas, Monsieur, habiter votre maison; mais je souviendrai toujours avec reconnoissance que vous me l'avez offerte; et je regretterai quelque foix de n'y être pas pour cultiver les bontés, et l'amitié du maître.

Agréez, Monsieur le Comte, je vous supplie, mes remerciments très sinceres, et mes très humbles salutations.

Translation of the above Letters.

I.

YOU will not be ſurpriſed at my writing you; for you know men are apt to have ſingularities: You have yours, and I have mine: theſe are things of courſe. My motive for writing you is not leſs ſo: I have obſerved you for ſome time going from place to place. I know the reaſons of this by public rumour; and perhaps I am miſinformed, as public rumour is not always true. I believe you are now in England with the Duke of Richmond; and I ſuppoſe that there you are happily ſituated. Nevertheleſs, I have taken it into my head to tell you, that I have an eſtate diſtant ſixty verſts, that is, about ten German miles, from St. Peterſburg, where the air is healthy, the water admirable, and the little hills ſurrounding the lakes form walks very well ſuited for contemplation. The inhabitants are ignorant both of Engliſh and French; and ſtill more ſo of Greek and Latin. The curate can neither argue nor preach; and his ſheep, in making the ſign of the

the cross, are satisfied in good earnest that they have done all that is needful. Now, Sir, if ever this place suit your taste, you may come here and live. You shall have your wants supplied, if you chuse. If not, you shall have hunting and fishing. If you tire of solitude, and chuse conversation, it is in your power. But in all, and above all, you shall suffer restraint in nothing, and have obligations to none. Besides, your retreat may be as secret as you incline: and, in that view, I would advise you, if you can bear the voyage, to come by sea. By taking that route, you will be less teized by inquisitive persons than if you came by land.

All this, Sir, I thought my duty to tell you, out of gratitude for the instruction which your books, though they were not written on my account, have afforded me: and am, Sir, with much respect, &c.

II.

Hatton, Feb. 23.

YOU would pass, Sir, for a person who has singularities. In truth, it is a singularity to be beneficent without ſelf-intereſt. It is much more ſo to be beneficent from ſo great a diſtance, and towards a perſon with whom you are not acquainted. Your obliging offers, the manner in which they are made, and the deſcription of the dwelling you intend for me, would be fully ſufficient to draw me thither, were I leſs infirm, better able to travel, and younger than I am, and if you were ſituated nearer the ſun. Beſides, I would be afraid, leſt, in ſeeing him whom you honour with an invitation, you ſhould feel ſome regret. You expect a ſort of learned man, a rare talker, who ought to repay your hoſpitality with wit and fine ſpeeches; and inſtead of this you would have but a very plain and ſimple man, whoſe taſte and misfortunes have rendered very ſolitary; and who has no other amuſement than to paſs the day in herbalizing; but who finds, in converſing with plants, that peace, ſo pleaſing to his heart, which men have refuſed him. I will not, therefore, go to live in the houſe you mention; but, Sir, I will always, with gratitude, remember the offer you have made me; and I ſhall ſometimes regret that I am

5 not

not there to enjoy the goodneſs and friendſhip of its owner.

I intreat you, Sir, to accept of my ſincereſt thanks.

LETTER XLIX.

Translation of an Easter Hymn, sometimes recited in the Churches of the Greek Communion.

To the Reverend Dr. L———d.

REV. DEAR SIR,

YOU know that, at Easter, in churches of the Greek communion, Priests, appointed for the purpose, represent the Resurrection of our Saviour. On that occasion, I have been informed, that the following Hymn, written originally in Greek by a Bishop of Thessalonica, is sometimes sung. You will easily observe, that it is intended to be recited in the interval between the burial and the resurrection.

O WHAT an awful, awful hour,
Beheld our Saviour die!
The Sun, in dire eclipse, withdrew
His radiance from the sky.

The

The waters of the troubled deep
    To their abyſſes fled:
The mountains, and the ſolid earth,
    Shook with exceſſive dread.

Amazement was in heav'n! But who
    The ſolemn myſt'ry ſaw,
That ſtruck, ev'n in the heav'n of heavens,
    Angelic hoſts with awe?

At that tremendous, awful hour,
    The gates of heav'n were clos'd:
The fabric of the rolling ſpheres
    With conſternation paus'd.

Meantime what deeds were done on earth!
    Deeds of atrocious ſtrife!
The powers of Death and Darkneſs ſtrove
    Againſt the Lord of Life!

And conquer'd—as they vainly deem'd!
    Nor, in their frenzy, knew,
That they ſhould, by that heinous act,
    Their own rebellion rue.

The darkneſs flies away! the gates
    Of heaven are open'd wide!
And ſudden, from the ſapphire throne,
    Burſts an effulgent tide.

Emerging

Emerging from the cloud of light,
With beaming harps, behold!
In bright attire, the Seraphin
Their radiant forms unfold.

On high their loud hoſannas flow:
Meſſiah's praiſe they ſing:
The nether orbs reſume their ſpeed,
And with hoſannas ring.

" Meſſiah triumphs," they proclaim,—
" Tho' in the grave he lies,
" Soon will he burſt the bonds of Death,
" And reaſcend the ſkies.

" Ten thouſand thouſand angels then
" Shall join the vocal lay;
" And hail, triumphant, his return
" To everlaſting day!

" To Him a crown of majeſty
" Amid the hoſts of heaven,
" Shall by Jehova be with power
" And wide dominion given.

" Far thro' the ſtarry realms of ſpace
" Blazing with beams of gold,
" His banner, at the gate of heaven,
" An angel ſhall unfold.

" Then

" Then pealing with tremendous voice
The Seraph of the Sun,
" Shall, as *his* flames expires, proclaim
" Meſſiah's reign begun.

" Rous'd by that voice, in white array,
" His Elect to the ſky
" Shall ſoar, and reign with glory crown'd
" In realms of bleſs on high.

" Glory to God, and to the Son,
" And to the Spirit pure!
" Their juſtice, goodneſs, and their power,
" Forever ſhall endure."

LETTER L.

The Seraſkier of Bender.

DEAR SIR, July 10th, 1771.

IT is ſaid here, that, except Conſtantinople, no city in Europe contains a greater variety of ſtrangers than St Peterſburg. In London and Paris you have Europeans of all nations; but you have not, additionally to theſe, different races of Tartars, Circaſſians, and Armenians.——The moſt beautiful Circaſſian I have ſeen here is the wife of an Armenian merchant; and her beauty ſeems of a kind ſomewhat ſingular. She is moſt gracefully formed; but has not the leaſt tint of complexion: nor does ſhe imitate the Ruſſian ladies, in ſummoning art to the aſſiſtance of nature. Her ſkin is as white as the driven ſnow; it is ſo tranſparent, as to ſhew the purple veins underneath; her features diſplay the beauties of Helen; her eyes are deep

deep blue; her eye-brows exquiſite; and her hair, flowing over her ivory neck, is as black as the wing of a raven This ſpecies of beauty, however, does not diſtinguiſh all the Circaſſians I have ſeen; ſome of them have black eyes, and a ruddy complexion.

In conſequence of the number of ſtrangers in St. Peterſburg, many perſons ſpeak a variety of different languages: nor would even the ladies think you were calling them bad names, if you were to ſay they were Polyglots. The Engliſh ladies here ſpeak French, German, and Ruſs, and ſome of them Italian. Their other graces and accompliſhments are proportioned to their gift of tongues.

The variety of ſtrangers here is diverſified at preſent, by the addition of a great many Turkiſh priſoners. They are remarkably well uſed; and go about the city with a great deal of freedom. The moſt diſtinguiſhed perſonage among them is the Seraſkier, who behaved ſo gallantly in the defence of Bender. He is an Emir; that is, a deſcendant of Mahomet; and, as a mark of his high lineage, the colour of his robe is green. The faſhion

of

of his dreſs, excepting that he wears a turban, is the ſame as that of the Hoſpodar of Wallachia. But he is a different perſon from the Hoſpodar. Gregorio Giko is rather tall, and of a dignified appearance: the Seraſkier is little, meagre, marked with the ſmall-pox, and of a mean appearance. But he is as valiant as the edge of his ſabre, ſteady to his truſt, active in the diſcharge of his duty, and determined in his tenor of conduct. Though conquered, and a captive, he is not ſubdued; but exhibits an unyielding, and even contemptuous ſternneſs, that ſurpriſes his conquerors. He inſiſted on having a numerous attendance of Turks, including a part of his ſeraglio, and a perſon of ſmall ſtature, who diſplays the antic geſtures of a buffoon: his requiſition was immediately granted. A Ruſſian nobleman aſked him to his houſe: "I am "your priſoner," he replied; "you may do "with me what you pleaſe; you may cut off "my head, if you will: but if I am free to "go to your houſe, or not; I will *not* go."— One of his baſhaws gave a blow with his fiſt to a Ruſſian officer. The officer complained to his General; and the General aſked the Seraſkier, "what would have been done to a "Ruſſian

"Ruſſian at Conſtantinople, who ſhould have "behaved in that manner to a Turk?" "They would have ſtrangled him," he replied. But the Turk was not ſtrangled.——The Seraſkier, however, paid a viſit, at his houſe in the country, to the Britiſh Ambaſſador. He came on horſe-back, with his green flowing garment, and his horſe moſt ſumptuouſly capariſoned. He ſpoke little; for, ſoon after his ſitting down, one of his attendants brought him a very long tobacco-pipe, and he continued ſmoking all the time of his viſit. His buffoon appears very often in parti-coloured garments in the ſtreets of the city; and endeavours, by his drolleries, to amuſe the paſſengers. The Turks themſelves appear ſo grave and ſolemn, that it is really amuſing to ſee a Turkiſh buffoon.——Adieu.

goodneſs, and all his other moral qualities. The creation of the world is then briefly treated of; and the following account given us of the origin of evil:——Every thing is ſaid to be created by God's wiſdom; nevertheleſs the beſt things may be abuſed; a ſword may be uſed to ſlay the innocent, and the human underſtanding may be employed in guile. Man is ſaid to have been made after the image of God, with a natural propenſity to good, and averſion to evil. The providence of God is alſo aſſerted; and that the utility reſulting to mankind, from the knowledge of God and of ourſelves, conſiſts in begetting in us confidence in God, and reſignation to his will; in ſtrengthening our moral principles, and in diſpoſing us to worſhip God. The worſhip of God is ſaid to be twofold; interior, conſiſting in love, fear, veneration, and gratitude to God; and, exterior, conſiſting in the external forms of devotion. Conſcience, however, is ſaid to inform us, that our utmoſt efforts to fulfil the will of God are imperfect; and that our only hope is in his mercy. No mention of original ſin.

PART

PART II.

TREATING of Revealed Religion, it is obſerved, that the light of nature is not alone ſufficient for our ſalvation; that ſalvation is only had by the goſpel, which contains the joyful tidings of our redemption; that religion is the receiving the goſpel in our hearts; that the great truths of the goſpel are contained in the Old and New Teſtament, and are ſummarily contained in the Apoſtles Creed; that by it we are inſtructed in all the great doctrines of Chriſtianity; that God is one in eſſence, but conſiſts of three perſons, the Father eternal, the Son, begot by the Father before all ages, and the Holy Ghoſt, proceeding from the Father; all three to be equally adored: that faith in Chriſt is of infinite uſe, by calming the terrors of conſcience, and repreſenting God as merciful as well as juſt; that it muſt be an active faith, turning us to repentance and the true worſhip of God; that all thoſe who truly believe, conſtitute the church; that thoſe who belong to the church, are initiated by baptiſm; a myſterious rite, by which the ſoul is waſhed from ſin; that the Euchariſt is another rite, by which we teſtify our faith, and by eating bread and wine, myſteriouſly converted into the body and blood of Chriſt, receive great ſpiritual advantages, and oblige ourſelves to live in union with the church; and that the care of imparting the Euchariſt is committed to the clergy; that the church poſſeſſes other ſacraments, unction at baptiſm, and extreme unction; that it hath other inſtitutions for the ſake of good order; and, finally, that all who act according to the goſpel, and believe, ſhall riſe to immortal life; and that all who act in a contrary manner, ſhall be eternally puniſhed.

PART III.

CONCERNING the ſubjects of the laws of God, it is aſſerted, that faith, without works, is ineffectual; that we muſt not only believe, but act agreeably to the law of God; that the will of God is contained in the Decalogue; that thoſe who ſin againſt the firſt commandment, are atheiſts; Epicureans, rejecting Providence; polytheiſts; ſorcerers, who divine by dreams, who obſerve omens, and aſcribe ſanctity to certain dreſſes and tonſures; heretics and ſchiſmatics; and thoſe who depend for all their welfare on their wealth or on human aid: that the invocation of ſaints is not forbid by this commandment, becauſe they are invoked as interceſſors with God and Chriſt. God is ſaid to be the maſter, and they are his principal ſervants; but that it is ſinful to honour them in their feſtivals equally with God. That the ſecond commandment is tranſgreſſed by thoſe who worſhip graven images; by uſurers and profligates; by hypocrites, who think they worſhip God by penances and feſtivity; by ſuperſtitious people, who pretend to have intercourſe with ghoſts; and, briefly, by all thoſe who hope to gain God's love otherwiſe than by faith and good works. That it is not ſinful to have pictures of Chriſt and of the ſaints, for the pictures are not themſelves worſhipped, they only aid the memory and imagination; but this practice is liable to be perverted to idolatry. That the third commandment is tranſgreſſed by blaſphemers, perjured perſons, habitual ſwearers falſe prophets, and by thoſe who make indecent requeſts to God. That the fourth commandment enjoins the obſervance of the Sabbath, and of feſtivals on religious occaſions; particularly it enjoins reſt from labour, and the going to church to pray; it enjoins the giving charity, the giving for the ſupport of the church and its miniſters, for hoſpitals, ſchools, and for the care of ſtrangers and priſoners; that all thoſe who act otherwiſe, whether laity or eccleſiaſtics, either through impiety, or negligence, or wantonneſs, or profligacy, or avarice, tranſgreſs the commandment. That the fifth commandment enjoins reverence and obedience to parents, rulers, clergy, teachers, benefactors, and old men; that the duty of parents is to educate and inſtruct their children; the duty of children is to ſupport their parents; and to act in like manner in all the other relations above-mentioned; that the duty of ſovereigns is to procure peace and happineſs to their ſubjects, to maintain juſtice, to puniſh the guilty, and reward the deſerving to ſupport the clergy, and be as fathers to their people; that the duty of ſubjects is to love their ſovereigns next to God,—to obey them without complaint, to pay tribute, and, in caſe of need, to give their lives for their ſafety; that the duty of paſtors is to inſtruct mildly by precept and example; the duty

duty of the flock to follow the shepherd with all due respect; that the duty of masters is to instruct their servants—not to overburthen them, nor to punish them too rigorously; that the duty of servants is to fear their masters with filial fear, to obey without sloth or murmuring, to put up with their ill-humours, and defend their honour; that the duty of the husband is to love his wife, to correct her faults *gently*; the duty of the wife to love and revere her husband; that fidelity is the duty of both; that the rich are bound not to be proud nor covetous, but liberal, and that the poor are bound to be honest and industrious; that, in general, we ought to love and consult the interest of all men. Against the sixth commandment those transgress who take away life from themselves or others, or who are accessory to such crimes, by aiding or concealing the guilty; also unjust judges; those who let the poor die of cold or hunger; those who punish and oppress their servants, so as *to kill them*; and all who encourage hatred, anger, malice, envy, inhumanity, the dispositions of mind tending to the destruction of mankind. Against the seventh commandment all those transgress who are impure in any manner in thought, word, or deed; and all who indulge in wanton discourse, dainty living, and debauchery, tending to encourage impurity. Against the eighth commandment all those transgress who rob, or steal; all superiors who enslave the free; force those to sell who do not chuse it; who exact more labour of workmen than they engaged for; who seize their neighbours goods, lands, &c. at their pleasure; who retain the labourers' hire; also all those who take advantage of a dearth to raise the price of provision: who exact unconscientious service of the poor in return for aiding them; all usurers; all those who, in selling, impose on the buyers, by vending damaged goods; all who rob or cheat the government or the church; all who having found what had been lost, keep it without seeking the owner; all who practise simony; who forge wills or accounts; who, being rich, pretend they are poor, that they may get charity; all hypocrites, who get money by pretending zeal; all flatterers, who get money by imposing on the weakness of others, &c. Against the ninth commandment all liars and dissemblers transgress. And the tenth commandment is a summary a ſummary of the preceding ones, and prohibits us even from thinking ſinfully. It is alſo aſſerted, that we cannot perform every thing required of us in theſe laws of ourſelves, without the grace of God, which is obtained by prayer; and that our prayers ought to be formed on the model of the Lord's Prayer.

LETTER LII.

Account of a Circassian Princess, the Widow of Donduc Ambo, Chan of the Calmuck Tartars.

DEAR SIR,

AGREEABLY to your desire, I have perused Dr. Cook's Travels *; and as you wish to have my opinion concerning them, I can assure you that, in so far as my knowledge of the facts he relates, or of the manners he describes, extends, he is a writer of strict veracity. I agree with you in thinking his account of the Circassian Princess very interesting; and also in regretting that he has not so united the different circumstances, as that the whole might be read as a continued story. I have endeavoured to supply this defect; and from such information as I have collected here, together with his anecdotes, I have formed the following uninterrupted

* Travels and Voyages through the Russian Empire, &c. by J. Cook, M. D.

Narrative.

Narrative. In an evening, during the bad weather, and your preſent ſolitude in the country, it may perhaps amuſe you.

THE CALMUCK TARTARS inhabit, or rather frequent, that country which lies between the Caſpian and Euxine Seas; bounded on the ſouth by Circaſſia, on the north by the dominions of Ruſſia, on the eaſt by the Caſpian Sea and the Volga, and on the weſt by the river Don and the Sea of Aſoph. They have no fixed habitation, but live chiefly in tents; and ſubſiſt by depredation, or by the paſturage of cattle. They pretend they are an independent nation; yet, if they are not abſolutely governed, their counſels are much influenced by the authority of the Ruſſians.

In the reign of the Empreſs Anna Ivanowna, the Court of Ruſſia, by endeavouring to prevail with the Calmucks to betake themſelves to agriculture, and live in fixed habitations, wanted to reduce them to ſtill greater ſubjection. In this attempt, Donduc Ambo, the Chan of the Tartars, gave them great oppoſition. The Russian ministry, therefore, resolved to deprive him of his sovereignty, and substitute Donduc Dashee, who, they conceived, would give them less opposition, in his place. But the wisdom and valour of the reigning prince rendered their plan abortive. He was, nevertheless, so sensible of his danger, and so justly apprehensive of the future machinations of the Russian Court, that he prevailed with his nation to leave the regions they had formerly occupied, and migrate into Cuban-Tartary. This country is situated on the south side of the Palus Mœotis or Sea of Asoph, is separated from Crimea by the Straits of Taman, and its inhabitants, the Cuban Tartars, are dependants on the Ottoman Porte.

The reception, however, which Donduc Ambo met with from the Turks, and the Tartars of Cuban, not having answered his expectations, he determined to embrace the first opportunity of re-uniting himself, on honourable terms, with Russia, and of returning to the banks of the Volga. This opportunity soon occurred. For a war having arisen between the Turks and the Russians, he he knew that the aſſiſtance of his nation would be of great importance on either ſide; and offered his friendſhip to the Empreſs of Ruſſia. An agreement took place between them: it was ſtipulated, that the Calmucks ſhould return to the neighbourhood of Aſtracan; that Donduc Ambo ſhould be their acknowledged ſovereign; and that he ſhould aſſiſt the Ruſſians with forty or fifty thouſand men. The Empreſs ratified the league by preſents ſent to the Calmuck Chan *.— Among theſe were two beautiful braſs cannon, of two or three pounders, and a ſcymeter with a hilt of gold, ſtudded with precious ſtones. He ſeized an early opportunity of putting his ſcymeter to the proof; for the Cuban Tartars, who had treated him with little friendſhip, during his ſojourn among them, having purſued him with hoſtile intentions at his departure, he fell upon them with great fury, and cut off the flower of their army.

Not long after, about the time peace was concluded between the Turks and the Ruſſians, Donduc Ambo died. On his deceaſe,

* Dr. Cook.

the Ruſſian Miniſtry reſumed their favourite deſign of abridging the independence of the Calmuck nation. For this purpoſe, they again attempted to inveſt Donduc Daſhee, whom Anna Ivanowna had maintained in a princely manner in the city of Caſan, with the ſovereign authority. But they met with unexpected reſiſtance in the widow of Donduc Ambo, the former Chan.

This Princeſs was a Circaſſian of illuſtrious lineage; and not more diſtinguiſhed for her beauty, which was eminent even in Circaſſia, than for her virtues. She was the mother of five children; and though they were yet in their infancy, ſhe determined to aſſert their right to the ſovereignty enjoyed by their father. Therefore, finding herſelf in danger from the ambition of Donduc Daſhee, and the contrivances of the Ruſſians, ſhe ſummoned the Calmuck chiefs to her tent. She repreſented to them the attempt made on their independence; the unworthy conduct of Donduc Daſhee, who would ſacrifice the intereſt of his people to his ambition; the magnanimous virtues of their former Chan; his attachment to the dignity of the Calmuck nation;

nation; the helpleſs ſtate of his family; and the confidence ſhe repoſed in the care they would have of her children. Her beauty, heightened by her diſtreſs, added force to her eloquence. The Tartar leaders entered warmly into her intereſts; and declared, that none but the progeny of Donduc Ambo ſhould be their Sovereigns. Thus the Princeſs, finding herſelf at the head of at leaſt forty thouſand men, who had fought the battles of her huſband, and were now devoted to her family, having encamped for ſome time nigh the banks of the Volga, retired, during the winter, to the borders of Circaſſia.

Meantime the Ruſſians in the ſouthern provinces became apprehenſive of a viſit from Kouli-chan, the tyrant of Perſia, no leſs famous for his conqueſts, than abhorred for his cruelty. Conſcious too, of their having irritated the Calmuck Princeſs, they were afraid, that, in caſe of an invaſion, the Tartars would co-operate with the Perſians. It was determined, therefore, that every engine ſhould be employed to deprive her of her authority; and Donduc Daſhee, with thoſe Tartars who adhered to him, entertained the

moſt

moſt ſanguine expectations of compaſſing their deſigns. For though the Empreſs Anna was now dead, her ſucceſſor, Elizabeth, entered in this particular into her views. But the vigilant Circaſſian was aware of her danger. She was apprehenſive leſt the Coſſacks on the river Don, uniting with ſome Circaſſians who had been brought over to the intereſts of her opponents, would either betray her into the hands of the Ruſſians, or oblige her to relinquiſh her authority. She therefore withdrew, very early in the ſpring, to the eaſtern ſide of the Volga. Here ſhe was in leſs danger of being ſurrounded by her adverſaries; and in caſe of their perſiſting in their oppreſſion, ſhe could betake herſelf for protection to the great nation of Black Calmucks, who frequent the vaſt continent between the Caſpian Sea and the Wall of China. She flattered herſelf with meeting with a more friendly reception from them, as they were probably of the ſame origin with the Weſtern Calmucks, and of ſimilar manners, particularly as to religious opinions, than her huſband had experienced among the Tartars of Cuban.

In the mean time Donduc Dashee having received many assurances that the Calmuck Princess was afraid of him, and would, on the first appearance of force, give up the contest, left Casan with an army of five thousand men, and pursued her into the desart. Having overtaken her in her march, he was advancing boldly to the Tartar camp. Here he was met by some Calmuck chiefs, who informed him, that the Princess insisted on his advancing no farther; but that she was willing to converse with any Commissioner whom he should appoint to treat of the interests of the Calmuck nation. He accordingly sent one of his friends, acquainting her, that the Empress expected she would resign her authority to him; and that she and her children might depend on having such provision made for them, as suited their high rank and condition. The Princess, who was only desirous of gaining time, and obtaining information concerning the force he had brought against her, answered, that it was then late, and that next morning "they should adjust their differences *." In the night she consulted with her

* If the Calmuck Princess be thought to incur blame in this part of her conduct, and if it can be removed or lessened by

her chieftains; ſhe found them reſolute; and next morning, by ſun-riſe, ſhe appeared on horſeback at the head of her army. She fell upon Donduc Daſhee. His five thouſand men made a gallant defence; but, overpowered by numbers, the greateſt part of them were put to the ſword. Intelligence of this fatal conflict was brought to Aſtracan by a Tartar attached to Donduc Daſhee. He was a perſon of ſome diſtinction: had with him neither bow nor ſcymeter, nor any other weapon than a battle-axe *. He ſhed a torrent of tears; and ſaid, his friends and the Calmuck Prince were certainly ſlain.

Vaſilee Nikitits Tatiſhoff was at that time Governor of Aſtracan. He was a conſummate politician; and had diſtinguiſhed himſelf at the acceſſion of the Empreſs Anna, by baffling the deſigns of the Ruſſian noblemen, who wanted to impoſe ſome terms on their Sovereign, and reſtrict her power. He was indeed well ſuited to promote the views of an abſolute Prince. Totally unprincipled, he laughed at every ſacred tie; and being ad-

by authority, an apologiſt may ſay for her, that the ſtratagem ſhe practiſed was ſimilar to one practiſed againſt the Carthaginians by Scipio Africanus.

* Dr. Cook.

dicted

dicted to study, he could support his immoral or irreligious maxims, by the reasonings of those writers who gave countenance to his opinions *. He possessed, at the same time, all the penetration, craft, and dexterity necessary for the services to which he was called.

After the discomfiture of Donduc Dashee, the Calmuck Princess returned to the country usually frequented by her nation, between the Don and the Volga; and there was reason to believe, that she intended, in case of any future assault, to put herself and her children under the protection of the Persian Monarch. It was necessary, therefore, that Tatishoff should lose no time in executing the designs of his Sovereign. He was fully satisfied, since the defeat of Donduc Dashee, that open violence was not to be attempted; and had recourse to such measures as were better suited to his character. Trusting to his address in discerning, and adapting himself to the weakness of the female constitution, he sent her magnificent presents; he said they were from the Russian Empress; he affected to disapprove of her rival; and, finally, he as-

* Dr. Cook.

ſured her, that his Sovereign, from the high opinion ſhe entertained of her merits, had appointed her governor of Aſtracan. He informed her, that he was ready to obey her commands; and that her power in that country would be inferior only to that of Elizabeth Petrowna. In order ſtill farther to impoſe on her credulity, he forged letters as from the Empreſs; and ſent ſome officers of diſtinction to aſſure her, that the great palace in the citadel, and the palace built in the neighbourhood of the city by Peter the Great, were ready for her reception. He told her, that all reſpect ſhould be ſhown her as if ſhe were Sovereign of the country; and that her new ſubjects were impatient to ſee her inveſted with the badges of her authority.

The Princeſs, in evil hour, was ſeduced. She quitted her retreat, and arrived in the neighbourhood of Aſtracan. Tatiſhoff waited upon her in her tent. He threw himſelf on his knees before her, and ſeemed to ratify, by the ardour of his proteſtations, the ſincerity of his profeſſions. Accordingly a day was fixed for her public entry into the city. Four thouſand men were drawn up in the ſtreet,

forming

forming a lane from the gate to the citadel. Cannons were fired, drums beat, bells rung, and the whole city seemed to be filled with joy and congratulation *. The Princess walked on foot, attended by forty Calmucks, the chief men of her nation. Tatishoff and his officers appeared in her retinue. The dignity of her person, and the beauty of her countenance, excited the admiration of the assembled multitude. The consciousness of her own integrity, and the belief that her spirited exertions, in behalf of her family, had procured her this distinction as the reward of her virtues, gave additional dignity to her appearance. She little knew that she had fallen into a treacherous snare.

A magnificent entertainment was provided for her in the great hall in the castle. She was seated at the head of the table; and while Tatishoff sat at the foot, her forty Calmucks took their places on each side of her. Every thing was conducted with the utmost splendour. Tatishoff was overjoyed; and the unsuspecting Princess was too soon in-

* Dr. Cook.

formed, that his joy arose from a very different cause than what she apprehended. For, after dinner, on pretence of some business, he requested her to go aside with him into an adjoining gallery. She went along with him unattended. The gallery had three doors; one at each end, and one from the hall. She had no sooner entered than the doors were shut: two grenadiers, with screwed bayonets, had been placed by every one of them on the inside: and she was informed, in their presence, of Tatishoff's perfidious purpose. He told her not to be alarmed, for that no harm was intended against her life, or that of her children; but that she must be prevailed with to resign her authority to Donduc Dashee; and that if her attending Calmucks made any resistance, it would prove fatal both to her and to them. The astonishment, the resentment, and the anguish of the Princess, were no doubt excessive. Yet these emotions did not deprive her of recollection, nor of the sense of her own dignity. Her conduct in this critical situation was such, as did not alter the circumstances of her fate, but very much lessened, if it did not entirely destroy, the triumph of her betrayer.

She

She upbraided him with his treachery; but absolved the Empress from any share in his guilt: she reasoned concerning the propriety of his political conduct; she represented to him that her children were not actually in his power; that she had given general instructions to the Calmucks, who had them in charge, never, even at her request, in whatsoever circumstance she might be, to give them out of their hands; and that any violence done to them would for ever alienate the Calmuck nation from the interests of Russia. She told him moreover, that she acquiesced in her fate; she saw it was in vain to contend; but that if she were allowed to confer with her army, she would be able to dispose them to such an accommodation as was equally consistent with their honour, and the interests of the Russian empire. She added more prevailing enticements—her tears flowed in abundance, and with effectual power. A sympathetic emotion seized the heart of Tatishoff; he was unprincipled—but not insensible: and in that susceptible moment he yielded to her entreaty. The Princess's attendants received no information concerning this unexpected business till they returned with her to the Calmuck camp—Tatiſhoff, in the mean time, was not ſo entirely overcome by his feelings, as not to attend to ſome prudential conſiderations; and he ſent along with the Princeſs a guard of above five hundred men. They were commanded by his ſon; and armed in the completeſt manner. It would appear, that the Tartar forces, on this occaſion, were not very numerous, elſe they would have reſcued the Princeſs from the hands of the Ruſſians. But this, upon the preſent occaſion, they were unable to execute.

The Princeſs on returning to her encampment, loſt no time in accompliſhing the flight of her children: ſhe herſelf was taking meaſures for her own eſcape; was mounting her horſe at midnight; was diſcovered; and kept afterwards in cloſer confinement. In this ſituation, however, exulting inwardly in the ſuppoſed ſafety of her children, ſhe appeared rather with the dignified ſilence of fallen majeſty, than with the plaintive ſorrow of afflicted weakneſs. By the dignity of her deportment ſhe awed the forwardneſs of young Tatiſhoff, who was ſuſpected of hav-

ing

ing offered her insult; and compelled him, by her indignant reserve, to behave with humiliating distance.

Meantime the Governor of Astracan repented him of his sensibility. The generality of mankind who suffer self-condemnation, are afflicted on account of their errors; but Tatishoff suffered self condemnation for having given indulgence to somewhat of a generous emotion. He argued, he intreated, he solicited his captive (for, though in the Tartar camp, she was still his captive), to learn from her what she had done with her children. He sent troops in pursuit of them; he scoured the desart with his Cossacks; but in vain. She smiled at his distress: she told him he might do with her what he pleased; but the children of Donduc Ambo were no longer in his power. His chagrin preyed on his constitution; his sleep and his appetite left him; he durst not, for fear of making the whole Calmuck nation revolt, use the Princess with inhumanity; yet he was deeply mortified, and covered with shame for his disappointment.

Nevertheless

Nevertheleſs he was too ſoon relieved from this merited affliction. The young Princes were indeed under the protection of a numerous body of Calmucks, who were determined to defend them. But they were no longer defended by the wiſdom, the vigilance, and affection of their mother. They fell at length into the hands of their enemy; and were ſent, along with the Princeſs, under a ſtrong guard, to Moſcow. They were treated there with the utmoſt reſpect. The Empreſs gave them ample poſſeſſions; ſhe viſited the Princeſs; and did every thing in her power to render her ſituation agreeable. Virtuous, amiable, and reſpected, the Calmuck Princeſs enjoyed as much felicity as was conſiſtent with the remembrance of her former condition. Some circumſtances of her ſtory reſemble that of Zenobia, the famous Queen of Palmyra; and thoſe particulars, in which there is any difference, do honour to the fair Circaſſian.

It does not appear that Donduc Daſhee was able, or perhaps entirely willing, to accompliſh the change ſo much deſired by the Ruſſians, in the manners of the Calmuck nation.

tion. Nor is it probable, that Tatishoff had much reason to rejoice in his impious maxims. Successful in one perfidious enterprize, he attempted others: and while he supported, as he apprehended, the interests of the empire, he was not inattentive to his own private emoluments. He became solicitous of amassing wealth. Selfish and unprincipled, he proceeded from injustice to violence and inhumanity. Among other enormities, he plundered and put to death an Armenian merchant. The affair was represented at St. Petersburgh. Enquiry was made; and his guilt appeared so manifest, that he was divested of his command, and confined to a village in the neighbourhood of Moscow. He endeavoured to get an audience of his Sovereign; and did not doubt but that his insinuation and address would procure him forgiveness. But those who were interested in his fall opposed the means of his restoration. Once, in the disguise of a soldier, he had almost reached the palace; but was detected, dragged away, and sent back to his place of confinement. He did not die a violent death; but, possessed of keen sensibility, he suffered pangs more excruciating than the

pain

pain perhaps of ſuch a death. Devoured with chagrin, he blaſphemed heaven, ſpoke treaſon againſt his Sovereign calumniated all men, pined in diſcontent, and died of vexation.

LETTER LIII.

A Peſtilential Diſtemper in Ruſſia.—The Maſſacre of the Archbiſhop of Moſcow.

DEAR SIR, St. Peterſburg, Dec. 3. 1771.

A PESTILENTIAL diſtemper has, for ſeveral months, been raging at Moſcow, and in the neighbourhood. It had been communicated from the army; and broke out in the rainy ſeaſon. Its ravages have been chiefly confined to the lower ranks; nor has it ever appeared very formidable where people have uſed the proper precautions of cleanlineſs and good air, to prevent it. I have not heard any good account of the ſymptoms, or nature of this dreadful diſorder, other than that the unfortunate perſons who are ſeized with it, are firſt affected with ſtartings and tremors in the ſkin; they are then afflicted with a violent fever; exhibit red ſpots in different parts of the body, which ſeldom ſuppurate; and are tormented with excruciating pain in the bowels. They uſually die in three or four days: and ſo furious was this diſtemper for above two months in the antient metropolis of this empire, that a thouſand perſons are ſaid to have periſhed daily.

Its progreſs was encouraged by the improper treatment of the diſeaſed. Hundreds of ſick perſons were unmercifully crowded into peſt-houſes, and there left to themſelves. Whenever any perſon was ſuſpected of having the plague, he was torn from his family, ſhut up with a multitude of loathſome wretches, and, thus abandoned by the world, he was given up to deſpair. Of conſequence, few that were confined ever recovered; and as no one, at the beginning of the diſorder, thought of burning the clothes of thoſe who died, the contagion ſpread very faſt.

Perſons of diſtinction, and even ſome perſons in authority, fled to the country. Numberleſs riots enſued; and inhuman robberies are ſaid to have been committed. One ſhocking ſpecies of oppreſſion is reported to have been practiſed by ſome inferior officers. If they bore

ill-will

ill-will againſt any one, or wanted a bribe, they threatened to accuſe him of having the plague. The plague itſelf was not more formidable to the poor people, than the inhumanity with which the ſick were treated; and rather than ſubmit to it, they gave all they had to ſatisfy the avarice of their rapacious tyrants. The conſequence of this was, that many perſons actually diſeaſed went about at large; and many in good health ſuffered dreadful confinement.

Meantime the peſtilence became more and more violent, ſo that the people were driven to diſtraction; and receiving little aſſiſtance from their rulers, they had recourſe to ſuperſtition. A certain image of the Virgin Mary was reported, by ſome mercenary prieſts, to poſſeſs ſingular efficacy in curing and preventing the diſtemper. Crowds both of healthy and diſeaſed perſons flocked to this hallowed phyſician; nor were they niggardly in their gifts and oblations. So that ſome of the inferior clergy, no leſs than the inferior officers, derived inhuman gains from the miſeries of their fellow citizens.

Ambrosius, Archbishop of Moscow, a man of great worth and liberality of sentiment, dreading the consequences, and shocked at the inhumanity of this infamous conduct, endeavoured, by removing the picture, to prevent it. This, however, produced an effect very different from what he expected. The people were enraged; their rage was exasperated by the instigation of the priests; they exclaimed that the archbishop was a Jew and a heretic; and that he was engaged in a hellish conspiracy with the physicians and surgeons, against whom their wrath was also kindled, to destroy them. In this furious state of mind, about ten thousand of them, with tumult and outcry, surrounded a church where the good archbishop was performing mass, and putting up prayers for their welfare. They insisted that he should come out, and restore to them their favourite idol. The venerable man appeared: he was arrayed in the solemn garb of his office; his grey hair was crowned with a mitre; he bore on his arm a cross; he stood on some steps on the outside of the church; and was about to address them. They fell upon him, and tore

him

him in pieces. Rendered frantic by this bloody deed, they were proceeding to ſet open all the peſt-houſes,—to let out the diſeaſed,—and maſſacre all obnoxious perſons.

Mean time a Ruſſian officer, named Yrepkin, with great reſolution and preſence of mind, collected about ſeventy ſoldiers: theſe were all he could muſter: he alſo got two pieces of cannon; and with theſe he poſted himſelf at the entry into one of the principal ſtreets. The mob advanced; he ordered his men to fire; they did ſo; ſome of the rioters were killed: his men looked diſcontented; they were inclined to mutiny: "is it pro-"per," ſaid one of them, aſſuming an arrogant tone, "that we ſhould embrue our hands in "the blood of our miſerable countrymen?" Yrepkin made no other reply than to plunge his ſword in his boſom. The reſt were confounded; they obeyed the orders of their ſpirited leader, and diſpelled the tumult: not, however, without the bloodſhed of many hundreds.

When the tidings came to St. Peterſburg, the conſternation was univerſal; the Empreſs

 cried

cried bitterly; and Count Orloff was immediately appointed, with full powers, to do every thing for the reſtoration of health, and the re-eſtabliſhment of the public tranquillity. He accepted of the office with the utmoſt alacrity; and I hear his labours are likely to prove effectual. He employs all the poor people in public works without the city; and by keeping them cleanly, and in freſh air, the violence of the diſorder is much abated. It is expected too, that much advantage will be derived from the ſeverity of the winter.

There is no appearance of any peſtilential diſtemper in this city. Every precaution, however, is uſed againſt it: the communication with Moſcow, and all ſuſpected places, is interrupted; vinegar is burnt in great quantities in every houſe; and the utmoſt attention is paid to the health of the lower ranks. Yet it is not very pleaſant to be within two or three days journey of ſo dreadful a neighbour. Adieu.

LETTER LIV. (EXTRACT.)

Anſwer to an Objection concerning the National Character of the Ruſſians.

* * * INDEED, Sir, I muſt ſtill retain my opinion, that the Ruſſians, in general, ſhew a great deal of ill-regulated ſenſibility. This is a character which you may often ſee exemplified in individuals: But I ſuppoſe Ruſſia is the only country where it is ſo general as to become a leading feature in the *national* character. It appears, I think, in the volatility of the Ruſſians, in their fickleneſs, and ſudden tranſitions from one affection, or one ſtate of mind, to another. They have been branded with perfidy; yet I am apt to believe, that the appearances, in favour of ſuch a charge, may often be traced to the changes and caprices of irregular feeling. Nor is it an objection, that, in many inſtances, they diſcover ſtrong ſymptoms of in-

humanity. You will agree with me, if you recollect, that feeling and sensibility may lead men to resentment and indignation; these emotions may appear quite proper; and if so in minds unaccustomed to reflection, their violent excesses will suffer little restraint; this is still more the case, when the manners of men are rude and undisciplined. Persons of great sensibility, or, in other words, persons very apt to be moved, even in periods of refinement, unless their passions be under due management, are more in danger of being transported by virulent and inhuman vehemence, than persons of a colder and less affectionate temper. The Greeks were a people of more sensibility than the Romans; yet a sagacious observer, and excellent judge of human nature, and withal an admirer of the Greeks, represents them as more sanguinary and inhuman. "*Hoc egit civis Romanus* "*ante te nemo. Externi isti sunt mores.* "*Usque ad sanguinem incitari solet odium aut* "*levium Græcorum, aut immanium barbarorum.* *"

The terms and phrases of endearment among the Russians are as extravagant, as

* Cicero pro Ligario.

they

they are groſs and violent in their abuſe. The ſoftneſs and copiouſneſs of their language too, are in favour of my opinion.— In a word, give them ſteadineſs, give them firmneſs of mind, either by moral conſiderations, or by a regard to their own intereſt; teach them to act from fixed principles, and as they are an animated, you would ſoon ſee them a reſpectable, people. * * *

LETTER LV.

Remarks on the preſent Situation of the Jews.

DEAR SIR,

I FLATTER myſelf I ſhall very ſoon have the pleaſure of ſeeing you in England. * * * *

Mean time, as you are a lover of hiſtorical enquiries, I ſend you incloſed ſome *Remarks on the preſent Situation of the Jews.* They were given me by a ſenſible and ingenious friend, in conſequence of ſome ſhort obſervations of mine on the ſame ſubject †.

THE FATE OF THE JEWS, ſince their conqueſt by the Romans, is one of the moſt ſingular events we meet with in the hiſtory of the world. A conquered people have generally been either extirpated by their conquerors, or have been left by them to enjoy certain laws and privileges, or, mixing with

† See Letter XV.

their

their conquerors, have united and been blended together. The Saxons, when they conquered England, extirpated the natives, and they ceafed to be a people. The Normans fpared the lives of the Saxons, and the two people uniting, the diftinction between them was quickly loft. But the Jews, after they were conquered by the Romans, being difperfed into the moft diftant countries, with out any affociation together, or without any common bond of union to attach them to one country, or to one form of government, have remained diftinct, feparate, and divided from the reft of world; and no where do they feem to have been blended with the nations in whofe country they have had their refidence. In vain would we account for this from the prophetic defcriptions of their fituation contained in the Sacred Scriptures. The bare prophecies could never produce the event. It is enough, if thofe prophecies have foretold an event, which it feems to have been beyond the utmoft power of human wit to forefee. To account for this event from any fupernatural caufe, muft be equally unfatisfactory. It is not probable that God, though he may, for wife purpofes, have in-

 tended

tended that the Jews ſhould remain in this ſituation, would chuſe to effectuate this by means different from his other operations in the world: and this is an account which no one, deſirous of a ſolution, can reſt upon with any tolerable degree of ſatisfaction.

But the circumſtance of the Jews having remained a ſeparate people, diſunited from every nation in whoſe country they lived, is not the only thing that is ſingular in their hiſtory. Another very particular circumſtance in their hiſtory is, their having been almoſt every where of the ſame profeſſion. The Jews, wherever ſituated, and in whatever country diſperſed, have conſtantly been merchants; and if you ſpeak of a Jew, the idea of a merchant is immediately called up along with it.

A third circumſtance very particular in the ſituation of the Jews is their number. It is obſerved by Mr. Addiſon, in a paper in the Spectator upon the ſubject, that the Jews are at preſent as numerous as they were formerly in the land of Canaan; and that this is very wonderful, when we conſider the dreadful ſlaughter

ſlaughter made of them under ſome of the Roman Emperors, their diſperſion, and the inumerable maſſacres and perſecutions they have ſince undergone.

A fourth circumſtance, which may be conſidered particular with regard to the Jews in their character. The Jews, wherever they have gone, have ever held one uniform character. They have conſtantly, without exception, been conſidered as a deceitful and a vile people.

To endeavour to give ſome account of thoſe peculiarities in the ſituation of the Jews, is propoſed in the following remarks; which ſhall be chiefly confined to the ſituation of thoſe Jews who have fixed their reſidence in Europe.

Firſt, with regard to their having remained a ſeparate and diſtinct people, never mingling or blending with thoſe nations among whom they lived. One principal cauſe of this appears to have ariſen from the peculiar nature of their religion. The religion of the Jews was ſuch, that they could

not

not poſſibly retain it, unleſs they remained ſeparate and diſtinct. The moment they intermingled, or intermarried with any other nation, it behoved them to abandon and forſake it. The religion of the Jews was peculiar to themſelves; it was peculiar to the twelve tribes of Iſrael; it was directed ſolely to the children of Abraham; and was a religion which could ſcarcely be adopted by any other people. Beſides, the government of the Jews was founded on their religion; nay, made a part of it; and, unleſs they retained that government, as inſtituted at firſt by Moſes, they could not retain their religious principles. The theocracy, the prieſthood, veſted in the Tribe of Levi; nay, every article of their private law, was an article of religion, and believed to be delivered by God to Moſes from the Mount. Hence the neceſſity this people lay under of remaining a diſtinct people, ſo long as they retained their religion. This is a circumſtance which diſtinguiſhes the Jewiſh from almoſt every other religion. A Proteſtant may remain a Proteſtant wherever he lives, whether he intermingle or unite with the people where he lives, or not. But a Jew, the moment he does this, gives up his religion,

religion, and forfeits all the bleſſings which are promiſed to his nation, or which belong to his particular tribe. God's choſen and well-beloved people reckon themſelves the only people on earth worthy his protection and defence. Upon this foundation they deſpiſe the Gentiles, they value themſelves as being the ſons of Abraham, Iſaac, and Jacob; and, in order to obtain the bleſſings promiſed to each particular ſect, they remain ſeparate and diſtinct, and every Jew can number up his anceſtors, in a direct line from himſelf to Abraham. Particular bleſſings were promiſed to them and them alone; and the long expected Meſſiah was propheſied to the Jewiſh nation only; and when he came, he was to be of the Tribe of Judah.

Another circumſtance which accounts for the Jews having never united or intermixed with the nations among whom they lived is, the averſion which, from the particularity of their ſituation, they muſt have entertained to all the nations among whom they inhabited, and which thoſe nations muſt, in their turn, have had to them. This mutual averſion muſt have ſeparated them more and more; and

and muſt have tended ſtill further to keep the Jews a ſeparate and diſtinct people. After the eſtabliſhment of Chriſtianity, it is by no means wonderful, that the Jews ſhould have been the objects of hatred and antipathy to the people among whom they lived. The Jewiſh religion being allowed by all Chriſtians to be of divine origin, though the only one, except their own, which could claim this privilege, they were naturally led to conſider the Jews as the moſt formidable antagoniſts to Chriſtianity. Both boaſting of a religion of a divine origin, the addition of a new and later revelation, being the only circumſtance by which the Chriſtians could ſupport their deviation from the principles and religion of the Jews, they were naturally apt to conſider thoſe as their greateſt enemies, who, coming ſo near themſelves, and allowing part of the religion which they poſſeſſed to be divine, refuſed to acknowledge theſe later articles which they deemed the moſt important. Beſides, being of the ſame country with the Author of Chriſtianity, having had opportunity of becoming acquainted with the miracles which he performed, and the other proofs which he gave of the divinity of his miſſion, it was natural that the Chriſtians

Christians should entertain an aversion to a people, who were not only of a religion different from their own, but who, favoured with all these circustances, continued to deny those mighty works which had been wrought among them. But, above all, it was the people of this nation who had brought to the most cruel and infamous death the Son of God, and the founder of the Christian system. The people concerned in this transaction were now, indeed, long since buried in their graves; but their children still remained a living example of their wretchedness; nay, they still persisted in approving of the deed, and continued to glory in what had been done. We may add to this, that the fury which formerly seized the Christians, of making crusades to the Holy Land, tended to keep up their antipathy to the Jews; and, at every new expedition, the Jews were sure to feel the effects of their religious zeal. The English history alone is a sufficient proof of the oppressions which the Jews suffered; and these were all laid to the charge of their difference in religion. It is no wonder then that the Jews should entertain an aversion to the religion and people with whom they lived; and that, in theſe circumſtances, they ſhould be more rivetted in their own religious principles and cuſtoms. Beſides, that ſtubbornneſs ſo natural to mankind in certain circumſtances, which makes them reſolved not to give up their opinions to ſuperior force, they would be apt to conſider thoſe oppreſſions as the effects of the greateſt depravity and blindneſs; and they would eſteem themſelves as ſuffering in the cauſe of God and religion. Had the Jews been treated like other people,—had they been allowed to enjoy the ſame privileges and immunities with the other inhabitants of the countries in which they lived, it is not probable that they would have remained ſo long a ſeparate and diſtinct people. Their own ancient manners would naturally have begun to have had leſs influence upon their minds; and they would have been gradually interchanged for the manners of their neighbours: but the bad treatment they met with, inſtead of aſſimilating them to the people among whom they lived, ſerved to preſerve that diſguſt and thoſe prejudices which it was natural for them at firſt to entertain againſt them, and to confirm them in their obſtinacy in maintaining their ancient errors.

errors. The Jews, ſeparated and diſperſed from one another, had no head, no regular ſociety or junction, to ſupport or confirm one another in their notions; but the bad treatment they met with ſerved the ſame end, and united more cloſely thoſe who inhabited the ſame country.

I now proceed to conſider thoſe circumſtances which may account for the Jews being all of one profeſſion; and this appears to have ariſen from the ſituation in which Europe was about the time, and for a conſiderable time after, the firſt ſettlements of the Jews. Europe, the greateſt part of it at leaſt, was for a long time rude and barbarous. War was the only profeſſion which was looked upon as honourable or reputable. Commerce, and every art connected with, or ſubſervient to it, was conſidered as mean and unworthy. No circumſtance tends to diſtinguiſh an early from an improved age, more than that ſuperior honour which is paid to thoſe who follow the art of war, and the diſgrace which is thrown upon every other. Men in early ages, accuſtomed to military atchievements, and filled with high ideas of heroiſm and honour, are naturally apt to conſider in a mean and deſpicable light the more peaceable and ſafe employments of the mechanic, the manufacturer, or the merchant; and the whole affair of commerce is conſidered as a profeſſion founded on injuſtice and oppreſſion, and by which men live by taking advantage of the wants and neceſſities of others.

Thus, among the Greeks and Romans, it was reckoned a diſgrace for a free man to be employed in a mechanical art. In the ſame manner, among all the nations in Europe, mechanics were held in contempt, and merchandize was in the greateſt diſrepute. The borrowing money upon intereſt, a thing without which trade cannot be carried on, was looked upon as the groſſeſt injuſtice. In early ages, before the introduction of commerce, men never borrowed but when in need of money to ſupply their neceſſities, or the common expences of life. To take advantage of theſe neceſſities, by refuſing to lend without a premium, was conſidered as an injuſtice by which men took advantage of the neceſſities of others. After commerce is introduced, when men begin to borrow money, not

not to ſupply their neceſſities, but with a view to profit and to increaſe their fortune, the lending money may then be defended upon all the principles of juſtice; yet men's prejudice againſt this ſpecies of traffic, from the influence of cuſtom, ſtill remains; and the taking of intereſt branded with the odious name of uſury, is ſtill prohibited and accounted injuſtice. The ſevereſt laws were made in Europe againſt it; the canon law, from the influence of the cauſes above-mentioned, which were increaſed by the authority of Ariſtotle's philoſophy, permitted no Chriſtian to receive intereſt; and the municipal ſeconded the prohibition of the canon law.

From theſe cauſes, the lending of money upon intereſt, the carrying on of every money tranſaction, and almoſt every branch of buſineſs, was taken out of the hands of the Chriſtians, and was engroſſed by the Jews. Hated already, and deſpiſed by the people among whom they lived, making light of any additional hatred or contempt which the profeſſion of a merchant could bring upon them, and taught by their religion that it was no crime to take uſury from a ſtranger, they engaged in thoſe branches of buſineſs which no other perſon in the country, who valued his reputation or character, would engage in. Devoid of the military ſpirit, becauſe they had nothing to rouſe it, and the more cloſely attached to their own intereſt, that they were ſecluded from the ſociety of the people among whom they lived, they were almoſt the only perſons, for a long time, who followed the profeſſion of a merchant; and by means thereof they generally amaſſed prodigious eſtates. Joined to their being the only perſons who enjoyed the advantage of this profeſſion, the high intereſt of money, which ſometimes even amounted to 50 *per cent.* contributed greatly to the vaſt fortunes which they were enabled to acquire.

The circumſtances which have been now mentioned, as they account for the Jews having been merchants, will likewiſe help to give ſome additional reaſons for the other peculiarity in their ſituation, viz. their having ſo long remained a ſeparate and diſtinct people. It has been ſhewn, that the Jews were the natural objects of odium to the people among whom

whom they lived; that this circumſtance, while it drew upon them many hardſhips and perſecutions, ſo it rendered them more and more averſe to unite and connect themſelves with thoſe people by whom they ſuffered theſe perſecutions. But this mal treatment of the Jews will not of itſelf ſufficiently account for their perſeverance in their religion, and their attachment to each other. Had their perſeverance only expoſed them to evils and calamities, it is not to be believed that it would have continued. Men may for a while perſiſt in their oppoſition to the crueleſt perſecutions; and inſtead of putting an end to their zeal, it may increaſe it; but the more cool views of intereſt will, in proceſs of time, get the better of the more violent, and, of conſequence, leſs permanent principle of zeal. The fathers may retain their ancient opinions, but the children will be apt to forſake them.

We have now ſeen, that evils and calamities were not the only things which attended the Jews, on account of their religion; but from their perſeverance therein, and in the doctrines of their fathers, they reaped many and ſignal advantages. By a fortuitous coincidence of circumſtances, the perſecution and ill-uſage which they met with, and the advantages which they reaped from their religion and country would both have the ſame effect, and would tend to make them continue attached to their religion and people, and averſe to mingle and unite with other nations. When they were haraſſed and oppreſſed by the Chriſtians, they would conſider themſelves as ſuffering in the cauſe of God, and the conſideration of this would attach them ſtrongly to their religion; when, from the circumſtance of their being of that religion, they amaſſed great fortunes, they would conſider theſe as the reward of their perſeverance; and ready to ſink under the ill-uſage they met with, they would comfort themſelves under the view of more proſperous circumſtances, and of amaſſing ſtill greater fortunes; not to mention that the Jews, having no other object to attract their attention or engage their thoughts, would naturally become intereſted, and put a high value on their riches. The perſecutions they met with, were likewiſe chiefly of that kind which

which made them put the greater value on the advantages they received from their religion. The aversion of the Christians to the Jews, while it led the Christians to oppress them, served at the same time to gratify another strong principle in the human mind, *their avarice.* The ill-will of the Christians was chiefly exerted in robbing and plundering the Jews of their great estates. This circumstance must have had a considerable influence in attaching them to their religion. It was the poverty or necessity of the Christians which led them to attack the fortunes of the Jews; it was the riches of the Jews which exposed them to these attacks. The continual comparison of those different situations would make the Jews always give the preference to their own. It was to their religion they owed being so much richer than the people about them; and the worst that could befal them was to be stripped of those possessions, and to be reduced to fortunes similar to those of their neighbours. By becoming converts to Christianity, they lost at once all the advantages of procuring large fortunes, whereas, by remaining in their antient persuasion, they had ſtill a chance of freeing themſelves from the plunder of their enemies. Attached to no one country more than another, if ever the perſecution raiſed againſt them became ſo hot as to deſtroy all the advantages of their remaining in the country where they reſided, they quickly left it; and finding means, by the invention of bills of exchange, to remove their effects, they ſettled in ſome other country where they could live with greater ſafety. This happened in England during the reign of one of the Edwards; and ſince that time, Mr. Hume obſerves, very few of that nation have ever lived in England.

Theſe remarks may give ſome account of the cauſes of the particular ſituation of the Jews. Their having ſo long remained a ſeparate and diſtinct people, and attached ſo cloſely to their religion, ſeems to have ariſen, firſt, from the nature of that religion, the very exiſtence of which depended on its votaries continuing a ſeparate people. 2dly, It ſeems to have ariſen from the averſion which took place between them and the people among whom they lived, and the hardſhips and perſecutions they met with, which increaſed that

that hatred and diſlike. 3dly, It appears, that it may be alſo in part accounted for, from certain advantages which they reaped from continuing attached to their religion and people.

The ſecond peculiarity mentioned in the ſituation of the Jews, has alſo been accounted for, viz. their having been merchants, from the particular ſituation of the countries in which they lived, which preven ed other men from being merchants, or laid them under great diſadvantages if they followed that profeſſion.

With regard to the third circumſtance, mentioned as ſingular in the ſituation of the Jews, viz. their great number, perhaps it may be aſcribed to their being merchants, and the wealth and opulence which the exerciſe of that profeſſion produced. It is an obſervation, the truth of which will not be diſputed, and which has been lately well illuſtrated by ſome eminent writers, that the populouſneſs of a people depends on its means of ſubſiſtence; and that, in ſhort, wherever people have enough to maintain a family, they will get a family; and that where this is the caſe, the nation muſt increaſe in its numbers. Now, the Jews becoming rich and wealthy, had ſubſiſtence ſufficient. They had more; they were richer than their neighbours around them; and, as they increaſed their connexions became, of courſe, more and more numerous.

The fourth circumſtance, which was mentioned as particular with regard to the Jews, was the unfavourable character uniformly given of them. The remarks which have been made, will help to give ſome account of this. To which may be added the juſt obſervation, that, to treat men with infamy; is the ſure way to make them deſerve it.

Upon the whole, theſe cauſes, if they cannot account for the events, may, at leaſt, give room for enquiry upon the ſubject. It muſt be confeſſed, however, that the *influence of theſe cauſes ſeems now to be near an end.* The principles of toleration that have now taken place, have, in ſome meaſure, moderated, at least, men's aversion to the Jews; and the improvements of a more enlightened age have made men form better and more worthy notions of all the transactions of commerce. These Remarks have chiefly been confined to the situation of the Jews who have settled in Europe. With regard to the Jews who have settled in other countries, it shall only be observed in general, that the same causes which account for the singular situation of the Jews in Europe, will account for it likewise elsewhere. The Jewish religion is opposite to the Mahometan and Pagan, as well as to the Christian; and there seems indeed to have been something, both in the religious and political institutions and customs of the Jews, peculiar to themselves, which served to detach them, and to render them odious to every other people in the world. The same causes will likewise account for their being merchants: besides, it ought to be observed, that Alexandria was the place to which most of the Jews, who did not inhabit Europe, resorted; but the situation of Alexandria was such as peculiarly fitted it for merchandize, and for inspiring into the minds of a people, who had no other

object

object to attach them, a fondneſs for this occupation. Alexandria, ſituated on the coaſt of the Levant, not far from the Red Sea, and near one of the mouths of the Nile, lay moſt conveniently for carrying on the merchandize of India and of all the Eaſt.

LETTER LVI. (EXTRACT.)

Journal of a Voyage from Cronſtadt to Copenhagen.

* * * * * *

Auguſt 16th, 1772. WE ſet ſail in the afternoon for England *. An agreeable evening; a briſk wind; the moonlight glancing upon the waves; gentle lightning darting at intervals from the boſom of a white cloud: the woody coaſt of Eſthonia calm and ſilent.

Why did my heart throb, and my tears ſtart, when I found myſelf in an Engliſh man of war? A thouſand images of friends and country ruſhed on my mind. O, Nature! with what exquiſite cords doſt thou bind our hearts, and makeſt them thrill with ineffable rapture! I leaned over the ſide of the ſhip, and thought of Britain.

* In the Flora, commanded by Mr. now Sir, George Collier, who diſtinguiſhed himſelf in the laſt war by his ſervices in America, and by the capture of the Leocadia.

Aug. 17th. We paſſed Hogland: a mountainous and heath-clad iſland.

Aug. 18th—29th. Croſs winds all the way from the Gulf of Finland: we run zig-zag from Abo to Dantzig, and from Dantzig to the Gulf of Bothnia. We paſs Gothland; its ſhores are involved in a ſtorm. Mean-time the ſailors are drowning cats and goats; performing ſacrifice, half in jeſt and half in earneſt, to the devil. There is more poly-theiſm in the world than is commonly thought.

Aug. 30th. A thouſand bleſſings on thy green hills and rocky ſhores, and on all thy ſons and daughters, fair and pleaſant Born-holm! Though thou canſt not boaſt of groves and trees, yet thy verdure is lovely: and ſtill, to the weary mariner, may it ſeem ſo! Still, as to us, may thy gentle gales come in place of impetuous tempeſts!

Sept. 1ſt. We paſſed the Iſle of Ween; and alſo a long neck of land that forms the Bay of Copenhagen. We left to the leeward fifty-two ſail of merchantmen. The ſcene delightful:

delightful: it exhibits Copenhagen lying at the bottom of the Bay, ornamented with ſeven conſiderable ſteeples, and a number of leſſer ſpires; behind it, a beautiful green eminence; the ſhore on each ſide flat, adorned with verdure corn fields, houſes, and villages; a multitude of veſſels, including eight ſhips of war, belonging to different nations, lying at anchor.

Sept. 2d. The city of Copenhagen is irregularly and too cloſely built. The ſtreets are narrow and ill paved; the houſes are of brick, and are covered with tiles. The palace is a heavy inelegant building: and the gardens of Roſenburg exhibit nothing but narrow lanes between high hedges, and dull canals. I do aſſure you, and the fact may be of ſervice to thoſe who gaze on the outſide of a palace with admiration, that in a room in the manſion of the Daniſh Princes, where we were told, the King and his Miniſters held councils of ſtate, we beheld—the Royal Game of the Gooſe.

The Muſeum contains a valuable collection of natural curioſities, and ſome good pictures. Here we were alſo ſhewn ſome ivory trinkets executed by a Danish King: the workmanship was indeed fine: but as we were looking at one piece that consisted of different parts linked together by little ivory rings, the person who shewed it accidently dropt it on the floor: it was shivered into a thousand fragments. We were filled with consternation: a monument of royal ingenuity! a palladium perhaps of the Danish state!—"Never mind it," said our good-natured guide, "I shall have another in its "place to-morrow."

The other curiosities which are shewn to strangers, are the dock-yard, which is indeed very noble; and the heads of Struensée and Brandt, which are very shocking. * * * * Adieu.

Cras ingens iterabimus æquor.

THE END.

ERRATA.

Page 25. line 10. *for* render *read* renders.
311. —— 6. *for* ſullen *read* fallen.
370. —— 8. *dele* or.
10. *for* without diſguiſe, *read* or without diſguiſe.
411. —— 3. *for* flames *read* flame.